HENRY THE FOURTH, *PART I*

An Annotated Text
Extracts from the Major Sources
Essays in Criticism

NORTON CRITICAL EDITIONS

※ A NORTON CRITICAL EDITION ※

WILLIAM SHAKESPEARE

HENRY THE FOURTH, *Part I*

AN ANNOTATED TEXT
EXTRACTS FROM THE MAJOR SOURCES
ESSAYS IN CRITICISM

※※

Edited by

JAMES L. SANDERSON
RUTGERS UNIVERSITY

W · W · NORTON & COMPANY · INC · *New York*

CONTENTS

PREFACE

Since its first appearance on the stage in 1597 and in print in 1598, *Henry IV, Part I*, has been one of Shakespeare's most popular plays. The dramatization of the struggle for a kingdom, focused in the climactic and mortal competition of two attractive heroes, Prince Henry and Harry Percy ("Hotspur"), still commands our attention more than five hundred years after the historical event. To the contemplation of those sterner realities upon which the fates of kingdoms and individuals depend is added the inexhaustibly entertaining Falstaff, one of Shakespeare's most complex and most debated creations. With something of Cleopatra's "infinite variety," Falstaff eludes attempts to confine him in too narrow interpretational categories as nimbly as he carried himself away to safety one memorable night on Gad's Hill. As a result, his power to amuse and interest us remains fresh after more than three centuries. Whether he is in our minds a "sanguine coward" and a "villainous abominable misleader of youth" or "sweet," "kind," "true," and "valiant Jack Falstaff," or perhaps something of all of these, it is impossible not to like the source of so much fun. And it is equally impossible not to surrender, momentarily one hopes, to his timeless invitation, as Charles Lamb said in another context, "to take an airing from the diocese of the strict conscience."

The play's success on the stage has been equaled, perhaps surpassed, by its success in the quiet of the study. It has been reprinted many times and has received a large amount of scholarly and critical comment. The purpose of this edition of the play is to provide an annotated text and a generous sampling of this comment. Placing the text and the critical essays in the same volume suggests a mode of approach in studying the play. The student's own reading of the play is, of course, basic. The reading of secondary comment cannot be a satisfying substitute for a great literary work itself. But understanding a play and getting at its meaning involve also a consideration of what it has meant to other responsible readers. The scholarly and critical insights of those who have devoted a lifetime to the study of Shakespeare and critics who are graced with a special alertness to literary values can add that keener pleasure to the student's experience which comes from a more nearly complete understanding and appreciation of the play. Such insights are to be gained from the essays selected for this anthology.

The essays are divided into two parts: those in the first part discuss the theme, characters, structure, and style of the play; those in the second part illustrate the variety of interpretation that has befallen the character of Falstaff during the last two centuries. The works listed in the Bibliography offer opportunity for a further study of these matters. For those who wish to use these secondary materials in documented reports, publication data are included. Unless otherwise specified, the materials have been reprinted exactly as they appeared in the sources from which they were drawn.

In addition to the text and criticism of the play, extracts are included from three of the more important works generally believed to have been sources which Shakespeare drew upon in writing *Henry IV, Part I*: Holinshed's *Chronicles of England*, Samuel Daniel's *The Civil Wars*, and *The Famous Victories of Henry the Fifth*.

I am chiefly indebted to the writers whose work appears in the anthology, but I also wish to acknowledge the help derived from the splendid *Variorum* edition of the play by the late Professor S. B. Hemingway and its equally useful *Supplement* by Professor G. Blakemore Evans. Thanks are due Professor M. H. Abrams for suggestions that I have incorporated in the book and the Master and Fellows of Trinity College, Cambridge, for permission to reproduce the title-page from the Trinity College Library copy of the first quarto. My wife, Rosamond, assisted as needed, in the proofreading and, as needed, in the maintaining of a sympathetic silence, for both of which I here extend "a liberal thanks."

Camden, New Jersey   James L. Sanderson
January 1962

A NOTE ON THE TEXT

The present text, with few departures, follows that of the first quarto (1598) edition of the play. Act and scene divisions are not indicated in the quarto; those of the first folio have been incorporated here with one exception: Scene ii of Act V has been divided into two scenes and the concluding scenes renumbered accordingly. Stage directions supplemental to those in the quarto have been placed in brackets. Aside from the adoption of modern conventions of spelling and punctuation, I have made only a few textual emendations. Words added have been placed in brackets; the other emendations are as follows:

I.ii.69. *similes*: smiles Q 137. *thou*: the Q 140. *Bardolph, Peto*: Haruey, Rossill Q 166. *to-night*: to morrow night Q I.iii.233. *I will*: ile Q II.ii.45. *Bardolph. What news?*: [Printed as part of Poins' preceding lines] Q 46–48. *assigned to Gadshill*: [assigned to Bard.] Q II.iii.3. *respect*: the respect Q II.iv.29. *precedent*: present Q 32. *Assigned to Poins*: [assigned to Prince] Q 157–60. *Parts assigned to Prince, Gadshill, Falstaff, Gadshill*: Gad, Ross., Falst., Ross. [respectively] Q 164–65. *Gadshill*: Ross Q 222. *eelskin*: elsskin Q 272. *Tell*: Faith tell Q 303. *Owen*: O Q 350. *tristful*: trustfull Q 357. *yet*: so Q 404. *reverend*: reverent Q III.i.100. *cantle*: scantle Q 116. *I will*: Ile Q 192. *She will*: sheele Q III.iii.29. *that's*: that Q 48. *tithe*: tight Q 89. *lose*: loose Q 175. *Poins*: Peto Q 182. *they or we*: we or they Q IV.i.20. *bear*: beares Q; *lord*: mind Q 108. *dropped*: drop Q 126. *cannot*: can Q 127. *yet*: it Q IV.ii.29. *that*: as Q 66. *on*: in Q IV.iii.21. *horse*: horses Q 82. *country's*: Countrey Q V.i.2. *busky*: bulky Q V.ii.3. *undone*: vnder one Q 10. *ne'er*: neuer Q 70. *Upon*: On Q V.iv.33. *So*: and Q 67. *Nor*: Now Q 153. *ours*: our Q 154. *let's*: let us Q

ABBREVIATED GENEALOGY OF THE MORTIMERS AND THE HOUSE OF LANCASTER

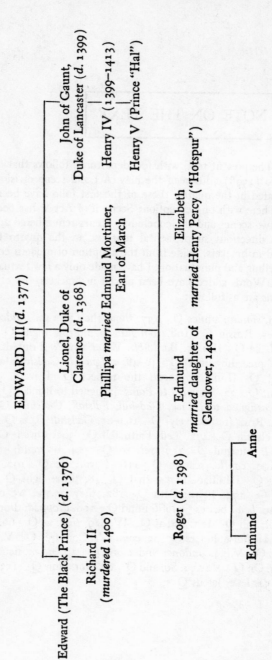

EDWARD III (*d.* 1377)

Edward (The Black Prince) (*d.* 1376)

Richard II (*murdered* 1400)

Lionel, Duke of Clarence (*d.* 1368)

Phillipa *married* Edmund Mortimer, Earl of March

Roger (*d.* 1398)

Edmund *married* daughter of Glendower, 1402

Elizabeth *married* Henry Percy ("Hotspur")

Edmund

Anne

John of Gaunt, Duke of Lancaster (*d.* 1399)

Henry IV (1399–1413)

Henry V (Prince "Hal")

THE TEXT OF HENRY THE FOURTH, PART I

THE
HISTORY OF
HENRIE THE
FOVRTH;

With the battell at Shrewsburie,
betweene the King and Lord
Henry Percy, surnamed
Henrie Hotspur of
the North.

With the humorous conceits of Sir
Iohn Falstalffe.

AT LONDON,
Printed by *P. S.* for *Andrew Wise*, dwelling
in Paules Churchyard, at the signe of
the Angell. 1598.

[DRAMATIS PERSONÆ

KING HENRY THE FOURTH
HENRY ("HAL"), *Prince of Wales* ⎫
PRINCE JOHN OF LANCASTER   ⎭ *sons of the* KING
EARL OF WESTMORELAND
SIR WALTER BLUNT
THOMAS PERCY, *Earl of Worcester*
HENRY PERCY, *Earl of Northumberland*
HENRY PERCY ("HOTSPUR"), *his son*
EDMUND MORTIMER, *Earl of March*
ARCHIBALD, *Earl of Douglas*   *enemies of the* KING
OWEN GLENDOWER
SIR RICHARD VERNON
RICHARD SCROOP, *Archbishop of York*
SIR MICHAEL, *friend of the Archbishop of York*
SIR JOHN FALSTAFF
POINS   ⎫
GADSHILL   ⎪
             ⎬ *companions of* FALSTAFF
PETO   ⎪
BARDOLPH   ⎭
LADY PERCY ("KATE"), *wife of* HOTSPUR *and sister of* MORTIMER
LADY MORTIMER, *daughter of* GLENDOWER *and wife of* EDMUND
MISTRESS QUICKLY, *hostess of the Boar's Head Tavern*

  *Lords, Carriers, Ostler, Chamberlain, Travellers, Vintner,
Drawers, Officers, Messengers, Sheriff, and Attendants*
                        TIME: 1402–1403]

The First Part of
KING HENRY THE FOURTH

[ACT I. SCENE I. *London. The Palace.*]

Enter the KING, LORD JOHN OF LANCASTER, EARL OF
WESTMORELAND, [SIR WALTER BLUNT], *with others.*

KING. So shaken as we are, so wan with care,
    Find we a time for frighted peace to pant,
    And breathe short-winded accents of new broils
    To be commenced in stronds afar remote.
    No more the thirsty entrance of this soil   5
    Shall daub her lips with her own children's blood,
    No more shall trenching war channel her fields,
    Nor bruise her flow'rets with the armed hoofs
    Of hostile paces; those opposed eyes
    Which, like the meteors of a troubled heaven,   10
    All of one nature, of one substance bred,
    Did lately meet in the intestine shock
    And furious close of civil butchery,
    Shall now, in mutual well-beseeming ranks,
    March all one way and be no more opposed   15
    Against acquaintance, kindred, and allies.
    The edge of war, like an ill-sheathed knife,
    No more shall cut his master. Therefore, friends,
    As far as to the sepulchre of Christ,
    Whose soldier now, under whose blessed cross   20
    We are impressed and engaged to fight,

2. **pant**: recover breath
3. **accents**: words
4. **stronds**: shores
7. **trenching**: cutting; **channel**: furrow
10. **meteors**: atmospheric conditions (hail, lightning, etc.)
12. **intestine**: internal
13. **close**: encounter
14. **mutual**: united
17. **edge**: sword
19. **sepulchre of Christ**: in Jerusalem
21. **impressed**: enlisted; **engaged**: pledged

Forthwith a power of English shall we levy,
Whose arms were moulded in their mother's womb
To chase these pagans in those holy fields
Over whose acres walked those blessed feet   25
Which fourteen hundred years ago were nailed
For our advantage on the bitter cross.
But this our purpose now is twelve month old,
And bootless 'tis to tell you we will go;
Therefore we meet not now. Then let me hear   30
Of you, my gentle cousin Westmoreland,
What yesternight our council did decree
In forwarding this dear expedience.
WESTMORELAND. My liege, this haste was hot in question
And many limits of the charge set down   35
But yesternight; when all athwart there came
A post from Wales, loaden with heavy news,
Whose worst was that the noble Mortimer,
Leading the men of Herefordshire to fight
Against the irregular and wild Glendower,   40
Was by the rude hands of that Welshman taken,
A thousand of his people butchered;
Upon whose dead corpse there was such misuse,
Such beastly shameless transformation,
By those Welshwomen done as may not be   45
Without much shame retold or spoken of.
KING. It seems then that the tidings of this broil
Brake off our business for the Holy Land.
WESTMORELAND. This matched with other did, my gracious lord;
For more uneven and unwelcome news   50
Came from the north, and thus it did import:

22. **power:** army
29. **bootless:** to no purpose
30. **Therefore . . . not:** we do not meet now concerning that matter
31. **cousin:** a friendly form of address
33. **dear expedience:** important enterprise
34. **hot in question:** being hotly discussed
35. **limits of the charge:** determination of responsibility
36. **athwart:** perversely
40. **irregular:** lawless
43. **corpse:** corpses
50. **uneven:** disconcerting

On Holy-rood Day the gallant Hotspur there,
Young Harry Percy, and Brave Archibald,
That ever-valiant and approved Scot,
At Holmedon met,   55
Where they did spend a sad and bloody hour;
As by discharge of their artillery
And shape of likelihood the news was told;
For he that brought them, in the very heat
And pride of their contention did take horse,   60
Uncertain of the issue any way.
KING. Here is [a] dear, a true industrious friend,
Sir Walter Blunt, new lighted from his horse,
Stained with the variation of each soil
Betwixt that Holmedon and this seat of ours,   65
And he hath brought us smooth and welcome news.
The Earl of Douglas is discomfited.
Ten thousand bold Scots, two and twenty knights,
Balked in their own blood, did Sir Walter see
On Holmedon's plains. Of prisoners, Hotspur took   70
Mordake Earl of Fife and eldest son
To beaten Douglas, and the Earl of Athol,
Of Murray, Angus, and Menteith.
And is not this an honorable spoil?
A gallant prize? Ha, cousin, is it not?   75
WESTMORELAND. In faith,
It is a conquest for a prince to boast of.
KING. Yea, there thou mak'st me sad, and mak'st me sin
In envy that my Lord Northumberland
Should be the father to so blest a son,   80
A son who is the theme of honor's tongue,
Amongst a grove the very straightest plant,
Who is sweet fortune's minion and her pride;
Whilst I, by looking on the praise of him,

52. **Holy-rood Day:** September 14
55. **Holmedon:** a town in Northumberland
58. **shape of likelihood:** probability
59. **them:** i.e., the news
60. **pride . . . contention:** height of their battle
61. **issue:** outcome
69. **Balked:** (1) heaped up in ridges (2) thwarted
83. **minion:** favorite

See riot and dishonor stain the brow   85
Of my young Harry. O that it could be proved
That some night-tripping fairy had exchanged
In cradle clothes our children where they lay,
And called mine Percy, his Plantagenet!
Then would I have his Harry, and he mine.   90
But let him from my thoughts. What think you, coz,
Of this young Percy's pride? The prisoners
Which he in this adventure hath surprised
To his own use he keeps, and sends me word
I shall have none but Mordake Earl of Fife.   95

WESTMORELAND. This is his uncle's teaching, this is Worcester,
Malevolent to you in all aspects,
Which makes him prune himself and bristle up
The crest of youth against your dignity.

KING. But I have sent for him to answer this;   100
And for this cause awhile we must neglect
Our holy purpose to Jerusalem.
Cousin, on Wednesday next our council we
Will hold at Windsor. So inform the lords;
But come yourself with speed to us again,   105
For more is to be said and to be done
Than out of anger can be uttered.

WESTMORELAND. I will, my liege.   *Exeunt.*

[SCENE II. *London. An apartment of the* PRINCE'S.]

Enter PRINCE OF WALES *and* SIR JOHN FALSTAFF.

FALSTAFF. Now, Hal, what time of day is it, lad?
PRINCE. Thou art so fat-witted with drinking of old sack, and un-
buttoning thee after supper, and sleeping upon benches after
noon, that thou hast forgotten to demand that truly which
thou wouldest truly know. What a devil hast thou to do with   5

89. **Plantagenet:** a dynasty of English kings founded by Geoffrey of Anjou
91. **coz:** cousin
93. **surprised:** captured
97. **Malevolent . . . aspects:** an astrological expression comparing Worcester to a star exerting an evil influence on the fortunes of Henry IV
98. **prune:** preen
2. **sack:** a white Spanish wine

the time of the day? Unless hours were cups of sack, and minutes capons, and clocks the tongues of bawds, and dials the
signs of leaping houses, and the blessed sun himself a fair hot
wench in flame-colored taffeta, I see no reason why thou
shouldst be so superfluous to demand the time of the day.   10

FALSTAFF. Indeed, you come near me now, Hal; for we that take
purses go by the moon and the seven stars, and not by Phoebus,
he, that wand'ring knight so fair. And I prithee, sweet wag,
when thou art a king, as, God save thy grace—majesty I
should say, for grace thou wilt have none—   15

PRINCE. What, none?

FALSTAFF. No, by my troth, not so much as will serve to be
prologue to an egg and butter.

PRINCE. Well, how then? Come, roundly, roundly.

FALSTAFF. Marry, then, sweet wag, when thou art king let not   20
us that are squires of the night's body be called thieves of the
day's beauty. Let us be Diana's foresters, gentlemen of the
shade, minions of the moon; and let men say we be men of
good government, being governed as the sea is, by our noble
and chaste mistress the moon, under whose countenance we   25
steal.

PRINCE. Thou sayest well, and it holds well too; for the fortune
of us that are the moon's men doth ebb and flow like the sea,
being governed, as the sea is, by the moon. As, for proof now:
a purse of gold most resolutely snatched on Monday night and   30
most dissolutely spent on Tuesday morning; got with swearing
"Lay by," and spent with crying "Bring in"; now in as low an
ebb as the foot of the ladder, and by and by in as high a flow
as the ridge of the gallows.

8. **leaping houses:** brothels
9. **flame-colored taffeta:** the kind of garb worn by prostitutes
12. **go:** (1) walk (2) tell time; **seven stars:** the Pleiades
13. **wag:** fellow
17. **troth:** faith
18. **prologue . . . butter:** prayer before a light meal
19. **roundly:** get to the point
20. **Marry:** to be sure
22. **Diana:** goddess of the moon and the hunt
32. **Lay by:** an outlaw's command to his victim; **Bring in: a tavern
expression, bring in the drinks
33. **ladder:** used to mount the gallows

FALSTAFF. By the Lord, thou say'st true, lad. And is not my hos- 35
tess of the tavern a most sweet wench?

PRINCE. As the honey of Hybla, my old lad of the castle. And is
not a buff jerkin a most sweet robe of durance?

FALSTAFF. How now, how now, mad wag? What, in thy quips
and thy quiddities? What a plague have I to do with a buff 40
jerkin?

PRINCE. Why, what a pox have I to do with my hostess of the
tavern?

FALSTAFF. Well, thou hast called her to a reckoning many a
time and oft.

PRINCE. Did I ever call for thee to pay thy part? 45

FALSTAFF. No, I'll give thee thy due; thou hast paid all there.

PRINCE. Yea, and elsewhere, so far as my coin would stretch;
and where it would not, I have used my credit.

FALSTAFF. Yea, and so used it that, were it not here apparent that 50
thou art heir apparent—But I prithee, sweet wag, shall there
be gallows standing in England when thou art king? and resolution thus fubbed as it is with the rusty curb of old father
antic the law? Do not thou, when thou art king, hang a thief.

PRINCE. No; thou shalt. 55

FALSTAFF. Shall I? O rare! By the Lord, I'll be a brave judge.

PRINCE. Thou judgest false already. I mean, thou shalt have the
hanging of the thieves and so become a rare hangman.

FALSTAFF. Well, Hal, well; and in some sort it jumps with my
humor as well as waiting in the court, I can tell you. 60

PRINCE. For obtaining of suits?

---

37. **Hybla:** a town in Sicily famous for its honey; **old lad . . . castle:**
(1) a roisterer (2) a pun on Falstaff's original name, Oldcastle. The
Castle was also the name of a London brothel.

38. **buff jerkin:** a leather jacket worn by sheriffs' sergeants; **durance:**
(1) durable material (2) imprisonment

40. **quiddities:** subtleties of wit

42. **a pox:** an expression of annoyance

44. **reckoning:** (1) totalling of a bill (2) giving an account of herself

52. **resolution:** courage

53. **fubbed:** cheated

54. **antic:** buffoon

56. **brave:** finely arrayed

59. **jumps:** agrees

61. **suits:** (1) petitions (2) clothes

FALSTAFF. Yea, for obtaining of suits, whereof the hangman hath no lean wardrobe. 'Sblood, I am as melancholy as a gib cat or a lugged bear.

PRINCE. Or an old lion, or a lover's lute.   65

FALSTAFF. Yea, or the drone of a Lincolnshire bagpipe.

PRINCE. What sayest thou to a hare, or the melancholy of Moor Ditch?

FALSTAFF. Thou hast the most unsavory similes, and art indeed the most comparative, rascalliest, sweet young prince. But, 70 Hal, I prithee trouble me no more with vanity. I would to God thou and I knew where a commodity of good names were to be bought. An old lord of the council rated me the other day in the street about you, sir, but I marked him not; and yet he talked very wisely, but I regarded him not; and yet he talked 75 wisely, and in the street too.

PRINCE. Thou didst well, for wisdom cries out in the streets, and no man regards it.

FALSTAFF. O, thou hast damnable iteration, and art indeed able to corrupt a saint. Thou hast done much harm upon me, Hal; 80 God forgive thee for it! Before I knew thee, Hal, I knew nothing; and now am I, if a man should speak truly, little better than one of the wicked. I must give over this life, and I will give it over! By the Lord, an I do not, I am a villain! I'll be damned for never a king's son in Christendom.   85

PRINCE. Where shall we take a purse to-morrow, Jack?

FALSTAFF. 'Zounds, where thou wilt, lad! I'll make one. An I

62–63. hangman . . . wardrobe: The hangman retained the clothing of his victims.

63. 'Sblood: an oath, by God's blood

63–64. gib cat: tomcat

64. lugged: baited

66. drone: bass pipe of a bagpipe

67. hare: considered a melancholy animal; Moor Ditch: an open drainage ditch in London cluttered with refuse

72. commodity: quantity

73. rated: chided

77–78. Cf. Proverbs I: 20–24: "Wisdom crieth without; she uttereth her voice in the streets . . . saying . . . 'I have stretched out my hand, and no man regarded.' "

79. iteration: repetition (of scripture)

84. an: if

87. 'Zounds: an oath, by God's wounds

do not, call me villain and baffle me.

PRINCE. I see a good amendment of life in thee: from praying
to purse-taking.   90

FALSTAFF. Why, Hal, 'tis my vocation, Hal. 'Tis no sin for a man
to labor in his vocation.

Enter POINS.

Poins! Now shall we know if Gadshill have set a match. O,
if men were to be saved by merit, what hole in hell were hot
enough for him? This is the most omnipotent villain that ever   95
cried "Stand!" to a true man.

PRINCE. Good morrow, Ned.

POINS. Good morrow, sweet Hal. What says Monsieur Remorse?
What says Sir John Sack and Sugar? Jack, how agrees the
devil and thee about thy soul, that thou soldest him on Good   100
Friday last for a cup of Madeira and a cold capon's leg?

PRINCE. Sir John stands to his word, the devil shall have his bargain; for he was never yet a breaker of proverbs. He will give
the devil his due.

POINS. Then art thou damned for keeping thy word with the   105
devil.

PRINCE. Else he had been damned for cozening the devil.

POINS. But, my lads, my lads, to-morrow morning, by four o'clock
early at Gad's Hill, there are pilgrims going to Canterbury with
rich offerings, and traders riding to London with fat purses.   110
I have vizards for you all; you have horses for yourselves.
Gadshill lies to-night in Rochester. I have bespoke supper to-
morrow night in Eastcheap. We may do it as secure as sleep.
If you will go, I will stuff your purses full of crowns; if you

88. **baffle**: disgrace
93. **set a match**: appoint a meeting (for the robbery)
96. **stand**: an outlaw's command, "Hands up!"
101. **Madeira**: a white wine
107. **cozening**: cheating
109. **pilgrims**: The pilgrims are taking gifts to the famous shrine of St.
Thomas à Becket at Canterbury.
111. **vizards**: masks
112. **Gadshill**: Gadshill is the name of one of the thieves and also the
site (on the road from London to Rochester) of the robbery. **Rochester:**
a town thirty-three miles east of London
113. **Eastcheap:** a street in London

will not, tarry at home and be hanged!   115

FALSTAFF. Hear ye, Yedward; if I tarry at home and go not I'll
    hang you for going.

PRINCE. You will, chops?

FALSTAFF. Hal, wilt thou make one?

PRINCE. Who, I rob? I a thief? Not I, by my faith.   120

FALSTAFF. There's neither honesty, manhood, nor good fellow-
    ship in thee, nor thou cam'st not of the blood royal if thou
    darest not stand for ten shillings.

PRINCE. Well then, once in my days I'll be a madcap.

FALSTAFF. Why, that's well said.   125

PRINCE. Well, come what will, I'll tarry at home.

FALSTAFF. By the Lord, I'll be a traitor then, when thou art king.

PRINCE. I care not.

POINS. Sir John, I prithee, leave the prince and me alone; I will
    lay him down such reasons for this adventure that he shall go. 130

FALSTAFF. Well, God give thee the spirit of persuasion and him
    the ears of profiting, that what thou speakest may move and
    what he hears may be believed, that the true prince may (for
    recreation sake) prove a false thief; for the poor abuses of the
    time want countenance. Farewell; you shall find me in East- 135
    cheap.

PRINCE. Farewell, thou latter spring! farewell, All-hallow sum-
    mer!   [Exit FALSTAFF.]

POINS. Now, my good sweet honey lord, ride with us to-morrow.
    I have a jest to execute that I cannot manage alone. Falstaff, 140
    Bardolph, Peto, and Gadshill shall rob those men that we
    have already waylaid; yourself and I will not be there, and
    when they have the booty, if you and I do not rob them, cut
    this head off from my shoulders.

PRINCE. How shall we part with them in setting forth?   145

POINS. Why, we will set forth before or after them and appoint
    them a place of meeting, wherein it is at our pleasure to fail;
    and then will they adventure upon the exploit themselves,

116. **Yedward:** Edward
118. **chops:** one with fat cheeks
122. **royal:** a play on the name of a coin worth 10 shillings
123. **stand:** fiight for
135. **want countenance:** lack encouragement
137. **All-hallown summer:** late autumn

which they shall have no sooner achieved, but we'll set upon
them.   150

PRINCE. Yea, but 'tis like that they will know us by our horses,
by our habits, and by every other appointment to be ourselves.

POINS. Tut, our horses they shall not see—I'll tie them in the
wood; our vizards we will change after we leave them; and,
sirrah, I have cases of buckram for the nonce, to immask our   155
noted outward garments.

PRINCE. Yea, but I doubt they will be too hard for us.

POINS. Well, for two of them, I know them to be as true-bred
cowards as ever turned back; and for the third, if he fight
longer than he sees reason, I'll forswear arms. The virtue of   160
this jest will be the incomprehensible lies that this same fat
rogue will tell us when we meet at supper: how thirty, at least,
he fought with; what wards, what blows, what extremities he
endured; and in the reproof of this lives the jest.

PRINCE. Well, I'll go with thee. Provide us all things necessary   165
and meet me to-night in Eastcheap; there I'll sup. Farewell.

POINS. Farewell, my lord.   *Exit* POINS.

PRINCE. I know you all, and will awhile uphold
The unyoked humor of your idleness.
Yet herein will I imitate the sun,   170
Who doth permit the base contagious clouds
To smother up his beauty from the world,
That, when he please again to be himself,
Being wanted, he may be more wondered at
By breaking through the foul and ugly mists   175
Of vapors that did seem to strangle him.
If all the year were playing holidays,
To sport would be as tedious as to work;
But when they seldom come, they wished-for come,
And nothing pleaseth but rare accidents.   180

152. **habits:** clothing; **appointment:** equipment
155. **sirrah:** a form of address usually applied to inferiors; **cases of buckram:** clothing of coarse linen; **for the nonce:** for the purpose
157. **doubt:** fear
163. **wards:** defensive postures
164. **reproof:** confutation
169. **unyoked:** undisciplined
171. **base:** low-lying; **contagious:** poisonous
180. **accidents:** incidents

So, when this loose behavior I throw off
And pay the debt I never promised,
By how much better than my word I am,
By so much shall I falsify men's hopes;
And like bright metal on a sullen ground,   185
My reformation, glitt'ring o'er my fault,
Shall show more goodly and attract more eyes
Than that which hath no foil to set it off.
I'll so offend to make offense a skill,
Redeeming time when men think least I will.   *Exit.* 190

[SCENE III. *London. The Palace.*]

Enter the KING, NORTHUMBERLAND, WORCESTER, HOTSPUR,
SIR WALTER BLUNT, *with others.*

KING. My blood hath been too cold and temperate,
Unapt to stir at these indignities,
And you have found me, for accordingly
You tread upon my patience; but be sure
I will from henceforth rather be myself,   5
Mighty and to be feared, than my condition,
Which hath been smooth as oil, soft as young down,
And therefore lost that title of respect
Which the proud soul ne'er pays but to the proud.
WORCESTER. Our house, my sovereign liege, little deserves   10
The scourge of greatness to be used on it;
And that same greatness, too, which our own hands
Have holp to make so portly.
NORTHUMBERLAND. My lord,—
KING. Worcester, get thee gone; for I do see   15
Danger and disobedience in thine eye.
O, sir, your presence is too bold and peremptory,
And majesty might never yet endure

185. **sullen:** dark
188. **foil:** contrasting background
189. **skill:** good strategy
190. **Redeeming time:** saving time from being wasted
3. **found me:** found me out
6. **condition:** disposition
13. **holp:** helped
16. **danger:** ungracious conduct

The moody frontier of a servant brow.
You have good leave to leave us; when we need   20
Your use and counsel, we shall send for you.

                                        Exit WORCESTER.

You were about to speak. [*to* NORTHUMBERLAND]
NORTHUMBERLAND.   Yea, my good lord.
Those prisoners in your highness' name demanded
Which Harry Percy here at Holmedon took,
Were, as he says, not with such strength denied   25
As is delivered to your majesty.
Either envy, therefore, or misprision
Is guilty of this fault, and not my son.
HOTSPUR. My liege, I did deny no prisoners.
But I remember, when the fight was done,   30
When I was dry with rage and extreme toil,
Breathless and faint, leaning upon my sword,
Came there a certain lord, neat and trimly dressed,
Fresh as a bridegroom, and his chin new reaped
Showed like a stubble land at harvest home.   35
He was perfumed like a milliner,
And 'twixt his finger and his thumb he held
A pouncet box, which ever and anon
He gave his nose, and took't away again;
Who therewith angry, when it next came there,   40
Took it in snuff; and still he smiled and talked;
And as the soldiers bore dead bodies by,
He called them untaught knaves, unmannerly,
To bring a slovenly unhandsome corse
Betwixt the wind and his nobility.   45
With many holiday and lady terms
He questioned me, amongst the rest demanded
My prisoners in your majesty's behalf.

19. frontier: forehead
27. envy: malice; misprision: misunderstanding
35. harvest-home: the close of harvesting
38. pouncet box: small container for perfumes
40. Who: i.e., the nose
41. Took . . . snuff: a play on the proverbial expression meaning to
take offense
46. holiday . . . terms: terms appropriate to a festive or sportive occasion

I then, all smarting with my wounds being cold,
To be so pestered with a popingay,   50
Out of my grief and my impatience
Answered neglectingly—I know not what—
He should, or he should not; for he made me mad
To see him shine so brisk, and smell so sweet,
And talk so like a waiting gentlewoman   55
Of guns and drums and wounds,—God save the mark!—
And telling me the sovereignest thing on earth
Was parmaceti for an inward bruise,
And that it was great pity, so it was,
This villainous saltpetre should be digged   60
Out of the bowels of the harmless earth,
Which many a good tall fellow had destroyed
So cowardly, and but for these vile guns,
He would himself have been a soldier.
This bald unjointed chat of his, my lord,   65
I answered indirectly, as I said,
And I beseech you, let not his report
Come current for an accusation
Betwixt my love and your high majesty.

BLUNT. The circumstance considered, good my lord,   70
Whate'er Lord Harry Percy then had said
To such a person, and in such a place,
At such a time, with all the rest retold,
May reasonably die, and never rise
To do him wrong, or any way impeach   75
What then he said, so he unsay it now.

KING. Why, yet he doth deny his prisoners,

50. **popingay:** parrot
51. **grief:** pain
54. **brisk:** smartly dressed
57. **sovereignest:** most excellent
58. **parmaceti:** spermaceti, a fatty substance found in the head of the sperm-whale and used in various medicinal preparations
62. **tall:** brave
65. **bald:** trivial; **unjointed:** incoherent
66. **indirectly:** negligently
68. **come current:** be accepted as genuine
75. **impeach:** disparage
77. **yet:** still

But with proviso and exception,
That we at our own charge shall ransom straight
His brother-in-law, the foolish Mortimer, 80
Who, on my soul, hath willfully betrayed
The lives of those that he did lead to fight
Against that great magician, damned Glendower,
Whose daughter, as we hear, that Earl of March
Hath lately married. Shall our coffers, then, 85
Be emptied to redeem a traitor home?
Shall we buy treason? and indent with fears
When they have lost and forfeited themselves?
No, on the barren mountains let him starve!
For I shall never hold that man my friend 90
Whose tongue shall ask me for one penny cost
To ransom home revolted Mortimer.
HOTSPUR. Revolted Mortimer!
He never did fall off, my sovereign liege,
But by the chance of war. To prove that true 95
Needs no more but one tongue for all those wounds,
Those mouthèd wounds, which valiantly he took
When on the gentle Severn's sedgy bank,
In single opposition hand to hand,
He did confound the best part of an hour 100
In changing hardiment with great Glendower.
Three times they breathed, and three times did they drink,
Upon agreement, of swift Severn's flood,
Who then, affrighted with their bloody looks,
Ran fearfully among the trembling reeds 105
And hid his crisp head in the hollow bank,
Bloodstained with these valiant combatants.
Never did bare and rotten policy
Color her working with such deadly wounds,

87. **indent:** enter into a compact
94. **fall off:** withdraw his allegiance
100. **confound:** consume
101. **changing hardiment:** exchanging blows
102. **breathed:** rested in their fighting
106. **crisp:** rippled
108. **policy:** dissimulation
109. **Color:** disguise

Nor never could the noble Mortimer   110
Receive so many, and all willingly.
Then let not him be slandered with revolt.
KING. Thou dost belie him, Percy, thou dost belie him!
He never did encounter with Glendower.
I tell thee,   115
He durst as well have met the devil alone
As Owen Glendower for an enemy.
Art thou not ashamed? But, sirrah, henceforth
Let me not hear you speak of Mortimer.
Send me your prisoners with the speediest means,   120
Or you shall hear in such a kind from me
As will displease you. My Lord Northumberland,
We license your departure with your son.
Send us your prisoners, or you will hear of it.

                    Exeunt KING, [BLUNT, *and* TRAIN].

HOTSPUR. An if the devil come and roar for them,   125
    I will not send them. I will after straight
    And tell him so, for I will ease my heart,
    Albeit I make a hazard of my head.
NORTHUMBERLAND. What, drunk with choler? Stay, and pause
        awhile.
    Here comes your uncle.

                    Enter WORCESTER.

HOTSPUR.   Speak of Mortimer?   130
    'Zounds, I will speak of him, and let my soul
    Want mercy if I do not join with him!
    Yea, on his part I'll empty all these veins,
    And shed my dear blood drop by drop in the dust,
    But I will lift the downtrod Mortimer   135
    As high in the air as this unthankful king,
    As this ingrate and cankered Bolingbroke.
NORTHUMBERLAND. Brother, the king hath made your nephew
        mad.

113. belie: lie about
128. make . . . of: gamble
129. choler: wrath
137. cankered: venomous; Bolingbroke: i.e., Henry IV

WORCESTER. Who struck this heat up after I was gone?

HOTSPUR. He will, forsooth, have all my prisoners;   140
   And when I urged the ransom once again
   Of my wife's brother, then his cheek looked pale,
   And on my face he turned an eye of death,
   Trembling even at the name of Mortimer.

WORCESTER. I cannot blame him. Was not he proclaimed   145
   By Richard that dead is, the next of blood?

NORTHUMBERLAND. He was; I heard the proclamation.
   And then it was when the unhappy king
   (Whose wrongs in us God pardon!) did set forth
   Upon his Irish expedition;   150
   From whence he intercepted did return
   To be deposed, and shortly murdered.

WORCESTER. And for whose death we in the world's wide mouth
   Live scandalized and foully spoken of.

HOTSPUR. But soft, I pray you. Did King Richard then   155
   Proclaim my brother Edmund Mortimer
   Heir to the crown?

NORTHUMBERLAND.   He did; myself did hear it.

HOTSPUR. Nay, then I cannot blame his cousin king,
   That wished him on the barren mountains starve.
   But shall it be that you, that set the crown   160
   Upon the head of this forgetful man,
   And for his sake wear the detested blot
   Of murtherous subornation—shall it be
   That you a world of curses undergo,
   Being the agents or base second means,   165
   The cords, the ladder, or the hangman rather?
   O, pardon me that I descend so low
   To show the line and the predicament
   Wherein you range under this subtle king!
   Shall it for shame be spoken in these days,   170

140. forsooth: in truth
145–46. proclaimed . . . blood: specified as the successor to the throne
156. brother: brother-in-law
163. murtherous subornation: encouraging one to commit murder
165. second: subordinate
168. line: degree; predicament: situation, position
169. range: occupy a position

Or fill up chronicles in time to come,
That men of your nobility and power
Did gage them both in an unjust behalf
(As both of you, God pardon it! have done)
To put down Richard, that sweet lovely rose,   175
And plant this thorn, this canker, Bolingbroke?
And shall it in more shame be further spoken
That you are fooled, discarded, and shook off
By him for whom these shames ye underwent?
No! yet time serves wherein you may redeem   180
Your banished honors and restore yourselves
Into the good thoughts of the world again;
Revenge the jeering and disdained contempt
Of this proud king, who studies day and night
To answer all the debt he owes to you   185
Even with the bloody payment of your deaths.
Therefore, I say—

WORCESTER.   Peace, cousin, say no more;
And now I will unclasp a secret book,
And to your quick-conceiving discontents
I'll read you matter deep and dangerous,   190
As full of peril and adventurous spirit
As to o'erwalk a current roaring loud
On the unsteadfast footing of a spear.

HOTSPUR. If he fall in, good night, or sink or swim!
Send danger from the east unto the west,   195
So honor cross it from the north to south,
And let them grapple. O, the blood more stirs
To rouse a lion than to start a hare!

NORTHUMBERLAND. Imagination of some great exploit
Drives him beyond the bounds of patience.   200

[HOTSPUR.] By heaven, methinks it were an easy leap
To pluck bright honor from the pale-faced moon,
Or dive into the bottom of the deep,
Where fathom-line could never touch the ground,
And pluck up drowned honor by the locks,   205

173. gage: pledge
187. Peace: calm down
196. So: so long as
198. start: startle

So he that doth redeem her thence might wear
Without corrival all her dignities;
But out upon this half-faced fellowship!

WORCESTER. He apprehends a world of figures here,
But not the form of what he should attend.   210
Good cousin, give me audience for a while.

HOTSPUR. I cry you mercy.

WORCESTER.   Those same noble Scots
That are your prisoners—

HOTSPUR.   I'll keep them all!
By God, he shall not have a Scot of them!
No, if a Scot would save his soul, he shall not.   215
I'll keep them, by this hand!

WORCESTER.   You start away
And lend no ear unto my purposes.
Those prisoners you shall keep.

HOTSPUR.   Nay, I will! That's flat!
He said he would not ransom Mortimer,
Forbade my tongue to speak of Mortimer,   220
But I will find him when he lies asleep,
And in his ear I'll holla "Mortimer!"
Nay, I'll have a starling shall be taught to speak
Nothing but "Mortimer," and give it him
To keep his anger still in motion.   225

WORCESTER. Hear you, cousin, a word.

HOTSPUR. All studies here I solemnly defy,
Save how to gall and pinch this Bolingbroke;
And that same sword-and-buckler Prince of Wales,
But that I think his father loves him not   230
And would be glad he met with some mischance,
I would have him poisoned with a pot of ale.

WORCESTER. Farewell, kinsman. I will talk to you
When you are better tempered to attend.

NORTHUMBERLAND. Why, what a wasp-stung and impatient fool   235
Art thou to break into this woman's mood,

208. out upon: an expression of indignation; **half-faced fellowship:**
imperfect partnership
212. **cry you mercy:** beg your pardon
227. **studies:** interests or pleasures; **defy:** reject
229. **sword-and-buckler:** roughneck

Tying thine ear to no tongue but thine own!
HOTSPUR. Why, look you, I am whipped and scourged with rods,
Nettled, and stung with pismires when I hear
Of this vile politician, Bolingbroke.   240
In Richard's time—what do you call the place?—
A plague upon it! it is in Gloucestershire;
'Twas where the madcap duke his uncle kept,
His uncle York—where I first bowed my knee
Unto this king of smiles, this Bolingbroke—   245
'Sblood!—when you and he came back from Ravenspurgh—
NORTHUMBERLAND. At Berkeley Castle.
HOTSPUR. You say true.
Why, what a candy deal of courtesy
This fawning greyhound then did proffer me!   250
Look, "when his infant fortune came to age,"
And "gentle Harry Percy," and "kind cousin"—
O, the devil take such cozeners! God forgive me!
Good uncle, tell your tale, [for] I have done.
WORCESTER. Nay, if you have not, to it again.   255
We will stay your leisure.
HOTSPUR.   I have done, i' faith.
WORCESTER. Then once more to your Scottish prisoners.
Deliver them up without their ransom straight,
And make the Douglas' son your only mean
For powers in Scotland—which, for divers reasons   260
Which I shall send you written, be assured
Will easily be granted. You, my lord, [to NORTHUMBERLAND]
Your son in Scotland being thus employed,
Shall secretly into the bosom creep
Of that same noble prelate well-beloved,   265
The archbishop.
HOTSPUR.   Of York, is it not?
WORCESTER. True; who bears hard
His brother's death at Bristow, the Lord Scroop.

239. pismires: ants
243. kept: lived
249. candy deal: sweet bit
253. cozeners: impostors
256. stay: wait for
268. Lord Scroop: William Scrope, Earl of Wiltshire, executed by
Henry IV in 1399

I speak not this in estimation,
As what I think might be, but what I know   270
Is ruminated, plotted, and set down,
And only stays but to behold the face
Of that occasion that shall bring it on.
HOTSPUR. I smell it. Upon my life, it will do well.
NORTHUMBERLAND. Before the game is afoot thou still let'st slip.   275
HOTSPUR. Why, it cannot choose but be a noble plot.
  And then the power of Scotland and of York
  To join with Mortimer, ha?
WORCESTER.   And so they shall.
HOTSPUR. In faith, it is exceedingly well aimed.
WORCESTER. And 'tis no little reason bids us speed   280
  To save our heads by raising of a head;
  For, bear ourselves as even as we can,
  The king will always think him in our debt,
  And think we think ourselves unsatisfied,
  Till he hath found a time to pay us home.   285
  And see already how he doth begin
  To make us strangers to his looks of love.
HOTSPUR. He does, he does! We'll be revenged on him!
WORCESTER. Cousin, farewell. No further go in this
  Than I by letters shall direct your course.   290
  When time is ripe, which will be suddenly,
  I'll steal to Glendower and Lord Mortimer,
  Where you and Douglas, and our pow'rs at once,
  As I will fashion it, shall happily meet,
  To bear our fortunes in our own strong arms,   295
  Which now we hold at much uncertainty.
NORTHUMBERLAND. Farewell, good brother. We shall thrive, I
      trust.
HOTSPUR. Uncle, adieu. O, let the hours be short
  Till fields and blows and groans applaud our sport!

                                          Exeunt.

274. **smell:** discern or discover
275. **Before . . . slip:** An expression from hunting: the dogs are
loosed before the game is afoot.
281. **head:** armed force
282. **even:** equably
285. **pay us home:** punish us severely
291. **suddenly:** very soon

[ACT II, SCENE I. *Rochester. An inn yard.*]

Enter a CARRIER *with a lantern in his hand.*

1 CARRIER. Heigh-ho! an it be not four by the day, I'll be hanged. Charles' wain is over the new chimney, and yet our horse not packed.—What, ostler!

OSTLER. [*within*] Anon, anon.

1 CARRIER. I prithee, Tom, beat Cut's saddle, put a few flocks 5 in the point. [The] poor jade is wrung in the withers out of all cess.

Enter another CARRIER.

2 CARRIER. Peas and beans are as dank here as a dog, and that is the next way to give poor jades the bots. This house is turned upside down since Robin Ostler died.   10

1 CARRIER. Poor fellow never joyed since the price of oats rose. It was the death of him.

2 CARRIER. I think this be the most villainous house in all London road for fleas. I am stung like a tench.

1 CARRIER. Like a tench? By the mass, there is ne'er a king chris- 15 ten could be better bit than I have been since the first cock.

2 CARRIER. Why, they will allow us ne'er a jordan, and then we leak in your chimney, and your chamber-lye breeds fleas like a loach.

1 CARRIER. What, ostler! come away and be hanged! come away! 20

s.d. **Carrier:** a transporter of goods
1. **four by the day:** four A. M.
2. **Charles' wain:** the constellation *Ursa Major*
3. **ostler:** groom
4. **Anon:** right away
5. **flocks:** tufts of wool (for padding)
6. **point:** part of the saddle; **jade:** worn-out horse; **wrung:** galled; **withers:** the juncture of the shoulder-bones and neck
6–7. **out . . . cess:** beyond measure
9. **next:** nearest; **bots:** worms
14. **tench:** a fish with red spots
15. **By the mass:** an oath
16. **first cock:** midnight
17. **jordan:** chamberpot
18. **chamber-lye:** urine
19. **loach:** a prolific fish

2 CARRIER. I have a gammon of bacon and two razes of ginger, to be delivered as far as Charing Cross.

1 CARRIER. God's body! the turkeys in my pannier are quite starved. What, ostler! A plague on thee! hast thou never an eye in thy head? Canst not hear? An 'twere not as good deed 25 as drink to break the pate on thee, I am a very villain. Come, and be hanged! Hast no faith in thee?

Enter GADSHILL.

GADSHILL. Good morrow, carriers. What's o'clock?

1 CARRIER. I think it be two o'clock.

GADSHILL. I prithee lend me thy lantern to see my gelding in the 30 stable.

1 CARRIER. Nay, by God, soft! I know a trick worth two of that, i' faith.

GADSHILL. I pray thee lend me thine.

2 CARRIER. Ay, when? canst tell? Lend me thy lantern, quoth he? 35 Marry, I'll see thee hanged first!

GADSHILL. Sirrah carrier, what time do you mean to come to London?

2 CARRIER. Time enough to go to bed with a candle, I warrant thee. Come, neighbor Mugs, we'll call up the gentlemen. They 40 will along with company, for they have great charge.

Exeunt [CARRIERS].

Enter CHAMBERLAIN.

GADSHILL. What, ho! chamberlain!

CHAMBERLAIN. At hand, quoth pickpurse.

GADSHILL. That's even as fair as "at hand, quoth the chamberlain"; for thou variest no more from picking of purses than giv- 45 ing direction doth from laboring; thou layest the plot how.

21. gammon: haunch; razes: roots
22. Charing Cross: i.e., the village of Charing, between London and Westminster
23. pannier: basket
26. pate: head
41. charge: baggage
42. chamberlain: room attendant at an inn
43. At hand . . . pickpurse: a proverbial expression, "near at hand"
44. even: just; fair: plausible

CHAMBERLAIN. Good morrow, Master Gadshill. It holds current
that I told you yesternight. There's a franklin in the Wild of
Kent hath brought three hundred marks with him in gold. I
heard him tell it to one of his company last night at supper; a 50
kind of auditor, one that hath abundance of charge too, God
knows what. They are up already and call for eggs and butter.
They will away presently.

GADSHILL. Sirrah, if they meet not with Saint Nicholas' clerks, I'll
give thee this neck.   55

CHAMBERLAIN. No, I'll none of it. I pray thee keep that for the
hangman; for I know thou worshippest Saint Nicholas as truly
as a man of falsehood may.

GADSHILL. What talkest thou to me of the hangman? If I hang,
I'll make a fat pair of gallows; for if I hang, old Sir John hangs 60
with me, and thou knowest he is no starveling. Tut! there are
other Trojans that thou dream'st not of, the which for sport
sake are content to do the profession some grace; that would,
if matters should be looked into, for their own credit sake
make all whole. I am joined with no foot land-rakers, no long- 65
staff six-penny strikers, none of these mad mustachio purple-
hued maltworms; but with nobility and tranquillity, burgomasters and great oneyers, such as can hold in, such as will strike
sooner than speak, and speak sooner than drink, and drink
sooner than pray; and yet, 'zounds, I lie; for they pray con- 70
tinually to their saint, the commonwealth, or rather, not pray
to her, but prey on her, for they ride up and down on her and
make her their boots.

CHAMBERLAIN. What, the commonwealth their boots? Will she
hold out water in foul way?   75

47. **holds current:** remains true
48. **franklin:** a landowner; **Wild:** weald, open country
49. **mark:** the equivalent of 13 shillings 4 pence
53. **presently:** right away
54. **Saint Nicholas' clerks:** highwaymen
62. **Trojans:** good fellows
65. **foot land-rakers:** highwaymen
66. **sixpenny strikers:** petty thieves
67. **maltworms:** topers
68. **oneyers:** ones; **hold in:** keep counsel
73. **boots:** spoils
75. **foul way:** muddy roads

GADSHILL. She will, she will! Justice hath liquored her. We steal
as in a castle, cocksure; we have the receipt of fernseed, we
walk invisible.

CHAMBERLAIN. Nay, by my faith, I think you are more beholding
to the night than to fernseed for your walking invisible.   80

GADSHILL. Give me thy hand. Thou shalt have a share in our purchase, as I am a true man.

CHAMBERLAIN. Nay, rather let me have it, as you are a false thief.

GADSHILL. Go to; *homo* is a common name to all men. Bid the
ostler bring my gelding out of the stable. Farewell, you muddy   85
knave.   [*Exeunt.*]

[SCENE II. *The Highway, near Gadshill.*]

Enter PRINCE, POINS, PETO, *and* [BARDOLPH].

POINS. Come, shelter, shelter! I have removed Falstaff's horse, and
he frets like a gummed velvet.

PRINCE. Stand close.   [*They step back.*]

Enter FALSTAFF.

FALSTAFF. Poins! Poins, and be hanged! Poins!

PRINCE. [*coming forward*] Peace, ye fat-kidneyed rascal! What a   5
brawling dost thou keep!

FALSTAFF. Where's Poins, Hal?

PRINCE. He is walked up to the top of the hill; I'll go seek him.
                                              [*Steps aside.*]

FALSTAFF. I am accursed to rob in that thief's company. The rascal hath removed my horse and tied him I know not where. If   10
I travel but four foot by the squire further afoot, I shall break
my wind. Well, I doubt not but to die a fair death for all this,
if I 'scape hanging for killing that rogue. I have forsworn his
company hourly any time this two and twenty years, and yet I
am bewitched with the rogue's company. If the rascal have not   15

76. **liquored:** water-proofed
77. **in a castle:** i.e., in safety; **receipt:** recipe; **fernseed:** It was popu-
larly believed that fernseed could render one invisible.
81. **purchase:** booty
85. **muddy:** dull
2. **frets . . . velvet:** Gum used to stiffen velvet peeled off ("fretted")
when it became hardened.
11. **squire:** rule

given me medicines to make me love him, I'll be hanged. It
could not be else; I have drunk medicines. Poins! Hal! A
plague upon you both! Bardolph! Peto! I'll starve ere I'll rob
a foot further. An 'twere not as good a deed as drink to turn
true man and to leave these rogues, I am the veriest varlet that 20
ever chewed with a tooth. Eight yards of uneven ground is
threescore and ten miles afoot with me, and the stony-hearted
villains know it well enough. A plague upon it when thieves
cannot be true one to another! (*They whistle.*) Whew! A
plague upon you all! Give me my horse, you rogues! give me 25
my horse and be hanged!

PRINCE. [*coming forward*] Peace, ye fat-guts! Lie down, lay thine
ear close to the ground, and list if thou canst hear the tread of
travellers.

FALSTAFF. Have you any levers to lift me up again, being down? 30
'Sblood, I'll not bear mine own flesh so far afoot again for all
the coin in thy father's exchequer. What a plague mean ye to
colt me thus?

PRINCE. Thou liest; thou art not colted, thou art uncolted.

FALSTAFF. I prithee, good Prince Hal, help me to my horse, good 35
king's son.

PRINCE. Out, ye rogue! Shall I be your ostler?

FALSTAFF. Hang thyself in thine own heir-apparent garters! If I
be ta'en, I'll peach for this. An I have not ballads made on you
all, and sung to filthy tunes, let a cup of sack be my poison. 40
When a jest is so forward, and afoot too, I hate it.

Enter GADSHILL.

GADSHILL. Stand!

FALSTAFF. So I do, against my will.

POINS. [*coming forward*] O, 'tis our setter; I know his voice.

BARDOLPH. What news? 45

GADSHILL. Case ye, case ye! On with your vizards! There's money

16. **medicines:** love potions
20. **veriest:** in the most extreme degree; **varlet:** rascal
33. **colt:** trick
38. **Hang . . . garters:** an adaptation of a proverbial expression
39. **peach:** turn king's evidence
44. **setter:** one who decoys persons to be robbed
46. **Case ye:** put on your disguises

of the king's coming down the hill; 'tis going to the king's exchequer.

FALSTAFF. You lie, ye rogue! 'Tis going to the king's tavern.

GADSHILL. There's enough to make us all.   50

FALSTAFF. To be hanged.

PRINCE. Sirs, you four shall front them in the narrow lane; Ned Poins and I will walk lower. If they 'scape from your encounter, then they light on us.

PETO. How many be there of them?   55

GADSHILL. Some eight or ten.

FALSTAFF. 'Zounds! will they not rob us?

PRINCE. What, a coward, Sir John Paunch?

FALSTAFF. Indeed, I am not John of Gaunt, your grandfather, but yet no coward, Hal.   60

PRINCE. Well, we leave that to the proof.

POINS. Sirrah Jack, thy horse stands behind the hedge; when thou need'st him, there thou shalt find him. Farewell and stand fast.

FALSTAFF. Now cannot I strike him, if I should be hanged.

PRINCE. [aside to POINS] Ned, where are our disguises?   65

POINS. [aside to PRINCE] Here, hard by. Stand close.

[Exeunt PRINCE and POINS.]

FALSTAFF. Now, my masters, happy man be his dole, say I. Every man to his business.

Enter the TRAVELLERS.

TRAVELLER. Come, neighbor. The boy shall lead our horses down the hill; we'll walk afoot awhile and ease our legs.   70

THIEVES. Stand!

TRAVELLER. Jesus bless us!

FALSTAFF. Strike! down with them! cut the villains' throats! Ah, whoreson caterpillars! bacon-fed knaves! they hate us youth. Down with them! Fleece them!   75

TRAVELLER. O, we are undone, both we and ours for ever!

FALSTAFF. Hang ye, gorbellied knaves, are ye undone? No, ye fat chuffs; I would your store were here! On, bacons, on! What,

66. **hard:** near
67. **happy . . . dole:** good luck
74. **whoreson:** bastard; **caterpillars:** parasites
77. **gorbellied:** fat-paunched
78. **chuffs:** churls; **store:** possessions; **bacons:** fat men

ye knaves! young men must live. You are grandjurors, are ye?
We'll jure ye, 'faith!   80

> *Here they rob them and bind them. Exeunt.*

Enter the PRINCE *and* POINS [*in buckram*].

PRINCE. The thieves have bound the true men. Now could thou
and I rob the thieves and go merrily to London, it would be
argument for a week, laughter for a month, and a good jest for
ever.

POINS. Stand close! I hear them coming.   85

> *Enter the* THIEVES *again.*

FALSTAFF. Come, my masters, let us share, and then to horse before day. An the prince and Poins be not two arrant cowards,
there's no equity stirring. There's no more valor in that Poins
than in a wild duck.

PRINCE. Your money! ⎧ *As they are sharing, the* PRINCE *and*
                      ⎪ POINS *set upon them. They all run*   90
POINS. Villains!   ⎨ *away, and* FALSTAFF, *after a blow or*
                      ⎪ *two, runs away too, leaving the booty*
                      ⎩ *behind them.*

PRINCE. Got with much ease. Now merrily to horse. The thieves
are all scattered, and possessed with fear so strongly that they
dare not meet each other; each takes his fellow for an officer.
Away, good Ned. Falstaff sweats to death and lards the lean   95
earth as he walks along. Were't not for laughing, I should pity
him.

POINS. How the [fat] rogue roared!   *Exeunt.*

[SCENE III. *Warkworth Castle.*]

Enter HOTSPUR *solus, reading a letter.*

HOTSPUR. "But, for mine own part, my lord, I could be well contented to be there, in respect of the love I bear your house."

79. **grandjurors:** people of sufficient importance to be selected as jurors
83. **argument:** subject for conversation
87. **arrant:** out-and-out
88. **equity:** impartiality
S.D. *solus:* alone
2. **house:** family

He could be contented: why is he not then? In respect of the
love he bears our house! He shows in this he loves his own
barn better than he loves our house. Let me see some more.   5
"The purpose you undertake is dangerous"—why, that's certain! 'Tis dangerous to take a cold, to sleep, to drink; but I tell
you, my lord fool, out of this nettle, danger, we pluck this
flower, safety. "The purpose you undertake is dangerous, the
friends you have named uncertain, the time itself unsorted,   10
and your whole plot too light for the counterpoise of so
great an opposition." Say you so, say you so? I say unto you
again, you are a shallow, cowardly hind, and you lie. What a
lack-brain is this! By the Lord, our plot is a good plot as ever
was laid; our friends true and constant: a good plot, good   15
friends, and full of expectation; an excellent plot, very good
friends. What a frosty-spirited rogue is this! Why, my Lord of
York commends the plot and the general course of the action.
'Zounds, an I were now by this rascal, I could brain him with
his lady's fan! Is there not my father, my uncle, and myself;   20
Lord Edmund Mortimer, my Lord of York, and Owen Glendower? Is there not, besides, the Douglas? Have I not all their
letters to meet me in arms by the ninth of the next month,
and are they not some of them set forward already? What a
pagan rascal is this! an infidel! Ha! you shall see now, in very   25
sincerity of fear and cold heart, will he to the king and lay
open all our proceedings. O, I could divide myself and go to
buffets for moving such a dish of skim milk with so honorable
an action! Hang him, let him tell the king! We are prepared.
I will set forward to-night.   30

Enter his LADY.

How now, Kate? I must leave you within these two hours.
LADY. O my good lord, why are you thus alone?
For what offense have I this fortnight been
A banished woman from my Harry's bed?
Tell me, sweet lord, what is't that takes from thee   35

10. **unsorted**: ill-chosen
13. **hind**: rustic
17. **Lord of York**: Archbishop of York
27–28. **divide . . . buffets**: strike myself

Thy stomach, pleasure, and thy golden sleep?
Why dost thou bend thine eyes upon the earth,
And start so often when thou sit'st alone?
Why hast thou lost the fresh blood in thy cheeks
And given my treasures and my rights of thee   40
To thick-eyed musing and cursed melancholy?
In thy faint slumbers I by thee have watched,
And heard thee murmur tales of iron wars,
Speak terms of manage to thy bounding steed,
Cry "Courage! to the field!" And thou hast talked   45
Of sallies and retires, of trenches, tents,
Of palisadoes, frontiers, parapets,
Of basilisks, of cannon, culverin,
Of prisoners' ransom, and of soldiers slain,
And all the currents of a heady fight.   50
Thy spirit within thee hath been so at war,
And thus hath so bestirred thee in thy sleep,
That beads of sweat have stood upon thy brow
Like bubbles in a late-disturbed stream,
And in thy face strange motions have appeared,   55
Such as we see when men restrain their breath
On some great sudden hest. O, what portents are these?
Some heavy business hath my lord in hand,
And I must know it, else he loves me not.

HOTSPUR. What, ho!

[Enter a SERVANT.]

                       Is Gilliams with the packet gone? 60
SERVANT. He is, my lord, an hour ago.
HOTSPUR. Hath Butler brought those horses from the sheriff?
SERVANT. One horse, my lord, he brought even now.

36. **stomach**: appetite
41. **thick-eyed**: dim-sighted
42. **faint**: light
47. **palisadoes**: fences made of stakes; **frontiers**: outlying defenses;
parapets: walls
48. **basilisks . . . culverin**: cannons
50. **currents**: tides; **heady**: violent
57. **hest**: determination
58. **heavy**: serious
60. **packet**: parcel of letters

HOTSPUR. What horse? [A] roan, a crop-ear, is it not?

SERVANT. It is, my lord.

HOTSPUR.   That roan shall be my throne.   65

    Well, I will back him straight. O esperance!

    Bid Butler lead him forth into the park.

                                 [*Exit* SERVANT.]

LADY. But hear you, my lord.

HOTSPUR. What say'st thou, my lady?

LADY. What is it carries you away?   70

HOTSPUR. Why, my horse, my love, my horse!

LADY. Out, you mad-headed ape!

    A weasel hath not such a deal of spleen

    As you are tossed with. In faith,

    I'll know your business, Harry; that I will!   75

    I fear my brother Mortimer doth stir

    About his title and hath sent for you

    To line his enterprise; but if you go—

HOTSPUR. So far afoot, I shall be weary, love.

LADY. Come, come, you paraquito, answer me   80

    Directly unto this question that I ask.

    In faith, I'll break thy little finger, Harry,

    An if thou wilt not tell me all things true.

HOTSPUR. Away, away, you trifler! Love? I love thee not;

    I care not for thee, Kate. This is no world   85

    To play with mammets and to tilt with lips.

    We must have bloody noses and cracked crowns,

    And pass them current too. God's me, my horse!

    What say'st thou, Kate? What wouldst thou have with me?

LADY. Do you not love me? do you not indeed?   90

    Well, do not then, for since you love me not,

---

66. esperance: hope (part of the Percy family motto: *Espérance en dieu*)

73. spleen: caprice

74. tossed with: agitated by

76. stir: cause commotion

78. line: strengthen

80. paraquito: small parrot

86. mammets: puppets

87. crowns: (1) heads (2) gold coins worth 5 shillings

88. pass them current: place them in circulation; God's me: God save me

I will not love myself. Do you not love me?
Nay, tell me if you speak in jest or no.
HOTSPUR. Come, wilt thou see me ride?
And when I am a-horseback, I will swear 95
I love thee infinitely. But hark you, Kate:
I must not have you henceforth question me
Whither I go, nor reason whereabout.
Whither I must, I must, and to conclude,
This evening must I leave you, gentle Kate. 100
I know you wise, but yet no farther wise
Than Harry Percy's wife; constant you are,
But yet a woman; and for secrecy,
No lady closer, for I well believe
Thou wilt not utter what thou dost not know, 105
And so far will I trust thee, gentle Kate.
LADY. How! so far?
HOTSPUR. Not an inch further. But hark you, Kate:
Whither I go, thither shall you go too;
To-day will I set forth, to-morrow you. 110
Will this content you, Kate?
LADY.   It must of force.   Exeunt.

[SCENE IV. *The Boar's Head Tavern in Eastcheap.*]

Enter PRINCE *and* POINS.

PRINCE. Ned, prithee, come out of that fat room and lend me
thy hand to laugh a little.
POINS. Where hast been, Hal?
PRINCE. With three or four loggerheads amongst three or four-
score hogsheads. I have sounded the very bass-string of hu- 5
mility. Sirrah, I am sworn brother to a leash of drawers and
can call them all by their christen names, as Tom, Dick, and
Francis. They take it already upon their salvation that, though
I be but Prince of Wales, yet I am the king of courtesy, and

111. of force: of necessity
1. fat: stuffy
4. loggerheads: blockheads
5. bass-string: i.e., the lowest degree
6. leash: three (the usual number of hounds coupled to one leash);
drawers: tapsters

tell me flatly I am no proud Jack like Falstaff, but a Corin-   10
thian, a lad of mettle, a good boy (by the Lord, so they call
me!), and when I am King of England I shall command all
the good lads in Eastcheap. They call drinking deep, dyeing
scarlet; and when you breathe in your watering, they cry
"hem!" and bid you play it off. To conclude, I am so good a   15
proficient in one quarter of an hour that I can drink with any
tinker in his own language during my life. I tell thee, Ned,
thou hast lost much honor that thou wert not with me in this
action. But, sweet Ned—to sweeten which name of Ned, I
give thee this pennyworth of sugar, clapped even now into   20
my hand by an under-skinker, one that never spake other
English in his life than "Eight shillings and sixpence," and
"You are welcome," with this shrill addition, "Anon, anon,
sir! Score a pint of bastard in the Half-moon," or so. But,
Ned to drive away the time till Falstaff come, I prithee do   25
thou stand in some by-room while I question my puny drawer
to what end he gave me the sugar; and do thou never leave
calling "Francis!" that his tale to me may be nothing but
"Anon!" Step aside, and I'll show thee a precedent.

POINS. Francis!   30
PRINCE. Thou art perfect.
POINS. Francis!   [Exit POINS.]

Enter [FRANCIS, *the*] DRAWER.

FRANCIS. Anon, anon, sir. Look down into the Pomgarnet, Ralph.
PRINCE. Come hither, Francis.
FRANCIS. My lord?   35
PRINCE. How long hast thou to serve, Francis?

10. **Corinthian:** gay fellow
13–14. **drinking . . . scarlet:** J. Dover Wilson (ed. 1946) notes that
the urine of topers was used in making scarlet dyes.
14. **breathe . . . watering:** take a breath while drinking
15. **play it off:** drink up
21. **under-skinker:** tapster
24. **Score:** charge; **bastard:** sweet Spanish wine; **Half-moon:** the name
of a room in the inn
26. **by-room:** private room; **puny:** novice
29. **precedent:** illustration
33. **Pomgarnet:** the Pomegranate, the name of another room
36. **serve:** i.e., as an apprentice

FRANCIS. Forsooth, five years, and as much as to—

POINS. [*within*] Francis!

FRANCIS. Anon, anon, sir.

PRINCE. Five year! by'r Lady, a long lease for the clinking of 40
pewter. But, Francis, darest thou be so valiant as to play the
coward with thy indenture and show it a fair pair of heels and
run from it?

FRANCIS. O Lord, sir, I'll be sworn upon all the books in England
I could find in my heart—   45

POINS. [*within*] Francis!

FRANCIS. Anon, sir.

PRINCE. How old art thou, Francis?

FRANCIS. Let me see—about Michaelmas next I shall be—

POINS. [*within*] Francis!   50

FRANCIS. Anon, sir. Pray stay a little, my lord.

PRINCE. Nay, but hark you, Francis: for the sugar thou gavest
me—'twas a pennyworth, was't not?

FRANCIS. O Lord, I would it had been two!

PRINCE. I will give thee for it a thousand pound. Ask me when 55
thou wilt, and thou shalt have it.

POINS. [*within*] Francis!

FRANCIS. Anon, anon.

PRINCE. Anon, Francis? No, Francis; but to-morrow, Francis; or,
Francis, a Thursday; or indeed, Francis, when thou wilt. But, 60
Francis—

FRANCIS. My lord?

PRINCE. Wilt thou rob this leathern-jerkin, crystal-button, not-
pated, agate-ring, puke-stocking, caddis-garter, smooth-tongue,
Spanish-pouch—   65

FRANCIS. O Lord, sir, who do you mean?

PRINCE. Why then, your brown bastard is your only drink; for
look you, Francis, your white canvas doublet will sully. In
Barbary, sir, it cannot come to so much.

42. **indenture:** a contract between an apprentice and his master
49. **Michaelmas:** September 29
63–65. **rob . . . Spanish-pouch:** i.e., steal from the innkeeper
63. **not-pated:** short-haired; **puke:** woolen
64. **caddis:** worsted tape
65. **Spanish-pouch:** a pouch made of Spanish leather
67–69. The obscurity of these lines was probably intended by Hal
further to confuse Francis.

FRANCIS. What, sir?   70
POINS. [*within*] Francis!
PRINCE. Away, you rogue! Dost thou not hear them call?

Here they both call him. The DRAWER *stands amazed,
not knowing which way to go.*

Enter VINTNER.

VINTNER. What! stand'st thou still, and hear'st such a calling?
[Lo]ok to the guests within. [*Exit* FRANCIS.] My lord, old Sir
John, with half-a-dozen more, are at the door. Shall I let   75
them in?
PRINCE. Let them alone awhile, and then open the door. [*Exit*
VINTNER.] Poins!
POINS. [*within*] Anon, anon, sir.

Enter POINS.

PRINCE. Sirrah, Falstaff and the rest of the thieves are at the   80
door. Shall we be merry?
POINS. As merry as crickets, my lad. But hark ye; what cunning
match have you made with this jest of the drawer? Come,
what's the issue?
PRINCE. I am now of all humors that have showed themselves   85
humors since the old days of goodman Adam to the pupil age
of this present twelve o'clock at midnight.

[*Enter* FRANCIS.]

What's o'clock, Francis?
FRANCIS. Anon, anon, sir.   [*Exit.*]
PRINCE. That ever this fellow should have fewer words than a   90
parrot, and yet the son of a woman! His industry is upstairs and
and downstairs, his eloquence the parcel of a reckoning. I am
not yet of Percy's mind, the Hotspur of the North, he that
kills me some six or seven dozen of Scots at a breakfast,
washes his hands, and says to his wife, "Fie upon this quiet   95
life! I want work." "O my sweet Harry," says she, "how many

85–87. I am now . . . midnight: "I am willing to indulge myself in
gayety and frolick, and try all the varieties of human life" (Johnson).
86. pupil age: youth

hast thou killed to-day?" "Give my roan horse a drench,"
says he, and answers, "Some fourteen," an hour after; "a trifle,
a trifle." I prithee call in Falstaff. I'll play Percy, and that
damned brawn shall play Dame Mortimer his wife. "Rivo!" 100
says the drunkard. Call in ribs, call in tallow.

Enter FALSTAFF, [GADSHILL, BARDOLPH, *and* PETO;
followed by FRANCIS *with wine*].

POINS. Welcome, Jack! Where hast thou been?
FALSTAFF. A plague of all cowards, I say, and a vengeance too!
Marry and amen! Give me a cup of sack, boy. Ere I lead this
life long, I'll sew netherstocks, and mend them and foot them 105
too. A plague of all cowards! Give me a cup of sack, rogue.
Is there no virtue extant?   *He drinketh*
PRINCE. Didst thou never see Titan kiss a dish of butter, pitiful-
hearted Titan, that melted at the sweet tale of the sun's? If
thou didst, then behold that compound.   110
FALSTAFF. You rogue, here's lime in this sack too! There is nothing but roguery to be found in villainous man; yet a coward
is worse than a cup of sack with lime in it—a villainous coward! Go thy ways, old Jack, die when thou wilt; if manhood, good manhood, be not forgot upon the fact of the earth, 115
then am I a shotten herring. There lives not three good men
unhanged in England; and one of them is fat and grows old.
God help the while! A bad world, I say. I would I were a
weaver; I could sing psalms or anything. A plague of all cowards, I say still!   120
PRINCE. How now, wool-sack? What mutter you?
FALSTAFF. A king's son! If I do not beat thee out of thy kingdom with a dagger of lath and drive all thy subjects afore thee

97. **drench:** dose of medicine
100. **brawn:** boar; **Rivo:** probably a drinker's exclamation
103. **of:** on
105. **netherstocks:** stockings
108. **Titan:** the sun
110. **compound:** mass
111. **lime:** added to clarify the wine
116. **shotten herring:** a herring that has shed its roe (and is thus thin)
118. **the while:** the present time
119. **weaver . . . psalms:** Weavers were noted for their singing while
working at their looms.
123. **dagger of lath:** an imitation weapon

like a flock of wild geese, I'll never wear hair on my face more.
You Prince of Wales!   125

PRINCE. Why, you whoreson round man, what's the matter?

FALSTAFF. Are not you a coward? Answer me to that, and Poins
there?

POINS. 'Zounds, ye fat paunch, an ye call me coward, by the Lord,
I'll stab thee.   130

FALSTAFF. I call thee coward? I'll see thee damned ere I call
thee coward, but I would give a thousand pound I could run
as fast as thou canst. You are straight enough in the shoulders;
you care not who sees your back. Call you that backing of
your friends? A plague upon such backing! Give me them that   135
will face me. Give me a cup of sack. I am a rogue if I drunk
to-day.

PRINCE. O villain! thy lips are scarce wiped since thou drunk'st
last.

FALSTAFF. All is one for that. (*He drinketh.*) A plague of all   140
cowards, still say I.

PRINCE. What's the matter?

FALSTAFF. What's the matter? There be four of us here have
ta'en a thousand pound this day morning.

PRINCE. Where is it, Jack? where is it?   145

FALSTAFF. Where is it? Taken from us it is. A hundred upon poor
four of us!

PRINCE. What, a hundred, man?

FALSTAFF. I am a rogue if I were not at half-sword with a dozen
of them two hours together. I have 'scaped by miracle. I   150
am eight times thrust through the doublet, four through the
hose; my buckler cut through and through, my sword hacked
like a handsaw—*ecce signum!* [*Shows his sword.*] I never
dealt better since I was a man. All would not do. A plague of
all cowards! Let them speak. If they speak more or less than   155
truth, they are villains and the sons of darkness.

PRINCE. Speak, sirs. How was it?

GADSHILL. We four set upon some dozen—

149. **at half-sword:** at close quarters
151. **doublet:** close-fitting body garment
152. **hose:** breeches; **buckler:** shield
153. *ecce signum:* behold the sign
154. **dealt:** fought

FALSTAFF. Sixteen at least, my lord.

GADSHILL. And bound them.   160

PETO. No, no, they were not bound.

FALSTAFF. You rogue, they were bound, every man of them, or
I am a Jew else, an Ebrew Jew.

GADSHILL. As we were sharing, some six or seven fresh men set
upon us—   165

FALSTAFF. And unbound the rest, and then come in the other.

PRINCE. What, fought you with them all?

FALSTAFF. All? I know not what you call all, but if I fought not
with fifty of them, I am a bunch of radish! If there were not
two or three and fifty upon poor old Jack, then am I no two- 170
legged creature.

PRINCE. Pray God you have not murdered some of them.

FALSTAFF. Nay, that's past praying for. I have peppered two of
them. Two I am sure I have paid, two rogues in buckram
suits. I tell thee what, Hal, if I tell thee a lie, spit in my face, 175
call me horse. Thou knowest my old ward. Here I lay, and
thus I bore my boint. Four rogues in buckram let drive at me.

PRINCE. What, four? Thou saidst but two even now.

FALSTAFF. Four, Hal. I told thee four.

POINS. Ay, ay, he said four.   180

FALSTAFF. These four came all afront and mainly thrust at me.
I made me no more ado but took all their seven points in my
target, thus.

PRINCE. Seven? Why, there were but four even now.

FALSTAFF. In buckram?   185

POINS. Ay, four, in buckram suits.

FALSTAFF. Seven, by these hilts, or I am a villain else.

PRINCE. [aside to POINS] Prithee let him alone. We shall have
more anon.

FALSTAFF. Dost thou hear me, Hal?   190

170. **three and fifty:** G. R. Stewart has noted that fifty-three was the
number of Spanish ships against which the *Revenge* heroically fought in
1591.

173. **peppered:** made it hot for

174. **paid:** killed

176. **horse:** a term of abuse; **ward:** fighting posture

183. **target:** shield

187. **by these hilts:** Falstaff swears by the cross-like shape made by
the handle and blade of his sword

PRINCE. Ay, and mark thee too, Jack.

FALSTAFF. Do so, for it is worth the listening to. These nine in
buckram that I told thee of—

PRINCE. So, two more already.

FALSTAFF. Their points being broken—   195

POINS. Down fell their hose.

FALSTAFF. Began to give me ground; but I followed me close,
came in, foot and hand, and with a thought seven of the eleven
I paid.

PRINCE. O monstrous! Eleven buckram men grown out of two!   200

FALSTAFF. But, as the devil would have it, three misbegotten
knaves in Kendal green came at my back and let drive at me,
for it was so dark, Hal, that thou couldst not see thy hand.

PRINCE. These lies are like their father that begets them—gross
as a mountain, open, palpable. Why, thou clay-brained guts,   205
thou knotty-pated fool, thou whoreson, obscene, greasy tallow-
catch—

FALSTAFF. What, art thou mad? art thou mad? Is not the truth
the truth?

PRINCE. Why, how couldst thou know these men in Kendal green   210
when it was so dark thou couldst not see thy hand? Come, tell
us your reason. What sayest thou to this?

POINS. Come, your reason, Jack, your reason.

FALSTAFF. What, upon compulsion? 'Zounds, an I were at the
strappado or all the racks in the world, I would not tell you 215
on compulsion. Give you a reason on compulsion? If reasons
were as plentiful as blackberries, I would give no man a reason
upon compulsion, I.

PRINCE. I'll be no longer guilty of this sin. This sanguine coward,
this bed-presser, this horseback-breaker, this huge hill of   220
flesh—

FALSTAFF. 'Sblood, you starveling, you eel-skin, you dried neat's-
tongue, you bull's pizzle, you stockfish! O for breath to utter
what is like thee! you tailor's yard, you sheath, you bowcase,

195. **points:** (1) sword-points (2) laces supporting the hose
206. **knotty-pated:** thick headed; **tallow-catch:** tub of tallow
212. **reason:** explanation
215. **strappado:** a torture machine
219. **sanguine:** red-faced
220. **bed-presser:** lazy fellow
223. **stockfish:** dried cod

you vile standing tuck!   225

PRINCE. Well, breathe awhile, and then to it again; and when
thou hast tired thyself in base comparisons, hear me speak
but this.

POINS. Mark, Jack.

PRINCE. We two saw you four set on four, and bound them and   230
were masters of their wealth. Mark now, how a plain tale shall
put you down. Then did we two set on you four and, with a
word, outfaced you from your prize, and have it; yea, and can
show it you here in the house. And, Falstaff, you carried your
guts away as nimbly, with as quick dexterity, and roared for   235
mercy, and still run and roared, as ever I heard bullcalf. What
a slave art thou to hack thy sword as thou hast done, and then
say it was in fight! What trick, what device, what starting hole
canst thou now find out to hide thee from this open and apparent shame?   240

POINS. Come, let's hear, Jack. What trick hast thou now?

FALSTAFF. By the Lord, I knew ye as well as he that made ye.
Why, hear you, my masters: Was it for me to kill the heir apparent? Should I turn upon the true prince? Why, thou knowest
I am as valiant as Hercules, but beware instinct. The lion will   245
not touch the true prince. Instinct is a great matter. I was
now a coward on instinct. I shall think the better of myself,
and thee, during my life; I for a valiant lion, and thou for a
true prince. But, by the Lord, lads, I am glad you have the
money. Hostess, clap to the doors. Watch to-night, pray to-   250
morrow. Gallants, lads, boys, hearts of gold, all the titles of
good fellowship come to you! What, shall we be merry? Shall
we have a play extempore?

PRINCE. Content—and the argument shall be thy running away.

FALSTAFF. Ah, no more of that, Hal, an thou lovest me!   255

Enter HOSTESS.

HOSTESS. O Jesu, my lord the Prince!

PRINCE. How now, my lady the hostess! What say'st thou to me?

225. **tuck:** rapier
233. **outfaced:** frightened
238. **starting hole:** loophole, escape
250–51. **watch . . . to-morrow:** Cf. Matthew 26:41: "Watch **and**
pray, that ye enter not into temptation. . . ."
254. **argument:** subject

HOSTESS. Marry, my lord, there is a noble man of the court at
door would speak with you. He says he comes from your father.

PRINCE. Give him as much as will make him a royal man, and 260
send him back again to my mother.

FALSTAFF. What manner of man is he?

HOSTESS. An old man.

FALSTAFF. What doth gravity out of his bed at midnight? Shall
I give him his answer?   265

PRINCE. Prithee do, Jack.

FALSTAFF. Faith, and I'll send him packing.   *Exit.*

PRINCE. Now, sirs, by'r Lady, you fought fair; so did you, Peto; so
did you, Bardolph. You are lions too: you ran away upon instinct, you will not touch the true prince; no, fie!   270

BARDOLPH. Faith, I ran when I saw others run.

PRINCE. Tell me now in earnest, how came Falstaff's sword so
hacked?

PETO. Why, he hacked it with his dagger, and said he would
swear truth out of England but he would make you believe 275
it was done in fight, and persuaded us to do the like.

BARDOLPH. Yea, and to tickle our noses with speargrass to make
them bleed, and then to beslubber our garments with it and
swear it was the blood of true men. I did that I did not this
seven year before. I blushed to hear his monstrous devices. 280

PRINCE. O villain! thou stolest a cup of sack eighteen years ago
and wert taken with the manner, and ever since thou hast
blushed extempore. Thou hadst fire and sword on thy side,
and yet thou ran'st away. What instinct hadst thou for it?

BARDOLPH. My lord, do you see these meteors? [*pointing to his* 285
own face] Do you behold these exhalations?

PRINCE. I do.

BARDOLPH. What think you they portend?

PRINCE. Hot livers and cold purses.

BARDOLPH. Choler, my lord, if rightly taken.   290

Enter FALSTAFF.

258–260. **noble . . . royal:** puns on court terms and names of coins:
noble (6s.8d) and royal (10s)

282. **wert . . . manner:** caught in the act

285–86. Bardolph is describing the eruptions on his face.

289. **Hot . . . purses:** drunkenness and poverty

290. **Choler:** anger

PRINCE. No, if rightly taken, halter. Here comes lean Jack; here comes bare-bone. How now, my sweet creature of bombast? How long is't ago, Jack, since thou sawest thine own knee?

FALSTAFF. My own knee? When I was about thy years, Hal, I was not an eagle's talon in the waist; I could have crept into 295 any alderman's thumb-ring. A plague of sighing and grief! It blows a man up like a bladder. There's villainous news abroad. Here was Sir John Bracy from your father. You must to the court in the morning. That same mad fellow of the north, Percy, and he of Wales that gave Amamon the bastinado, and 300 made Lucifer cuckold, and swore the devil his true liegeman upon the cross of a Welsh hook—what a plague call you him?

POINS. Owen Glendower.

FALSTAFF. Owen, Owen, the same; and his son-in-law Mortimer, and old Northumberland, and that sprightly Scot of Scots, 305 Douglas, that runs a-horseback up a hill perpendicular—

PRINCE. He that rides at high speed and with his pistol kills a sparrow flying.

FALSTAFF. You have hit it.

PRINCE. So did he never the sparrow.   310

FALSTAFF. Well, that rascal hath good metal in him; he will not run.

PRINCE. Why, what a rascal art thou then, to praise him so for running!

FALSTAFF. A-horseback, ye cuckoo! but afoot he will not budge 315 a foot.

PRINCE. Yes, Jack, upon instinct.

FALSTAFF. I grant ye, upon instinct. Well, he is there too, and one Mordake, and a thousand bluecaps more. Worcester is stolen away to-night; thy father's beard is turned white with 320 the news; you may buy land now as cheap as stinking mackerel.

PRINCE. Why then, it is like, if there come a hot June, and this

291. **taken**: (1) construed (2) apprehended; **halter**: the hangman's noose, i.e., a "collar" with a pun on "choler" above
292. **bombast**: cotton padding
300. **Amamon**: the name of a devil; **bastinado**: beating
301. **made . . . cuckhold**: i.e., caused horns to grow on Lucifer's head; **liegeman**: vassal sworn to the service of his lord
302. **Welsh hook**: a pike with a curved blade ending in a hook
319. **bluecaps**: Scots

civil buffeting hold, we shall buy maidenheads as they buy
hobnails, by the hundreds.

FALSTAFF. By the mass, lad, thou sayest true; it is like we shall ₃₂₅
have good trading that way. But tell me, Hal, art not thou
horrible afeared? Thou being heir apparent, could the world
pick thee out three such enemies again as that fiend Douglas,
that spirit Percy, and that devil Glendower? Art thou not horribly afraid? Doth not thy blood thrill at it?   ₃₃₀

PRINCE. Not a whit, i' faith. I lack some of thy instinct.

FALSTAFF. Well, thou wilt be horribly chid to-morrow when thou
comest to thy father. If thou love me, practice an answer.

PRINCE. Do thou stand for my father and examine me upon the
particulars of my life.   ₃₃₅

FALSTAFF. Shall I? Content. This chair shall be my state, this
dagger my sceptre, and this cushion my crown.

PRINCE. Thy state is taken for a joined-stool, thy golden sceptre
for a leaden dagger, and thy precious rich crown for a pitiful
bald crown.   ₃₄₀

FALSTAFF. Well, an the fire of grace be not quite out of thee,
now shalt thou be moved. Give me a cup of sack to make my
eyes look red, that it may be thought I have wept; for I must
speak in passion, and I will do it in King Cambyses' vein.

PRINCE. Well, here is my leg.   ₃₄₅

FALSTAFF. And here is my speech. Stand aside, nobility.

HOSTESS. O Jesu, this is excellent sport, i' faith!

FALSTAFF. Weep not, sweet queen, for trickling tears are vain.

HOSTESS. O, the Father, how he holds his countenance!

FALSTAFF. For God's sake, lords, convey my tristful queen! For ₃₅₀
tears do stop the floodgates of her eyes.

HOSTESS. O Jesu, he doth it as like one of these harlotry players
as ever I see!

330. thrill: tingle (with fear)
336. state: chair of state
338. joined-stool: a common piece of furniture
344. King Cambyses: a character in *Cambyses, King of Persia* (1570),
an old play noted for its bombast
345. leg: obeisance
349. holds his countenance: maintains a dignified appearance or, perhaps, strikes a pose
350. convey: escort; tristful: sad
352. harlotry: worthless

FALSTAFF. Peace, good pintpot. Peace, good tickle-brain. Harry,
I do not only marvel where thou spendest thy time, but also ₃₅₅
how thou art accompanied. For though the camomile, the
more it is trodden on, the faster it grows, yet youth, the more it
is wasted, the sooner it wears. That thou art my son I have
partly thy mother's word, partly my own opinion, but chiefly
a villainous trick of thine eye and a foolish hanging of thy ₃₆₀
nether lip that doth warrant me. If then thou be son to me,
here lies the point: why, being son to me, art thou so pointed
at? Shall the blessed sun of heaven prove a micher and eat
blackberries? A question not to be asked. Shall the son of England prove a thief and take purses? A question to be asked. ₃₆₅
There is a thing, Harry, which thou hast often heard of, and
it is known to many in our land by the name of pitch. This
pitch, as ancient writers do report, doth defile; so doth the
company thou keepest. For, Harry, now I do not speak to thee
in drink, but in tears; not in pleasure, but in passion; not in ₃₇₀
words only, but in woes also; and yet there is a virtuous man
whom I have often noted in thy company, but I know not his
name.

PRINCE. What manner of man, an it like your majesty?

FALSTAFF. A goodly portly man i' faith, and a corpulent; of a ₃₇₅
cheerful look, a pleasing eye, and a most noble carriage; and, as
I think, his age some fifty, or, by'r Lady, inclining to threescore; and now I remember me, his name is Falstaff. If that
man should be lewdly given, he deceiveth me; for, Harry, I
see virtue in his looks. If then the tree may be known by the ₃₈₀
fruit, as the fruit by the tree, then, peremptorily I speak it,
there is virtue in that Falstaff. Him keep with, the rest banish.
And tell me now, thou naughty varlet, tell me where hast thou

354. **pintpot**: a nickname for a seller of beer; **tickle-brain**: strong
liquor
360. **trick**: characteristic expression
361. **warrant**: assure
363. **micher**: truant
363–64. **eat blackberries**: i.e., wander here and there
369–71. **now . . . also**: a parody of the style of *Euphues* (1578),
a popular novel by John Lyly
379. **lewdly given**: accustomed to vile practices
380–81. **the tree . . . fruit**: Cf. Matthew 12:33.
381. **peremptorily**: positively

been this month?

PRINCE. Dost thou speak like a king? Do thou stand for me, 385 and I'll play my father.

FALSTAFF. Depose me? If thou dost it half so gravely, so majestically, both in word and matter, hang me up by the heels for a rabbit-sucker or a poulter's hare.

PRINCE. Well, here I am set.   390

FALSTAFF. And here I stand. Judge, my masters.

PRINCE. Now, Harry, whence come you?

FALSTAFF. My noble lord, from Eastcheap.

PRINCE. The complaints I hear of thee are grievous.

FALSTAFF. 'Sblood, my lord, they are false! Nay, I'll tickle ye for 395 a young prince, i' faith.

PRINCE. Swearest thou, ungracious boy? Henceforth ne'er look on me. Thou art violently carried away from grace. There is a devil haunts thee in the likeness of an old fat man; a tun of man is thy companion. Why dost thou converse with that trunk of 400 humors, that bolting hutch of beastliness, that swollen parcel of dropsies, that huge bombard of sack, that stuffed cloakbag of guts, that roasted Manningtree ox with the pudding in his belly, that reverend vice, that grey iniquity, that father ruffian, that vanity in years? Wherein is he good, but to taste sack 405 and drink it? wherein neat and cleanly, but to carve a capon and eat it? wherein cunning, but in craft? wherein crafty, but in villainy? wherein villainous, but in all things? wherein worthy, but in nothing?

FALSTAFF. I would your grace would take me with you. Whom 410 means your grace?

PRINCE. That villainous abominable misleader of youth, Falstaff, that old white-bearded Satan.

FALSTAFF. My lord, the man I know.

389. **rabbit-sucker:** suckling rabbit

395–96. **I'll tickle . . . prince:** Falstaff offers to amuse Hal by acting the part of a young prince.

401. **humors:** body fluids; **bolting hutch:** sifting bin

402. **bombard:** leather jug for liquor

403. **Manningtree:** a town in Essex at whose annual fairs oxen, famous for their size, were roasted.

404. **vice:** a mischievous character in the morality play

407. **cunning:** knowing

410. **take . . . you:** let me understand you

PRINCE. I know thou dost. 415

FALSTAFF. But to say I know more harm in him than in myself
were to say more than I know. That he is old, the more the
pity, his white hairs do witness it; but that he is, saving your
reverence, a whoremaster, that I utterly deny. If sack and sugar
be a fault, God help the wicked! If to be old and merry be a 420
sin, then many an old host that I know is damned. If to be fat
be to be hated, then Pharaoh's lean kine are to be loved. No,
my good lord: banish Peto, banish Bardolph, banish Poins;
but for sweet Jack Falstaff, kind Jack Falstaff, true Jack Falstaff, valiant Jack Falstaff, and therefore more valiant being, 425
as he is, old Jack Falstaff, banish not him thy Harry's company, banish not him thy Harry's company. Banish plump
Jack, and banish all the world!

PRINCE. I do, I will.

[A great knocking heard. Exeunt HOSTESS, FRANCIS, and BARDOLPH.]

Enter BARDOLPH, running.

BARDOLPH. O, my lord, my lord! the sheriff with a most monstrous 430
watch is at the door.

FALSTAFF. Out, ye rogue! Play out the play. I have much to say
in the behalf of that Falstaff.

Enter the HOSTESS.

HOSTESS. O Jesu, my lord, my lord!

PRINCE. Heigh, heigh, the devil rides upon a fiddlestick! What's 435
the matter?

HOSTESS. The sheriff and all the watch are at the door. They are
come to search the house. Shall I let them in?

FALSTAFF. Dost thou hear, Hal? Never call a true piece of gold
a counterfeit. Thou art essentially made without seeming so. 440

PRINCE. And thou a natural coward without instinct.

FALSTAFF. I deny your major. If you will deny the sheriff, so; if
not, let him enter. If I become not a cart as well as another

418. saving: with all respect to
422. Pharaoh's lean kine: see Genesis 41:19–21
435. the devil . . . fiddlestick: proverbial, much ado about nothing
440. essentially made: made of genuine substance
442. major: major premise
443. cart: used to transport prisoners to their execution

man, a plague on my bringing up! I hope I shall as soon be
strangled with a halter as another.   445

PRINCE. Go hide thee behind the arras. The rest walk up above.
Now, my masters, for a true face and good conscience.

FALSTAFF. Both which I have had; but their date is out, and therefore I'll hide me.   *[Exit.]*

PRINCE. Call in the sheriff.   450

[Exeunt all but the PRINCE and PETO.]

Enter SHERIFF and the CARRIER.

Now, master sheriff, what is your will with me?

SHERIFF. First, pardon me, my lord. A hue and cry
Hath followed certain men into this house.

PRINCE. What men?

SHERIFF. One of them is well known, my gracious lord,   455
A gross fat man.

CARRIER.   As fat as butter.

PRINCE. The man, I do assure you, is not here,
For I myself at this time have employed him.
And, Sheriff, I will engage my word to thee
That I will by to-morrow dinner time   460
Send him to answer thee, or any man,
For anything he shall be charged withal;
And so let me entreat you leave the house.

SHERIFF. I will, my lord. There are two gentlemen
Have in this robbery lost three hundred marks.   465

PRINCE. It may be so. If he have robbed these men,
He shall be answerable; and so farewell.

SHERIFF. Good night, my noble lord.

PRINCE. I think it is good morrow, is it not?

SHERIFF. Indeed, my lord, I think it be two o'clock.   470

Exeunt [SHERIFF and CARRIER].

PRINCE. This oily rascal is known as well as Paul's. Go call him
forth.

PETO. Falstaff! Fast asleep behind the arras, and snorting like a

446. **arras:** tapestry
447. **true:** honest-looking
448. **date is out:** term has expired
459. **engage:** pledge
471. **Paul's:** St. Paul's Cathedral, London

horse.

PRINCE. Hark how hard he fetches breath. Search his pockets.   475
    He searcheth his pocket[s] and findeth certain papers.
    What hast thou found?

PETO. Nothing but papers, my lord.

PRINCE. Let's see what they be. Read them.

[PETO.] [*reads*]
> "Item, A capon . . . .   2s. 2d.
> Item, Sauce 4d.   480
> Item, Sack two gallons . . . .   5s. 8d.
> Item, Anchovies and sack after supper   2s. 6d.
> Item, Bread . . . .   ob."

[PRINCE.] O monstrous! but one halfpennyworth of bread to this
    intolerable deal of sack! What there is else, keep close; we'll   485
    read it at more advantage. There let him sleep till day. I'll
    to the court in the morning. We must all to the wars, and thy
    place shall be honorable. I'll procure this fat rogue a charge
    of foot, and I know his death will be a march of twelve score.
    The money shall be paid back again with advantage. Be with   490
    me betimes in the morning, and so good morrow, Peto.

PETO. Good morrow, good my lord.   *Exeunt.*

[ACT III. SCENE I. *Wales.* GLENDOWER'S *Castle.*]

Enter HOTSPUR, WORCESTER, LORD MORTIMER, OWEN GLENDOWER.

MORTIMER. These promises are fair, the parties sure,
    And our induction full of prosperous hope.

HOTSPUR. Lord Mortimer, and cousin Glendower,
    Will you sit down?
    And uncle Worcester,—a plague upon it!   5
    I have forgot the map.

GLENDOWER.   No, here it is.
    Sit, cousin Percy; sit, good cousin Hotspur,

483. **ob.**: halfpenny
485. **deal**: large quantity
488–89. **charge of foot**: infantry command
489. **twelve score**: twelve score yards
490. **advantage**: interest
491. **betimes**: early
2. **induction**: initial step

For by that name as oft as Lancaster
Doth speak of you, his cheek looks pale and with
A rising sigh he wisheth you in heaven.   10
HOTSPUR. And you in hell, as oft as he hears Owen
   Glendower spoke of.
GLENDOWER. I cannot blame him. At my nativity
   The front of heaven was full of fiery shapes
   Of burning cressets, and at my birth   15
   The frame and huge foundation of the earth
   Shaked like a coward.
HOTSPUR. Why, so it would have done at the same
   season if your mother's cat had but kittened,
   though yourself had never been born.   20
GLENDOWER. I say the earth did shake when I was born.
HOTSPUR. And I say the earth was not of my mind,
   If you suppose as fearing you it shook.
GLENDOWER. The heavens were all on fire, the earth did tremble.
HOTSPUR. O, then the earth shook to see the heavens on fire,   25
   And not in fear of your nativity.
   Diseased nature oftentimes breaks forth
   In strange eruptions; oft the teeming earth
   Is with a kind of colic pinched and vexed
   By the imprisoning of unruly wind   30
   Within her womb, which, for enlargement striving,
   Shakes the old beldame earth and topples down
   Steeples and mossgrown towers. At your birth
   Our grandam earth, having this distemp'rature
   In passion shook.
GLENDOWER.   Cousin, of many men   35
   I do not bear these crossings. Give me leave
   To tell you once again that at my birth
   The front of heaven was full of fiery shapes,
   The goats ran from the mountains, and the herds
   Were strangely clamorous to the frighted fields.   40

8. **Lancaster:** i.e., Henry IV
14. **front:** forehead
15. **cressets:** fire baskets used as beacons
31. **enlargement:** release from confinement
32. **beldame:** grandmother
34. **distemp'rature:** disease
36. **bear . . . crossings:** tolerate these contradictions

These signs have marked me extraordinary;
And all the courses of my life do show
I am not in the roll of common men.
Where is he living, clipped in with the sea
That chides the banks of England, Scotland, Wales,   45
Which calls me pupil or hath read to me?
And bring him out that is but woman's son
Can trace me in the tedious ways of art
And hold me pace in deep experiments.

HOTSPUR. I think there's no man speaks better Welsh.   50
    I'll to dinner.

MORTIMER. Peace, cousin Percy; you will make him mad.

GLENDOWER. I can call spirits from the vasty deep.

HOTSPUR. Why, so can I, or so can any man;
    But will they come when you do call for them?   55

GLENDOWER. Why, I can teach you, cousin, to command
    The devil.

HOTSPUR. And I can teach thee, coz, to shame the devil
    By telling truth. Tell truth and shame the devil.
    If thou have power to raise him, bring him hither,   60
    And I'll be sworn I have power to shame him hence.
    O, while you live, tell truth and shame the devil!

MORTIMER. Come, come, no more of this unprofitable chat.

GLENDOWER. Three times hath Henry Bolingbroke made head
    Against my power; thrice from the banks of Wye   65
    And sandy-bottomed Severn have I sent him
    Booteless home and weather-beaten back.

HOTSPUR. Home without boots, and in foul weather too?
    How 'scapes he agues, in the devil's name?

GLENDOWER. Come, here is the map. Shall we divide our right   70
    According to our threefold order ta'en?

MORTIMER. The archdeacon hath divided it
    Into three limits very equally:

44. **clipped in with**: encircled by
45. **chides**: lashes
46. **read to**: taught
48. **art**: magic
49. **hold me pace**: keep up with me
64. **made head**: raised an army
67. **Booteless**: profitless
69. **agues**: fevers and chills

England, from Trent and Severn hitherto,
By south and east is to my part assigned;   75
All westward, Wales beyond the Severn shore,
And all the fertile land within that bound,
To Owen Glendower; and, dear coz, to you
The remnant northward lying off from Trent.
And our indentures tripartite are drawn,   80
Which being sealed interchangeably
(A business that this night may execute),
To-morrow, cousin Percy, you and I
And my good Lord of Worcester will set forth
To meet your father and the Scottish power,   85
As is appointed us, at Shrewsbury.
My father Glendower is not ready yet,
Nor shall we need his help these fourteen days.
Within that space you may have drawn together
Your tenants, friends, and neighboring gentlemen.   90
GLENDOWER. A shorter time shall send me to you, lords;
And in my conduct shall your ladies come,
From whom you now must steal and take no leave,
For there will be a world of water shed
Upon the parting of your wives and you.   95
HOTSPUR. Methinks my moiety, north from Burton here,
In quantity equals not one of yours.
See how this river comes me cranking in
And cuts me from the best of all my land
A huge half-moon, a monstrous cantle out.   100
I'll have the current in this place dammed up,
And here the smug and silver Trent shall run
In a new channel fair and evenly.
It shall not wind with such a deep indent
To rob me of so rich a bottom here.   105
GLENDOWER. Not wind? It shall, it must! You see it doth.

80. **indentures tripartite:** three-party compact
87. **father:** father-in-law
96. **moiety:** share
98. **cranking:** winding
100. **cantle:** piece
102. **smug:** smooth

MORTIMER. Yea, but
    Mark how he bears his course, and runs me up
    With like advantage on the other side,
    Gelding the opposed continent as much   110
    As on the other side it takes from you.
WORCESTER. Yea, but a little charge will trench him here
    And on this north side win this cape of land;
    And then he runs straight and even.
HOTSPUR. I'll have it so. A little charge will do it.   115
GLENDOWER. I will not have it altered.
HOTSPUR.   Will not you?
GLENDOWER. No, nor you shall not.
HOTSPUR.   Who shall say me nay?
GLENDOWER. Why, that will I.
HOTSPUR. Let me not understand you then; speak it in Welsh.
GLENDOWER. I can speak English, lord, as well as you;   120
    For I was trained up in the English court,
    Where, being but young, I framed to the harp
    Many an English ditty lovely well,
    And gave the tongue a helpful ornament,
    A virtue that was never seen in you.   125
HOTSPUR. Marry, and I am glad of it with all my heart!
    I had rather be a kitten and cry mew
    Than one of these same metre ballet-mongers.
    I had rather hear a brazen canstick turned
    Or a dry wheel grate on the axletree,   130
    And that would set my teeth nothing on edge,
    Nothing so much as mincing poetry.
    'Tis like the forced gait of a shuffling nag.
GLENDOWER. Come, you shall have Trent turned.
HOTSPUR. I do not care. I'll give thrice so much land   135
    To any well-deserving friend;
    But in the way of bargain, mark ye me,
    I'll cavil on the ninth part of a hair.
    Are the indentures drawn? Shall we be gone?

110. **opposed continent:** opposite shore
112. **charge:** cost
128. **ballet-mongers:** those who sang and sold ballads in the streets
129. **canstick:** candlestick; **turned:** shaped on a lathe

GLENDOWER. The moon shines fair; you may away by night. 140
    I'll haste the writer, and withal
    Break with your wives of your departure hence.
    I am afraid my daughter will run mad,
    So much she doteth on her Mortimer. *Exit.*

MORTIMER. Fie, cousin Percy! how you cross my father! 145

HOTSPUR. I cannot choose. Sometimes he angers me
    With telling me of the moldwarp and the ant,
    Of the dreamer Merlin and his prophecies,
    And of a dragon and a finless fish,
    A clip-winged griffin and a moulten raven, 150
    A couching lion and a ramping cat,
    And such a deal of skimble-skamble stuff
    As puts me from my faith. I tell you what:
    He held me last night at least nine hours
    In reckoning up the several devils' names 155
    That were his lackeys. I cried "hum," and "Well, go to!"
    But marked him not a word. O, he is as tedious
    As a tired horse, a railing wife;
    Worse than a smoky house. I had rather live
    With cheese and garlic in a windmill far 160
    Than feed on cates and have him talk to me
    In any summer house in Christendom.

MORTIMER. In faith, he is a worthy gentleman,
    Exceedingly well read, and profited
    In strange concealments, valiant as a lion, 165
    And wondrous affable, and as bountiful
    As mines of India. Shall I tell you, cousin?
    He holds your temper in a high respect
    And curbs himself even of his natural scope

141. **withal:** at the same time
142. **Break with:** tell
147. **moldwarp:** mole
148. **Merlin:** famous magician of Celtic legend
150. **griffin:** fabulous animal half lion, half eagle
151. **ramping:** rearing
152. **skimble-skamble:** nonsensical
153. **puts . . . faith:** makes me forget I am a Christian
156. **go to:** an expression of derisive disbelief
161. **cates:** dainties
164–65. **profited . . . concealments:** skilled in magic
169. **natural scope:** disposition

When you come 'cross his humor. Faith, he does.   170
I warrant you that man is not alive
Might so have tempted him as you have done
Without the taste of danger and reproof;
But do not use it oft, let me entreat you.

WORCESTER. In faith, my lord, you are too willful-blame,   175
And since your coming hither have done enough
To put him quite besides his patience.
You must needs learn, lord, to amend this fault.
Though sometimes it show greatness, courage, blood—
And that's the dearest grace it renders you—   180
Yet oftentimes it doth present harsh rage,
Defect of manners, want of government,
Pride, haughtiness, opinion, and disdain;
The least of which haunting a nobleman
Loseth men's hearts, and leaves behind a stain   185
Upon the beauty of all parts besides,
Beguiling them of commendation.

HOTSPUR. Well, I am schooled. Good manners be your speed!
Here come our wives, and let us take our leave.

Enter GLENDOWER *with the* LADIES..

MORTIMER. This is the deadly spite that angers me: 190
My wife can speak no English, I no Welsh.

GLENDOWER. My daughter weeps; she will not part with you;
She'll be a soldier too, she'll to the wars.

MORTIMER. Good father, tell her that she and my aunt Percy
Shall follow in your conduct speedily.   195

GLENDOWER *speaks to her in Welsh, and she
answers him in the same.*

GLENDOWER. She is desperate here. A peevish self-willed harlotry,
One that no persuasion can do good upon.

172. **tempted:** defied
175. **willful-blame:** obstinately blamable
179. **blood:** mettle
182. **government:** becoming conduct
183. **opinion:** arrogance
187. **Beguiling:** depriving
188. **be your speed:** give you success
190. **spite:** vexation
196. **peevish:** obstinate; **harlotry:** silly wench

The LADY *speaks in Welsh.*

MORTIMER. I understand thy looks. That pretty Welsh
  Which thou pourest down from these swelling heavens
  I am too perfect in; and, but for shame,   200
  In such a parley should I answer thee.

The LADY *again in Welsh.*

  I understand thy kisses, and thou mine,
  And that's a feeling disputation.
  But I will never be a truant, love,
  Till I have learnt thy language; for thy tongue   205
  Makes Welsh as sweet as ditties highly penned,
  Sung by a fair queen in a summer's bow'r,
  With ravishing division, to her lute.

GLENDOWER. Nay, if you melt, then will she run mad.

The LADY *speaks again in Welsh.*

MORTIMER. O, I am ignorance itself in this!   210

GLENDOWER. She bids you on the wanton rushes lay you down
  And rest your gentle head upon her lap,
  And she will sing the song that pleaseth you
  And on your eyelids crown the god of sleep,
  Charming your blood with pleasing heaviness,   215
  Making such difference 'twixt wake and sleep
  As is the difference betwixt day and night
  The hour before the heavenly-harnessed team
  Begins his golden progress in the east.

MORTIMER. With all my heart I'll sit and hear her sing.   220
  By that time will our book, I think, be drawn.

GLENDOWER.   Do so,
  And those musicians that shall play to you
  Hang in the air a thousand leagues from hence,
  And straight they shall be here. Sit, and attend.

HOTSPUR. Come, Kate, thou art perfect in lying down.   225

  201. **such a parley:** i.e., language of tears
  203. **disputation:** conversation
  206. **highly penned:** written in a lofty style
  208. **division:** melody
  211. **wanton:** luxuriant; **rushes:** used for floor covering
  215. **blood:** disposition
  221. **book:** i.e., the rebel compact
  224. **attend:** listen
  225. **perfect:** well-instructed

Come, quick, quick, that I may lay my head in thy lap.

LADY PERCY. Go, ye giddy goose.   *The music plays.*

HOTSPUR. Now I perceive the devil understands Welsh.

And 'tis no marvel he is so humorous,

By'r Lady, he is a good musician.   230

LADY PERCY. Then should you be nothing but musical, for you
are altogether governed by humors. Lie still ye thief, and hear
the lady sing in Welsh.

HOTSPUR. I had rather hear Lady, my brach, howl in Irish.

LADY PERCY. Wouldst thou have thy head broken?   235

HOTSPUR. No.

LADY PERCY. Then be still.

HOTSPUR. Neither! 'Tis a woman's fault.

LADY PERCY. Now God help thee!

HOTSPUR. To the Welsh lady's bed.   240

LADY PERCY. What's that?

HOTSPUR. Peace! she sings.

Here the LADY *sings a Welsh song.*

Come, Kate, I'll have your song too.

LADY PERCY. Not mine, in good sooth.

HOTSPUR. Not yours in good sooth? Heart, you swear like a   245
comfit-maker's wife. "Not you in good sooth!" and "as true as
I live!" and "as God shall mend me!" and "as sure as day!"

And givest such sarcenet surety for thy oaths

As if thou never walk'st further than Finsbury.

Swear me, Kate, like a lady as thou art,   250

A good mouth-filling oath, and leave "in sooth"

And such protest of pepper gingerbread

To velvet guards and Sunday citizens.

Come, sing.

LADY PERCY. I will not sing.   255

229. **humorous:** capricious
232. **humors:** whims
234. **brach:** bitch-hound
244. **sooth:** truth
246. **comfit-maker's:** confectioner's
248. **sarcenet:** a finely-woven silk
249. **Finsbury:** a popular place of recreation near London
253. **velvet guards:** wearers of clothing trimmed with velvet; **Sunday citizens:** citizens in their Sunday finery (and perhaps on their Sunday behavior)

HOTSPUR. 'Tis the next way to turn tailor or be redbreast–teacher.
    An the indentures be drawn, I'll away within these two hours;
    and so come in when ye will.   *Exit.*
GLENDOWER. Come, come, Lord Mortimer. You are as slow
    As hot Lord Percy is on fire to go.   260
    By this our book is drawn; we'll but seal,
    And then to horse immediately.
MORTIMER.   With all my heart.
                                Exeunt.

[SCENE II. *London. The Palace.*]

Enter the KING, PRINCE OF WALES, *and others.*

KING. Lords, give us leave: the Prince of Wales and I
    Must have some private conference; but be near at hand,
    For we shall presently have need of you.   *Exeunt* LORDS.
    I know not whether God will have it so
    For some displeasing service I have done,   5
    That, in his secret doom, out of my blood
    He'll breed revengement and a scourge for me;
    But thou dost in thy passages of life
    Make me believe that thou art only marked
    For the hot vengeance and the rod of heaven   10
    To punish my mistreadings. Tell me else,
    Could such inordinate and low desires,
    Such poor, such bare, such lewd, such mean attempts,
    Such barren pleasures, rude society,
    As thou art matched withal and grafted to,   15
    Accompany the greatness of thy blood
    And hold their level with thy princely heart?
PRINCE. So please your majesty, I would I could

256. **tailor:** tailors were noted for their singing
261. **this:** this time
6. **doom:** judgment
8. **passages:** actions
9–10. **marked for:** appointed as an instrument of
13. **bare:** wretched; **lewd:** base

Quit all offenses with as clear excuse
As well as I am doubtless I can purge   20
Myself of many I am charged withal.
Yet such extenuation let me beg
As, in reproof of many tales devised,
Which oft the ear of greatness needs must hear
By smiling pickthanks and base newsmongers,   25
I may, for some things true wherein my youth
Hath faulty wandered and irregular,
Find pardon on my true submission.
KING. God pardon thee! Yet let me wonder, Harry,
At thy affections, which do hold a wing   30
Quite from the flight of all thy ancestors.
Thy place in council thou hast rudely lost,
Which by thy younger brother is supplied,
And art almost an alien to the hearts
Of all the court and princes of my blood.   35
The hope and expectation of thy time
Is ruined, and the soul of every man
Prophetically do forethink thy fall.
Had I so lavish of my presence been,
So common-hackneyed in the eyes of men,   40
So stale and cheap to vulgar company,
Opinion, that did help me to the crown,
Had still kept loyal to possession
And left me in reputeless banishment,
A fellow of no mark nor likelihood.   45
By being seldom seen, I could not stir
But like a comet I was wondered at;
That men would tell their children, "This is he!"
Others would say, "Where? Which is Bolingbroke?"

19. **Quit:** acquit
23. **reproof:** refutation
25. **pickthanks:** flatterers
30. **affections:** inclinations
32. **rudely:** by violent behavior
36. **time:** youth
38. **forethink:** predict
40. **common-hackneyed:** vulgarized
42. **Opinion:** public opinion
43. **Had . . . possession:** i.e., remained loyal to Richard II

And then I stole all courtesy from heaven,   50
And dressed myself in such humility
That I did pluck allegiance from men's hearts,
Loud shouts and salutations from their mouths
Even in the presence of the crowned king.
Thus did I keep my person fresh and new,   55
My presence like a robe pontifical,
Ne'er seen but wondered at; and so my state,
Seldom but sumptuous, showed like a feast
And won by rareness such solemnity.
The skipping king, he ambled up and down   60
With shallow jesters and rash bavin wits,
Soon kindled and soon burnt; carded his state;
Mingled his royalty with cap'ring fools;
Had his great name profaned with their scorns
And gave his countenance, against his name,   65
To laugh at gibing boys and stand the push
Of every beardless vain comparative;
Grew a companion to the common streets,
Enfeoffed himself to popularity;
That, being daily swallowed by men's eyes,   70
They surfeited with honey and began
To loathe the taste of sweetness, whereof a little
More than a little is by much too much.
So, when he had occasion to be seen,
He was but as the cuckoo is in June,   75
Heard, not regarded; seen, but with such eyes
As, sick and blunted with community,
Afford no extraordinary gaze
Such as is bent on sunlike majesty
When it shines seldom in admiring eyes;   80
But rather drowsed and hung their eyelids down,

60. **skipping:** flighty; **king:** i.e., Richard II
61. **bavin:** brushwood
62. **carded:** mixed with something base
66. **stand the push:** tolerate the (verbal) jostling
67. **vain comparative:** foolish scoffer
69. **Enfeoffed:** surrendered; **popularity:** common people
77. **community:** commonness

Slept in his face, and rendered such aspect
As cloudy men use to their adversaries,
Being with his presence glutted, gorged, and full.
And in that very line, Harry, standest thou;   85
For thou hast lost thy princely privilege
With vile participation. Not an eye
But is a-weary of thy common sight,
Save mine, which hath desired to see thee more,
Which now doth that I would not have it do: 90
Make blind itself with foolish tenderness.   [*Weeping*]
PRINCE. I shall hereafter, my thrice gracious lord,
Be more myself.
KING.   For all the world,
As thou art to this hour was Richard then
When I from France set foot at Ravenspurgh;   95
And even as I was then is Percy now.
Now, by my sceptre, and my soul to boot,
He hath more worthy interest to the state
Than thou, the shadow of succession;
For of no right, nor color like to right,   100
He doth fill fields with harness in the realm,
Turns head against the lion's armed jaws,
And, being no more in debt to years than thou,
Leads ancient lords and reverend bishops on
To bloody battles and to bruising arms.   105
What never-dying honor hath he got
Against renowned Douglas! whose high deeds,
Whose hot incursions, and great name in arms
Holds from all soldiers chief majority

82. **Slept . . . face:** insulted him by going to sleep in his presence;
aspect: look
83. **cloudy:** sullen
85. **line:** i.e., line of descent
87. **vile participation:** fellowship with the low in rank
98. **interest:** title
99. **shadow:** mere name without a man to correspond to it
100. **color:** semblance
101. **harness:** men in armor
103. Historically, Hal was actually twenty-three years Hotspur's junior.
109. **majority:** superiority

And military title capital   110
Through all the kingdoms that acknowledge Christ.
Thrice hath this Hotspur, Mars in swathling clothes,
This infant warrior, in his enterprises
Discomfited great Douglas; ta'en him once,
Enlarged him, and made a friend of him,   115
To fill the mouth of deep defiance up
And shake the peace and safety of our throne.
And what say you to this? Percy, Northumberland,
The Archbishop's grace of York, Douglas, Mortimer
Capitulate against us and are up.   120
But wherefore do I tell these news to thee?
Why, Harry, do I tell thee of my foes
Which art my nearest and dearest enemy?
Thou that art like enough, through vassal fear,
Base inclination, and the start of spleen,   125
To fight against me under Percy's pay,
To dog his heels and curtsy at his frowns,
To show how much thou art degenerate.
PRINCE. Do not think so. You shall not find it so.
And God forgive them that so much have swayed   130
Your majesty's good thoughts away from me.
I will redeem all this on Percy's head,
And in the closing of some glorious day
Be bold to tell you that I am your son,
When I will wear a garment all of blood,   135
And stain my favors in a bloody mask,
Which, washed away, shall scour my shame with it.
And that shall be the day, whene'er it lights,
That this same child of honor and renown,
This gallant Hotspur, this all-praised knight,   140
And your unthought-of Harry chance to meet.

110. **capital:** chief
115. **Enlarged:** set at liberty
116. **To . . . up:** make defiance more vociferous
120. **Capitulate:** draw up articles of agreement; **up:** in arms
123. **dearest:** most beloved (with a possible play on "direst")
125. **start of spleen:** impulse
132. **redeem:** make up for
136. **favors:** facial features
138. **lights:** (1) dawns (2) happens

For every honor sitting on his helm,
Would they were multitudes, and on my head
My shames redoubled! For the time will come
That I shall make this northern youth exchange   145
His glorious deeds for my indignities.
Percy is but my factor, good my lord,
To engross up glorious deeds on my behalf;
And I will call him to so strict account
That he shall render every glory up,   150
Yea, even the slightest worship of his time;
Or I will tear the reckoning from his heart.
This in the name of God I promise here;
The which if He be pleased I shall perform,
I do beseech your majesty, may salve   155
The long-grown wounds of my intemperance.
If not, the end of life cancels all bands,
And I will die a hundred thousand deaths
Ere break the smallest parcel of this vow.
KING. A hundred thousand rebels die in this!   160
Thou shalt have charge and sovereign trust herein.

Enter BLUNT [*hastily*].

How now, good Blunt? Thy looks are full of speed.
BLUNT. So hath the business that I come to speak of.
Lord Mortimer of Scotland hath sent word
That Douglas and the English rebels met   165
The eleventh of this month at Shrewsbury.
A mighty and a fearful head they are,
If promises be kept on every hand,
As ever offered foul play in a state.
KING. The Earl of Westmoreland set forth to-day,   170
With him my son, Lord John of Lancaster,
For this advertisement is five days old.

146. **indignities:** unworthy traits
147. **factor:** agent
148. **engross:** buy up
151. **worship:** honor; **time:** lifetime
156. **intemperance:** intemperateness
159. **parcel:** portion
167. **head:** armed force
172. **advertisement:** information

On Wednesday next, Harry, you shall set forward;
On Thursday we ourselves will march. Our meeting
Is Bridgenorth; and, Harry, you shall march   175
Through Gloucestershire; by which account,
Our business valued, some twelve days hence
Our general forces at Bridgenorth shall meet.
Our hands are full of business. Let's away;
Advantage feeds him fat while men delay.   *Exeunt.* 180

[SCENE III. *Eastcheap. The Boar's Head Tavern.*]

Enter FALSTAFF *and* BARDOLPH.

FALSTAFF. Bardolph, am I not fallen away vilely since this last
action? Do I not bate? Do I not dwindle? Why, my skin hangs
about me like an old lady's loose gown. I am withered like an
old apple-john. Well, I'll repent, and that suddenly, while I am
in some liking. I shall be out of heart shortly, and then I shall   5
have no strength to repent. An I have not forgotten what the
inside of a church is made of, I am a peppercorn, a brewer's
horse. The inside of a church! Company, villainous company,
hath been the spoil of me.

BARDOLPH. Sir John, you are so fretful you cannot live long.   10

FALSTAFF. Why, there is it; come, sing me a bawdy song; make
me merry. I was as virtuously given as a gentleman need to be,
virtuous enough: swore little, diced not above seven times a
week, went to a bawdy house not above once in a quarter of an
hour, paid money that I borrowed three or four times, lived   15
well, and in good compass; and now I live out of all order, out
of all compass.

BARDOLPH. Why, you are so fat, Sir John, that you must needs be
out of all compass, out of all reasonable compass, Sir John.

FALSTAFF. Do thou amend thy face, and I'll amend my life; thou   20

174. meeting: meeting-place
175. Bridgenorth: a market town twenty miles from Shrewsbury.
177. Our . . . valued: considering how long our business will take
1–2. last action: i.e., the robbery at Gad's Hill
2. bate: shrink, decrease
4. apple-john: a shrivelled and withered apple
7–8. brewer's horse: an emaciated nag
16. in good compass: orderly
19. compass: circumference

art our admiral: thou bearest the lantern in the poop, but 'tis
in the nose of thee. Thou art the Knight of the Burning Lamp.

BARDOLPH. Why, Sir John, my face does you no harm.

FALSTAFF. No, I'll be sworn; I make as good use of it as many a
man doth of a death's-head or a *memento mori*. I never see 25
thy face but I think upon hellfire and Dives that lived in purple, for there he is in his robes, burning, burning. If thou wert
any way given to virtue, I would swear by thy face; my oath
should be "By this fire, that's God's angel." But thou art altogether given over, and wert indeed, but for the light in thy face, 30
the son of utter darkness. When thou ran'st up Gad's Hill in
the night to catch my horse, if I did not think thou hadst been
an *ignis fatuus* or a ball of wildfire, there's no purchase in
money. O, thou art a perpetual triumph, an everlasting bonfire-
light! Thou hast saved me a thousand marks in links and 35
torches, walking with thee in the night betwixt tavern and
tavern; but the sack that thou has drunk me would have bought
me lights as good cheap at the dearest chandler's in Europe. I
have maintained that salamander of yours with fire any time
this two and thirty years. God reward me for it! 40

BARDOLPH. 'Sblood, I would my face were in your belly!

FALSTAFF. God-a-mercy! so should I be sure to be heartburned.

Enter HOST[ESS].

How now, Dame Partlet the hen? Have you inquired yet who
picked my pocket?

HOSTESS. Why, Sir John, what do you think, Sir John? Do you 45
think I keep thieves in my house? I have searched, I have in-

21. admiral: flagship; poop: stern
25. death's head: skull; *memento mori*: reminder of death
26. Dives: for the parable of Dives and Lazarus, see Luke 16:19–31
29. By . . . angel: Cf. Exodus 3:2: "And the Angel of the Lord appeared to him in a flame of fire out of the midst of a bush. . . ."
30. given over: abandoned
33. *ignis fatuus:* will-o'-the-wisp; wildfire: fireworks; purchase: advantage
34. triumph: public festivity
35. links: torches
38. good cheap: cheaply; chandler: seller of candles
39. salamander: a kind of lizard believed able to live in fire
43. Dame Partlet: a talkative, advice-giving hen in Chaucer's *Nun's
Priest's Tale*

quired, so has my husband, man by man, boy by boy, servant
by servant. The tithe of a hair was never lost in my house before.

FALSTAFF. Ye lie, hostess. Bardolph was shaved and lost many a 50
hair, and I'll be sworn my pocket was picked.
Go to, you are a woman, go!

HOSTESS. Who, I? No; I defy thee! God's light, I was never called
so in mine own house before!

FALSTAFF. Go to, I know you well enough. 55

HOSTESS. No, Sir John; you do not know me, Sir John. I know
you, Sir John; you owe me money, Sir John, and now you pick
a quarrel to beguile me of it. I bought you a dozen of shirts to
your back.

FALSTAFF. Dowlas, filthy dowlas. I have given them away to 60
bakers' wives; they have made bolters of them.

HOSTESS. Now, as I am a true woman, holland of eight shillings
an ell. You owe money here besides, Sir John, for your diet and
by-drinkings, and money lent you, four and twenty pound.

FALSTAFF. He had his part of it; let him pay. 65

HOSTESS. He? Alas, he is poor; he hath nothing.

FALSTAFF. How? Poor? Look upon his face. What call you rich?
Let them coin his nose; let them coin his cheeks. I'll not pay a
denier. What, will you make a younker of me? Shall I not take
mine ease in mine inn but I shall have my pocket picked? I 70
have lost a seal-ring of my grandfather's worth forty mark.

HOSTESS. O Jesu, I have heard the prince tell him, I know not
how oft, that that ring was copper!

FALSTAFF. How? the prince is a Jack, a sneak-up.

---

48. **tithe:** tenth part
50. **shaved:** contracted venereal disease
50–51. **lost . . . hair:** baldness was considered a symptom of venereal
disease
52. **woman:** mistress
60. **Dowlas:** a coarse linen
61. **bolters:** flour-sieves
62. **holland:** a linen fabric
63. **ell:** a cloth measure of forty-five inches
64. **by-drinkings:** drinks at odd times
69. **denier:** a French coin worth one-twelfth of a sou; **younker:**
youngster
74. **Jack:** knave; **sneak-up:** servile person

'Sblood, an he were here, I would cudgel him like a dog if 75
would say so.

Enter the PRINCE [*and* POINS], *marching, and* FALSTAFF *meets*
[*them*], *playing upon his truncheon like a fife.*

How now, lad? Is the wind in that door, i' faith? Must we all
march?

BARDOLPH. Yea, two and two, Newgate fashion.

HOSTESS. My lord, I pray you hear me. 80

PRINCE. What sayest thou, Mistress Quickly? How doth thy husband? I love him well; he is an honest man.

HOSTESS. Good my lord, hear me.

FALSTAFF. Prithee let her alone and list to me.

PRINCE. What sayest thou, Jack? 85

FALSTAFF. The other night I fell asleep here behind the arras and
had my pocket picked. This house is turned bawdy house; they
pick pockets.

PRINCE. What didst thou lose, Jack?

FALSTAFF. Wilt thou believe me, Hal, three or four bonds of forty 90
pound apiece and a seal-ring of my grandfather's.

PRINCE. A trifle, some eight-penny matter.

HOSTESS. So I told him, my lord, and I said I heard your grace say
so; and, my lord, he speaks most vilely of you, like a foul-
mouthed man as he is, and said he would cudgel you. 95

PRINCE. What? he did not.

HOSTESS. There's neither faith, truth, nor womanhood in me else.

FALSTAFF. There's no more faith in thee than in a stewed prune,
nor no more truth in thee than in a drawn fox; and for womanhood, Maid Marian may be the deputy's wife of the ward to 100
thee. Go, you thing, go!

HOSTESS. Say, what thing? what thing?

s.d. truncheon: cudgel
79. Newgate fashion: as prisoners shackled together; Newgate: a prison
in London
98. stewed prune: bawd
99. drawn fox: a fox lured (i.e., "drawn") by hunters from his lair
would exercise his proverbial cunning to escape his pursuers; hence, a
cunning creature; womanhood: womanly qualities
100. Maid Marian: A female companion of Robin Hood in the legends
of that outlaw; hence a light, not very respectable woman; Maid Marian
. . . thee: even Maid Marian would be a model matron compared to you

FALSTAFF. What thing? Why, a thing to thank God on.

HOSTESS. I am no thing to thank God on, I would thou shouldst know it! I am an honest man's wife, and, setting thy knight- 105 hood aside, thou art a knave to call me so.

FALSTAFF. Setting thy womanhood aside, thou art a beast to say otherwise.

HOSTESS. Say, what beast, thou knave, thou?

FALSTAFF. What beast? Why, an otter. 110

PRINCE. An otter, Sir John? Why an otter?

FALSTAFF. Why, she's neither fish nor flesh; a man knows not where to have her.

HOSTESS. Thou art an unjust man in saying so. Thou or any man knows where to have me, thou knave, thou! 115

PRINCE. Thou say'st true, hostess, and he slanders thee most grossly.

HOSTESS. So he doth you, my lord, and said this other day you ought him a thousand pound.

PRINCE. Sirrah, do I owe you a thousand pound? 120

FALSTAFF. A thousand pound, Hal? A million! Thy love is worth a million; thou owest me thy love.

HOSTESS. Nay, my lord, he called you Jack and said he would cudgel you.

FALSTAFF. Did I, Bardolph? 125

BARDOLPH. Indeed, Sir John, you said so.

FALSTAFF. Yea, if he said my ring was copper.

PRINCE. I say 'tis copper. Darest thou be as good as thy word now?

FALSTAFF. Why, Hal, thou knowest, as thou art but man, I dare; but as thou art prince, I fear thee as I fear the roaring of the 130 lion's whelp.

PRINCE. And why not as the lion?

FALSTAFF. The king himself is to be feared as the lion. Dost thou think I'll fear thee as I fear thy father? Nay, an I do, I pray God my girdle break. 135

PRINCE. O, if it should, how would thy guts fall about thy knees! But, sirrah, there's no room for faith, truth, nor honesty in this bosom of thine. It is all filled up with guts and midriff. Charge an honest woman with picking thy pocket! Why, thou whore-

130–31. Cf. Proverbs, 20:2: "The fear of a king is as the roaring of a lion."
135. **girdle:** belt

son, impudent, embossed rascal, if there were anything in thy 140
pocket but tavern reckonings, memorandums of bawdy houses,
and one poor pennyworth of sugar candy to make thee long-
winded, if thy pocket were enriched with any other injuries
but these, I am a villain. And yet you will stand to it; you will
not pocket up wrong. Art thou not ashamed? 145

FALSTAFF. Dost thou hear, Hal? Thou knowest in the state of innocency Adam fell, and what should poor Jack Falstaff do in
the days of villainy? Thou seest I have more flesh than another
man, and therefore more frailty. You confess then, you picked
my pocket? 150

PRINCE. It appears so by the story.

FALSTAFF. Hostess, I forgive thee. Go make ready breakfast, love
thy husband, look to thy servants, cherish thy guests. Thou
shalt find me tractable to any honest reason. Thou seest I am
pacified still. Nay, prithee be gone. 155

Exit HOSTESS.

Now, Hal, to the news at court: for the robbery, lad—how is
that answered?

PRINCE. O my sweet beef, I must still be good angel to thee; the
money is paid back again.

FALSTAFF. O, I do not like that paying back; 'tis a double labor. 160

PRINCE. I am good friends with my father and may do anything.

FALSTAFF. Rob me the exchequer the first thing thou doest and
do it with unwashed hands too.

BARDOLPH. Do, my lord.

PRINCE. I have procured thee, Jack, a charge of foot. 165

FALSTAFF. I would it had been of horse. Where shall I find one
that can steal well? O for a fine thief of the age of two and
twenty or thereabouts! I am heinously unprovided. Well, God
be thanked for these rebels. They offend none but the virtuous.
I laud them, I praise them. 170

PRINCE. Bardolph!

140. **embossed**: swollen
144. **stand to it**: i.e., maintain this deception
144-45. **you . . . wrong**: Proverbial: you will not accept it without
protest.
153. **cherish**: entertain kindly
163. **with unwashed hands**: quickly, without taking time to wash your
hands
165. **charge of foot**: an infantry command

BARDOLPH. My lord?

PRINCE. Go bear this letter to Lord John of Lancaster,
To my brother John; this to my Lord of Westmoreland.
[*Exit* BARDOLPH.]
Go Poins, to horse, to horse; for thou and I   175
Have thirty miles to ride yet ere dinner time.
[*Exit* POINS.]
Jack, meet me to-morrow in the Temple Hall
At two o'clock in the afternoon.
There shalt thou know thy charge, and there receive
Money and order for their furniture.   180
The land is burning; Percy stands on high;
And either they or we must lower lie.   [*Exit.*]

FALSTAFF. Rare words! brave world! Hostess, my breakfast, come.
O, I could wish this tavern were my drum!   [*Exit.*]

[ACT IV, SCENE I. *The Rebel camp near Shrewsbury.*]

[*Enter* HOTSPUR, WORCESTER, *and* DOUGLAS.]

HOTSPUR. Well said, my noble Scot. If speaking truth
In this fine age were not thought flattery,
Such attribution should the Douglas have
As not a soldier of this season's stamp
Should go so general current through the world.   5
By God, I cannot flatter; I do defy
The tongues of soothers; but a braver place
In my heart's love hath no man than yourself.
Nay, task me to my word; approve me, lord.

DOUGLAS. Thou art the king of honor.   10
No man so potent breathes upon the ground
But I will beard him.

180. **furniture:** equipment
183. **brave:** excellent
4. **stamp:** coinage
5. **go . . . current:** be widely circulated
6. **defy:** despise
7. **soothers:** flatterers; **braver:** better
9. **task . . . word:** challenge me to be as good as my word; **approve:** try
12. **beard:** oppose with boldness

Enter one with letters.

HOTSPUR.   Do so and 'tis well.—
What letters hast thou there?—I can but thank you.
MESSENGER. These letters come from your father.
HOTSPUR. Letters from him? Why comes he not himself?   15
MESSENGER. He cannot come, my lord; he is grievous sick.
HOTSPUR. 'Zounds! how has he the leisure to be sick
    In such a justling time? Who leads his power?
    Under whose government come they along?
MESSENGER. His letters bear his mind, not I, my lord.   20
WORCESTER. I prithee tell me, doth he keep his bed?
MESSENGER. He did, my lord, four days ere I set forth,
    And at the time of my departure thence
    He was much feared by his physicians.
WORCESTER. I would the state of time had first been whole   25
    Ere he by sickness had been visited.
    His health was never better worth than now.
HOTSPUR. Sick now? droop now? This sickness doth infect
    The very life blood of our enterprise.
    'Tis catching hither, even to our camp.   30
    He writes me here that inward sickness—
    And that his friends by deputation could not
    So soon be drawn; nor did he think it meet
    To lay so dangerous and dear a trust
    On any soul removed but on his own.   35
    Yet doth he give us bold advertisement
    That with our small conjunction we should on
    To see how fortune is disposed to us;
    For, as he writes, there is no quailing now,
    Because the king is certainly possessed   40
    Of all our purposes. What say you to it?
WORCESTER. Your father's sickness is a maim to us.

18. **justling:** contentious
25. **time:** the present state of affairs
33. **drawn:** brought together; **meet:** suitable
35. **removed:** not immediately concerned
36. **advertisement:** advice
37. **conjunction:** united force; **on:** go ahead
40. **possessed:** informed

HOTSPUR. A perilous gash, a very limb lopped off.
 And yet, in faith, it is not! His present want
 Seems more than we shall find it. Were it good 45
 To set the exact wealth of all our states
 All at one cast? to set so rich a main
 On the nice hazard of one doubtful hour?
 It were not good, for therein should we read
 The very bottom and the soul of hope, 50
 The very list, the very utmost bound
 Of all our fortunes.
DOUGLAS.   Faith, and so we should.
 Where now remains a sweet reversion,
 We may boldly spend upon the hope
 Of what is to come in. 55
 A comfort of retirement lives in this.
HOTSPUR. A rendezvous, a home to fly unto,
 If that the devil and mischance look big
 Upon the maidenhead of our affairs.
WORCESTER. But yet I would your father had been here. 60
 The quality and hair of our attempt
 Brooks no division. It will be thought
 By some that know not why he is away,
 That wisdom, loyalty, and mere dislike
 Of our proceedings kept the earl from hence. 65
 And think how such an apprehension
 May turn the tide of fearful faction
 And breed a kind of question in our cause.
 For well you know we of the off'ring side
 Must keep aloof from strict arbitrement, 70

44. **His want:** our present lack of him
46. **set:** stake; **exact:** entire
47. **main:** stake
48. **nice:** doubtful; **hazard:** (1) risk (2) a game of chance
51. **list:** limit
53. **reversion:** hope of future possession
58. **big:** haughtily, boastfully
61. **hair:** nature
62. **Brooks:** tolerates, permits
64. **mere:** downright
67. **faction:** conspiracy
69. **off'ring:** attacking
70. **strict:** accurately determined; **arbitrement:** investigation

And stop all sight-holes, every loop from whence
The eye of reason may pry in upon us.
This absence of your father's draws a curtain
That shows the ignorant a kind of fear
Before not dreamt of.

HOTSPUR.   You strain too far.   75
I rather of his absence make this use:
It lends a lustre and more great opinion,
A larger dare to our great enterprise,
Than if the earl were here; for men must think,
If we, without his help, can make a head   80
To push against a kingdom, with his help
We shall o'erturn it topsy-turvy down.
Yet all goes well; yet all our joints are whole.

DOUGLAS. As heart can think. There is not such a word
Spoke of in Scotland as this term of fear.   85

Enter SIR RI[CHARD] VERNON.

HOTSPUR. My cousin Vernon! welcome, by my soul.
VERNON. Pray God my news be worth a welcome, lord.
The Earl of Westmoreland, seven thousand strong,
Is marching hitherwards; with him Prince John.
HOTSPUR. No harm. What more?
VERNON.   And further, I have learned,   90
The king himself in person is set forth,
Or hitherwards intended speedily,
With strong and mighty preparation.
HOTSPUR. He shall be welcome too. Where is his son,
The nimble-footed madcap Prince of Wales,   95
And his comrades, that daffed the world aside
And bid it pass?
VERNON.   All furnished, all in arms;
All plumed like estridges that with the wind
Bated like eagles having lately bathed;

75. **strain:** exaggerate
77. **opinion:** reputation
92. **intended:** purposed to come
96. **daffed:** thrust
98. **estridges:** ostriches
99. **Bated:** fluttered their wings

Glittering in golden coats like images;   100
As full of spirit as the month of May
And gorgeous as the sun at midsummer;
Wanton as youthful goats, wild as young bulls.
I saw young Harry with his beaver on,
His cushes on his thighs, gallantly armed,   105
Rise from the ground like feathered Mercury,
And vaulted with such ease into his seat
As if an angel dropped down from the clouds
To turn and wind a fiery Pegasus
And witch the world with noble horsemanship.   110

HOTSPUR. No more, no more! Worse than the sun in March
This praise doth nourish agues. Let them come.
They come like sacrifices in their trim,
And to the fire-eyed maid of smoky war
All hot and bleeding will we offer them.   115
The mailed Mars shall on his altar sit
Up to the ears in blood. I am on fire
To hear this rich reprisal is so nigh,
And yet not ours. Come, let me taste my horse,
Who is to bear me like a thunderbolt   120
Against the bosom of the Prince of Wales.
Harry to Harry shall, hot horse to horse,
Meet, and ne'er part till one drop down a corse.
O that Glendower were come!

VERNON.   There is more news.
I learned in Worcester, as I rode along,   125
He cannot draw his power this fourteen days.

DOUGLAS. That's the worst tidings that I hear of yet.

100. **images:** statues
103. **Wanton:** frolicsome
104. **beaver:** face-guard of a helmet
105. **cushes:** armor for the thighs
106. **Mercury:** the speedy messenger of the gods
109. **wind:** wheel; **Pegasus:** the winged horse of Greek mythology
112. **agues:** fevers
113. **trim:** fine trappings
114. **maid:** Bellona, Roman goddess of war
116. **mailed:** in armor; **Mars:** Roman god of war
118. **reprisal:** prize
126. **draw:** bring together

WORCESTER. Ay, by my faith, that bears a frosty sound.
HOTSPUR. What may the king's whole battle reach unto?
VERNON. To thirty thousand.
HOTSPUR.   Forty let it be.   130
My father and Glendower being both away,
The powers of us may serve so great a day.
Come, let us take a muster speedily.
Doomsday is near. Die all, die merrily.
DOUGLAS. Talk not of dying. I am out of fear   135
Of death or death's hand for this one half-year.

                                        Exeunt.

[SCENE II. A *public road near Coventry.*]

Enter FALSTAFF [*and*] BARDOLPH.

FALSTAFF. Bardolph, get thee before to Coventry; fill me a bottle
of sack. Our soldiers shall march through. We'll to Sutton
Cophill to-night.
BARDOLPH. Will you give me money, captain?
FALSTAFF. Lay out, lay out.   5
BARDOLPH. This bottle makes an angel.
FALSTAFF. An if it do, take it for thy labor; and if it make twenty,
take them all; I'll answer the coinage. Bid my lieutenant Peto
meet me at town's end.
BARDOLPH. I will, captain. Farewell.   *Exit.* 10
FALSTAFF. If I be not ashamed of my soldiers, I am a soused gur-
net. I have misused the king's press damnably. I have got, in
exchange of a hundred and fifty soldiers, three hundred and
odd pounds. I press me none but good householders, yeomen's

129. battle: army
2–3. Sutton Cophill: Sutton-Coldfield, a town in northern Warwickshire on the road to Shrewsbury
5. Lay out: i.e., you pay for it
6. makes an angel: this purchase makes an angel (10 shillings) I have
spent
7. An . . . labor: Falstaff puns on "make," saying if the bottle can
be made into an angel Bardolph may keep the money for his labor.
8. answer: be responsible for
11. soused gurnet: pickled fish
12. press: conscription of soldiers; Falstaff has accepted money from
the hundred and fifty *not* to draft them.

sons; inquire me out contracted bachelors, such as had been 15
asked twice on the banns, such a commodity of warm slaves as
had as lieve hear the devil as a drum, such as fear the report
of a caliver worse than a struck fowl or a hurt wild duck. I
pressed me none but such toasts-and-butter, with hearts in
their bellies no bigger than pins' heads, and they have bought 20
out their services; and now my whole charge consists of ancients, corporals, lieutenants, gentlemen of companies—slaves
as ragged as Lazarus in the painted cloth, where the glutton's
dogs licked his sores; and such as, indeed, were never soldiers,
but discarded unjust serving-men, younger sons to younger 25
brothers, revolted tapsters, and ostlers trade-fallen; the cankers
of a calm world and a long peace; ten times more dishonorable
ragged than an old fazed ancient; and such have I to fill up the
rooms of them that have bought out their services that you
would think that I had a hundred and fifty tattered prodigals 30
lately come from swine-keeping, from eating draff and husks.
A mad fellow met me on the way, and told me I had unloaded
all the gibbets and pressed the dead bodies. No eye hath seen
such scarecrows. I'll not march through Coventry with them,
that's flat. Nay, and the villains march wide betwixt the legs, 35
as if they had gyves on, for indeed I had the most of them out
of prison. There's not a shirt and a half in all my company, and
the half-shirt is two napkins tacked together and thrown over
the shoulders like a herald's coat without sleeves; and the shirt,
to say the truth, stolen from my host at Saint Alban's, or the 40

15–16. contracted . . . banns: i.e., those on the very verge of matri-
mony
  16. commodity: parcel; warm: well-off
  18. caliver: musket; struck: wounded
  19. toasts-and-butter: delicate fellows
  21. ancients: standard bearers
  22. gentlemen of companies: soldiers above the rank of regular enlisted men
  23. Lazarus: see Luke 16:19–31; painted cloth: a decorative hanging
for a room
  26. revolted: faithless; trade-fallen: unemployed
  28. fazed ancient: ragged flag
  31. draff: swill
  33. gibbets: gallows
  36. gyves: shackles
  40–41. Saint Albans . . . Daventry: towns on the road from London
to Coventry

red-nose innkeeper of Daventry. But that's all one; they'll find linen enough on every hedge.

Enter the PRINCE [*and the*] LORD OF WESTMORELAND.

PRINCE. How now, blown Jack? How now, quilt?

FALSTAFF. What, Hal? How now, mad wag? What a devil dost thou in Warwickshire? My good Lord of Westmoreland, I cry you mercy. I thought your honor had already been at Shrewsbury.

WESTMORELAND. Faith, Sir John, 'tis more than time that I were there, and you too, but my powers are there already. The king, I can tell you, looks for us all. We must away all night.

FALSTAFF. Tut, never fear me; I am as vigilant as a cat to steal cream.

PRINCE. I think, to steal cream indeed, for thy theft hath already made thee butter. But tell me, Jack, whose fellows are these that come after?

FALSTAFF. Mine, Hal, mine.

PRINCE. I did never see such pitiful rascals.

FALSTAFF. Tut, tut! good enough to toss; food for powder, food for powder. They'll fill a pit as well as better. Tush, man, mortal men, mortal men.

WESTMORELAND. Ay, but, Sir John, methinks they are exceeding poor and bare, too beggarly.

FALSTAFF. Faith, for their poverty, I know not where they had that, and for their bareness, I am sure they never learned that of me.

PRINCE. No, I'll be sworn, unless you call three fingers on the ribs bare. But, sirrah, make haste. Percy is already in the field.

Exit.

FALSTAFF. What, is the king encamped?

WESTMORELAND. He is, Sir John. I fear we shall stay too long.

FALSTAFF. Well, to the latter end of a fray and the beginning of a feast fits a dull fighter and a keen guest.   *Exeunt.*

41–42. **they'll . . . hedge:** i.e., they will steal laundry placed on the hedges to dry
43. **blown:** inflated
50. **away:** march
58. **to toss:** to carry aloft on the point of a pike

[SCENE III. *The rebel camp near Shrewsbury*.]

Enter HOTSPUR, WORCESTER, DOUGLAS, VERNON.

HOTSPUR. We'll fight with him to-night.

WORCESTER.   It may not be.

DOUGLAS. You give him then advantage.

VERNON.   Not a whit.

HOTSPUR. Why say you so? Looks he not for supply?

VERNON. So do we.

HOTSPUR.   His is certain, ours is doubtful.

WORCESTER. Good cousin, be advised; stir not to-night.   5

VERNON. Do not, my lord.

DOUGLAS.   You do not counsel well.
  You speak it out of fear and cold heart.

VERNON. Do me no slander, Douglas. By my life,
  And I dare well maintain it with my life,
  If well-respected honor bid me on,   10
  I hold as little counsel with weak fear
  As you, my lord, or any Scot that this day lives.
  Let it be seen to-morrow in the battle
  Which of us fears.

DOUGLAS.   Yea, or to-night.

VERNON.   Content.

HOTSPUR. To-night, say I.   15

VERNON. Come, come, it may not be. I wonder much,
  Being men of such great leading as you are,
  That you foresee not what impediments
  Drag back our expedition. Certain horse
  Of my cousin Vernon's are not yet come up.   20
  Your uncle Worcester's horse came but to-day;
  And now their pride and mettle is asleep,
  Their courage with hard labor tame and dull,
  That not a horse is half the half of himself.

HOTSPUR. So are the horses of the enemy   25
  In general journey-bated and brought low.

3. **supply:** reinforcements
10. **well-respected:** well-considered
19. **expedition:** haste; **horse:** cavalry
26. **journey-bated:** travel-wearied

The better part of ours are full of rest.
WORCESTER. The number of the king exceedeth ours.
For God's sake, cousin, stay till all come in.

The trumpet sounds a parley. Enter SIR WALTER BLUNT.

BLUNT. I come with gracious offers from the king,   30
If you vouchsafe me hearing and respect.
HOTSPUR. Welcome, Sir Walter Blunt; and would to God
You were of our determination.
Some of us love you well; and even those some
Envy your great deservings and good name,   35
Because you are not of our quality,
But stand against us like an enemy.
BLUNT. And God defend but still I should stand so.
So long as out of limit and true rule
You stand against anointed majesty.   40
But to my charge. The king hath sent to know
The nature of your griefs, and whereupon
You conjure from the breast of civil peace
Such bold hostility, teaching his duteous land
Audacious cruelty. If that the king   45
Have any way your good deserts forgot,
Which he confesseth to be manifold,
He bids you name your griefs, and with all speed
You shall have your desires with interest,
And pardon absolute for yourself and these   50
Herein misled by your suggestion.
HOTSPUR. The king is kind, and well we know the king
Knows at what time to promise, when to pay.
My father and my uncle and myself
Did give him that same royalty he wears;   55
And when he was not six and twenty strong,
Sick in the world's regard, wretched and low,
A poor unminded outlaw sneaking home,
My father gave him welcome to the shore;
And when he heard him swear and vow to God   60

31. **respect:** attention
33. **determination:** way of thinking
36. **quality:** party
38. **defend:** forbid

He came but to be Duke of Lancaster,
To sue his livery and beg his peace,
With tears of innocency and terms of zeal,
My father, in kind heart and pity moved,
Swore him assistance, and performed it too.   65
Now when the lords and barons of the realm
Perceived Northumberland did lean to him,
The more and less came in with cap and knee,
Met him in boroughs, cities, villages,
Attended him on bridges, stood in lanes,   70
Laid gifts before him, proffered him their oaths,
Gave him their heirs as pages, followed him
Even at the heels in golden multitudes.
He presently, as greatness knows itself,
Steps me a little higher than his vow   75
Made to my father, while his blood was poor,
Upon the naked shore at Ravenspurgh;
And now, forsooth, takes on him to reform
Some certain edicts and some strait decrees
That lie too heavy on the commonwealth;   80
Cries out upon abuses, seems to weep
Over his country's wrongs; and by this face,
This seeming brow of justice, did he win
The hearts of all that he did angle for;
Proceeded further, cut me off the heads   85
Of all the favorites that the absent king
In deputation left behind him here
When he was personal in the Irish war.
BLUNT. Tut! I came not to hear this.
HOTSPUR.   Then to the point.
In short time after, he deposed the king,   90

62. **sue his livery:** seek possession of his inheritance
63. **zeal:** ardent affection
72. **pages:** court attendants
73. **golden:** well-dressed
74. **as greatness knows itself:** i.e., as greatness becomes aware of its
own greatness
79. **strait:** strict
82. **face:** pretence
87. **In deputation:** as his deputies
88. **personal:** in person

Soon after that deprived him of his life,
And in the neck of that tasked the whole state;
To make that worse, suffered his kinsman March
(Who is, if every owner were well placed,
Indeed his king) to be engaged in Wales,   95
There without ransom to lie forfeited,
Disgraced me in my happy victories,
Sought to entrap me by intelligence,
Rated mine uncle from the council board,
In rage dismissed my father from the court,   100
Broke oath on oath, committed wrong on wrong,
And in conclusion drove us to seek out
This head of safety, and withal to pry
Into his title, the which we find
Too indirect for long continuance.   105

BLUNT. Shall I return this answer to the king?

HOTSPUR. Not so, Sir Walter. We'll withdraw awhile.
Go to the king; and let there be impawned
Some surety for a safe return again,
And in the morning early shall mine uncle   110
Bring him our purposes; and so farewell.

BLUNT. I would you would accept of grace and love.

HOTSPUR. And may be so we shall.

BLUNT.   Pray God you do.   [Exeunt.]

[SCENE IV. York, The Archbishop's palace.]

Enter ARCHBISHOP OF YORK [and] SIR MICHAEL.

ARCHBISHOP. Hie, good Sir Michael; bear this sealed brief
With winged haste to the lord marshal;
This to my cousin Scroop; and all the rest
To whom they are directed. If you knew
How much they do import, you would make haste.   5

92. in . . . that: immediately after; tasked: taxed
95. engaged: held as hostage
98. intelligence: espionage
99. Rated: scolded
103. withal: at the same time
108. impawned: pledged
1. brief: letter

SIR MICHAEL. My good lord,
  I guess their tenor.
ARCHBISHOP.   Like enough you do.
  To-morrow, good Sir Michael, is a day
  Wherein the fortune of ten thousand men
  Must bide the touch; for, sir, at Shrewsbury,   10
  As I am truly given to understand,
  The king with mighty and quick-raised power
  Meets with Lord Harry; and I fear, Sir Michael,
  What with the sickness of Northumberland,
  Whose power was in the first proportion,   15
  And what with Owen Glendower's absence thence,
  Who with them was a rated sinew too
  And comes not in, overruled by prophecies—
  I fear the power of Percy is too weak
  To wage an instant trial with the king.   20
SIR MICHAEL. Why, my good lord, you need not fear;
  There is Douglas and Lord Mortimer.
ARCHBISHOP. No, Mortimer is not there.
SIR MICHAEL. But there is Mordake, Vernon, Lord Harry Percy,
  And there is my Lord of Worcester, and a head   25
  Of gallant warriors, noble gentlemen.
ARCHBISHOP. And so there is; but yet the king hath drawn
  The special head of all the land together:
  The Prince of Wales, Lord John of Lancaster,
  The noble Westmoreland and warlike Blunt,   30
  And many mo corrivals and dear men
  Of estimation and command in arms.
SIR MICHAEL. Doubt not, my lord, they shall be well opposed.
ARCHBISHOP. I hope no less, yet needful 'tis to fear;
  And, to prevent the worst, Sir Michael, speed.   35
  For if Lord Percy thrive not, ere the king
  Dismiss his power, he means to visit us,
  For he hath heard of our confederacy,

7. **tenor**: import
10. **Must . . . touch**: must be put to the test
15. **proportion**: magnitude
17. **rated sinew**: esteemed strength
31. **mo**: more; **corrivals**: companions; **dear**: worthy
36. **thrive**: succeed

And 'tis but wisdom to make strong against him.
Therefore make haste. I must go write again   40
To other friends; and so farewell, Sir Michael.   *Exeunt.*

[ACT V, SCENE I. *The King's camp near Shrewsbury.*]

Enter the KING, PRINCE OF WALES, LORD JOHN OF LANCASTER,
SIR WALTER BLUNT, FALSTAFF.

KING. How bloodily the sun begins to peer
  Above yon busky hill! The day looks pale
  At his distemp'rature.
PRINCE.   The southern wind
  Doth play the trumpet to his purposes
  And by his hollow whistling in the leaves   5
  Foretells a tempest and a blust'ring day.
KING. Then with the losers let it sympathize,
  For nothing can seem foul to those that win.

  The trumpet sounds. Enter WORCESTER [*and* VERNON].

  How now, my Lord of Worcester! 'Tis not well
  That you and I should meet upon such terms   10
  As now we meet. You have deceived our trust
  And made us doff our easy robes of peace
  To crush our old limbs in ungentle steel.
  This is not well, my lord; this is not well.
  What say you to it? Will you again unknit   15
  This churlish knot of all-abhorred war,
  And move in that obedient orb again
  Where you did give a fair and natural light,
  And be no more an exhaled meteor,
  A prodigy of fear, and a portent   20
  Of broached mischief to the unborn times?

2. **busky**: bushy, wooded
3. **his**: the sun's; **distemp'rature**: discomposure
4. **trumpet**: trumpeter; **his purposes**: what the sun portends by its
unusual appearance
16. **churlish**: hard
17. **orb**: sphere of action
19. **exhaled**: evaporated
20. **prodigy of fear**: fearful omen
21. **broached**: set running

WORCESTER. Hear me, my liege.
  For mine own part, I could be well content
  To entertain the lag-end of my life
  With quiet hours, for I [do] protest   25
  I have not sought the day of this dislike.
KING. You have not sought it! How comes it then?
FALSTAFF. Rebellion lay in his way, and he found it.
PRINCE. Peace, chewet, peace!
WORCESTER. It pleased your majesty to turn your looks   30
  Of favor from myself and all our house;
  And yet I must remember you, my lord,
  We were the first and dearest of your friends.
  For you my staff of office did I break
  In Richard's time, and posted day and night   35
  To meet you on the way and kiss your hand
  When yet you were in place and in account
  Nothing so strong and fortunate as I,
  It was myself, my brother, and his son
  That brought you home and boldly did outdare   40
  The dangers of the time. You swore to us,
  And you did swear that oath at Doncaster,
  That you did nothing purpose 'gainst the state,
  Nor claim no further than your new-fall'n right,
  The seat of Gaunt, dukedom of Lancaster.   45
  To this we swore our aid. But in short space
  It rained down fortune show'ring on your head,
  And such a flood of greatness fell on you,
  What with our help, what with the absent king,
  What with the injuries of a wanton time,   50
  The seeming sufferances that you had borne,
  And the contrarious winds that held the king
  So long in his unlucky Irish wars
  That all in England did repute him dead;
  And from this swarm of fair advantages   55

24. lag-end: latter part
29. chewet: chatterer
32. remember: remind
35. posted: rode fast
40. outdare: defy
51. sufferances: distresses
52. contrarious: adverse

You took occasion to be quickly wooed
To gripe the general sway into your hand;
Forgot your oath to us at Doncaster;
And, being fed by us, you used us so
As that ungentle gull, the cuckoo's bird,   60
Useth the sparrow, did oppress our nest;
Grew by our feeding to so great a bulk
That even our love durst not come near your sight
For fear of swallowing; but with nimble wing
We were enforced for safety sake to fly   65
Out of your sight and raise this present head;
Whereby we stand opposed by such means
As you yourself have forged against yourself
By unkind usage, dangerous countenance,
And violation of all faith and troth   70
Sworn to us in your younger enterprise.

KING. These things, indeed, you have articulate,
Proclaimed at market crosses, read in churches,
To face the garment of rebellion
With some fine color that may please the eye   75
Of fickle changelings and poor discontents,
Which gape and rub the elbow at the news
Of hurlyburly innovation.
And never yet did insurrection want
Such water colors to impaint his cause,   80
Nor moody beggars, starving for a time
Of pell-mell havoc and confusion.

PRINCE. In both your armies there is many a soul
Shall pay full dearly for this encounter,
If once they join in trial. Tell your nephew   85
The Prince of Wales doth join with all the world

57. **gripe**: grasp firmly
60–61. The cuckoo lays its eggs in the nest of another bird.
69. **dangerous**: threatening
70. **troth**: truth
72. **articulate**: spelled out
73. **market crosses**: places of prominence at the markets
74. **face**: trim
76. **changelings**: inconstant persons
77. **rub the elbow**: show oneself pleased
78. **hurlyburly**: tumultuous; **innovation**: revolution

In praise of Henry Percy. By my hopes,
This present enterprise set off his head,
I do not think a braver gentleman,
More active-valiant or more valiant-young,   90
More daring or more bold, is now alive
To grace this latter age with noble deeds.
For my part, I may speak it to my shame,
I have a truant been to chivalry;
And so I hear he doth account me too.   95
Yet this before my father's majesty—
I am content that he shall take the odds
Of his great name and estimation,
And will, to save the blood on either side,
Try fortune with him in a single fight.   100
KING. And, Prince of Wales, so dare we venture thee,
    Albeit considerations infinite
    Do make against it. No, good Worcester, no!
    We love our people well; even those we love
    That are misled upon your cousin's part;   105
    And, will they take the offer of our grace,
    Both he, and they, and you, yea, every man
    Shall be my friend again, and I'll be his.
    So tell your cousin, and bring me word
    What he will do. But if he will not yield,   110
    Rebuke and dread correction wait on us,
    And they shall do their office. So be gone.
    We will not now be troubled with reply.
    We offer fair; take it advisedly.

                    Exit WORCESTER [*and* VERNON].

PRINCE. It will not be accepted, on my life.   115
    The Douglas and the Hotspur both together
    Are confident against the world in arms.
KING. Hence, therefore, every leader to his charge;

88. set . . . head: not laid to his charge
94. chivalry: the duties of knighthood
98. estimation: reputation
111. wait on us: are in our service

For, on their answer, will we set on them,
And God befriend us as our cause is just!   120

Exeunt. Manent PRINCE, FALSTAFF.

FALSTAFF. Hal, if thou see me down in the battle and bestride
me, so! 'Tis a point of friendship.

PRINCE. Nothing but a colossus can do thee that friendship. Say
thy prayers, and farewell.

FALSTAFF. I would 'twere bedtime, Hal, and all well.   125

PRINCE. Why, thou owest God a death.   [*Exit.*]

FALSTAFF. 'Tis not due yet: I would be loath to pay him before
his day. What need I be so forward with him that calls not on
me? Well, 'tis no matter; honor pricks me on. Yea, but how if
honor prick me off when I come on? How then? Can honor set 130
to a leg? No. Or an arm? No. Or take away the grief of a
wound? No. Honor hath no skill in surgery then? No. What is
honor? A word. What is in that word honor? What is that
honor? Air. A trim reckoning! Who hath it? He that died a
Wednesday. Doth he feel it? No. Doth he hear it? No. 'Tis 135
insensible then? Yea, to the dead. But will [it] not live with
the living? No. Why? Detraction will not suffer it. Therefore
I'll none of it. Honor is a mere scutcheon—and so ends my
catechism.   *Exit.*

[SCENE II. *The rebel camp.*]

Enter WORCESTER [*and*] SIR RICHARD VERNON.

WORCESTER. O no, my nephew must not know, Sir Richard,
The liberal and kind offer of the king.

VERNON. 'Twere best he did.

s.d. *Manent:* remain
122. so: good
130. prick: select a name (i.e., check his name off as a casualty)
130–31. set to: mend
131. grief: pain
134. trim: fine
136. insensible: not perceptible to the senses
137. Detraction: slander
138. scutcheon: escutcheon, a painted representation of a shield bearing a coat of arms

WORCESTER.   Then are we all undone.
It is not possible, it cannot be,
The king should keep his word in loving us.   5
He will suspect us still and find a time
To punish this offense in other faults.
Supposition all our lives shall be stuck full of eyes;
For treason is but trusted like the fox,
Who, ne'er so tame, so cherished and locked up,   10
Will have a wild trick of his ancestors.
Look how we can, or sad or merrily,
Interpretation will misquote our looks,
And we shall feed like oxen at a stall,
The better cherished still the nearer death.   15
My nephew's trespass may be well forgot;
It hath the excuse of youth and heat of blood
And an adopted name of privilege,
A hare-brained Hotspur, governed by a spleen.
All his offenses live upon my head   20
And on his father's. We did train him on;
And, his corruption being ta'en from us,
We, as the spring of all, shall pay for all.
Therefore, good cousin, let not Harry know,
In any case, the offer of the king.   25

                    Enter HOTSPUR [*and* DOUGLAS].

VERNON. Deliver what you will, I'll say 'tis so.
Here comes your cousin.
HOTSPUR.   My uncle is returned.
Deliver up my Lord of Westmoreland.
Uncle, what news?
WORCESTER. The king will bid you battle presently.   30
DOUGLAS. Defy him by the Lord of Westmoreland.
HOTSPUR. Lord Douglas, go you and tell him so.

    8. **Supposition:** suspicion
    12. **or** [1]: either
    19. **spleen:** fiery temper
    21. **train:** lure
    23. **spring:** source
    28. **Westmoreland:** the hostage given by the king
    30. **presently:** immediately

DOUGLAS. Marry, and shall, and very willingly.   *Exit.*
WORCESTER. There is no seeming mercy in the king.
HOTSPUR. Did you beg any? God forbid!   35
WORCESTER. I told him gently of our grievances,
   Of his oath-breaking, which he mended thus,
   By now forswearing that he is forsworn.
   He calls us rebels, traitors, and will scourge
   With haughty arms this hateful name in us.   40

                    Enter DOUGLAS.

DOUGLAS. Arm, gentlemen, to arms! for I have thrown
   A brave defiance in King Henry's teeth,
   And Westmoreland, that was engaged, did bear it;
   Which cannot choose but bring him quickly on.
WORCESTER. The Prince of Wales stepped forth before the king   45
   And, nephew, challenged you to single fight.
HOTSPUR. O, would the quarrel lay upon our heads,
   And that no man might draw short breath to-day
   But I and Harry Monmouth! Tell me, tell me,
   How showed his tasking? Seemed it in contempt?   50
VERNON. No, by my soul. I never in my life
   Did hear a challenge urged more modestly,
   Unless a brother should a brother dare
   To gentle exercise and proof of arms.
   He gave you all the duties of a man;   55
   Trimmed up your praises with a princely tongue;
   Spoke your deservings like a chronicle;
   Making you ever better than his praise
   By still dispraising praise valued with you;
   And, which became him like a prince indeed,   60
   He made a blushing cital of himself,

37. **mended:** atoned for
38. **forswearing . . . forsworn:** falsely denying that he has broken his
word
43. **engaged:** pledged as a hostage
49. **Harry Monmouth:** i.e., Hal
50. **tasking:** challenge
54. **proof:** trial
55. **duties of:** respects pertaining to
59. **valued . . . you:** compared with you in respect of worth
61. **cital:** citation

And chid his truant youth with such a grace
As if he mastered there a double spirit
Of teaching and of learning instantly.
There did he pause; but let me tell the world,   65
If he outlive the envy of this day,
England did never owe so sweet a hope,
So much misconstrued in his wantonness.

HOTSPUR. Cousin, I think thou art enamored
Upon his follies. Never did I hear   70
Of any prince so wild a liberty.
But be he as he will, yet once ere night
I will embrace him with a soldier's arm,
That he shall shrink under my courtesy.
Arm, arm with speed! and, fellows, soldiers, friends,   75
Better consider what you have to do
Than I, that have not well the gift of tongue,
Can lift your blood up with persuasion.

Enter a MESSENGER.

MESSENGER. My lord, here are letters for you.
HOTSPUR. I cannot read them now.   80
O gentlemen, the time of life is short!
To spend that shortness basely were too long
If life did ride upon a dial's point,
Still ending at the arrival of an hour.
An if we live, we live to tread on kings;   85
If die, brave death, when princes die with us!
Now for our consciences, the arms are fair,
When the intent of bearing them is just.

Enter another [MESSENGER].

MESSENGER. My lord, prepare. The king comes on apace.
HOTSPUR. I thank him that he cuts me from my tale,   90
For I profess not talking. Only this—
Let each man do his best; and here draw I

66. **envy:** malice
67. **owe:** own
83. **dial's point:** hand of a clock
84. **Still:** always
86. **brave:** excellent
89. **apace:** speedily

A sword whose temper I intend to stain
With the best blood that I can meet withal
In the adventure of this perilous day.   95
Now, Esperance! Percy! and set on.
Sound all the lofty instruments of war,
And by that music let us all embrace;
For, heaven to earth, some of us never shall
A second time do such a courtesy.   100

    Here they embrace. The trumpets sound. [Exeunt.]

    [SCENE III. *A Plain between the camps.*]

The KING *enters with his power [and passes over].*
Alarum to the battle. Then enter DOUGLAS *and*
SIR WALTER BLUNT.

BLUNT. What is thy name, that in battle thus
  Thou crossest me? What honor dost thou seek
  Upon my head?
DOUGLAS.   Know then my name is Douglas,
  And I do haunt thee in the battle thus
  Because some tell me that thou art a king.   5
BLUNT. They tell thee true.
DOUGLAS. The Lord of Stafford dear to-day hath bought
  Thy likeness, for instead of thee, King Harry,
  This sword hath ended him. So shall it thee,
  Unless thou yield thee as my prisoner.   10
BLUNT. I was not born a yielder, thou proud Scot;
  And thou shalt find a king that will revenge
  Lord Stafford's death.

    They fight. DOUGLAS *kills* BLUNT. *Then enter* HOTSPUR.

HOTSPUR. O Douglas, hadst thou fought at Holmedon thus,
  I never had triumphed upon a Scot.   15
DOUGLAS. All's done, all's won. Here breathless lies the king.
HOTSPUR. Where?
DOUGLAS. Here.

95. **adventure:** chance
96. **Esperance:** motto of the Percy family used here as a battle cry
97. **lofty instruments:** drums and trumpets
S.D. *Alarum:* call to arms

HOTSPUR. This, Douglas? No. I know this face full well.
A gallant knight he was, his name was Blunt;   20
Semblably furnished like the king himself.
DOUGLAS. Ah fool, go with thy soul, whither it goes!
A borrowed title hast thou bought too dear:
Why didst thou tell me that thou wert a king?
HOTSPUR. The king hath many marching in his coats.   25
DOUGLAS. Now, by my sword, I will kill all his coats;
I'll murder all his wardrobe, piece by piece,
Until I meet the king.
HOTSPUR.   Up and away!
Our soldiers stand full fairly for the day.   [*Exeunt.*]

Alarum. Enter FALSTAFF *solus.*

FALSTAFF. Though I could 'scape shot-free at London, I fear the   30
shot here. Here's no scoring but upon the pate. Soft! who are
you? Sir Walter Blunt. There's honor for you! Here's no
vanity! I am as hot as molten lead, and as heavy too. God
keep lead out of me. I need no more weight than mine own
bowels. I have led my ragamuffins where they are peppered.   35
There's not three of my hundred and fifty left alive, and they
are for the town's end, to beg during life. But who comes here?

Enter the PRINCE.

PRINCE. What, stand'st thou idle here? Lend me thy sword.
Many a nobleman lies stark and stiff
Under the hoofs of vaunting enemies,
Whose deaths are yet unrevenged. I prithee   40
Lend me thy sword.
FALSTAFF. O Hal, I prithee give me leave to breathe awhile. Turk
Gregory never did such deeds in arms as I have done this day.
I have paid Percy; I have made him sure.
    45

21. **Semblably furnished:** similarly dressed
29. **fairly:** favorable
30. **shot-free:** without having to pay the bill
31. **scoring:** (1) making a reckoning of a bill (2) cutting
35. **peppered:** done for
43–44. **Turk Gregory:** Possibly Pope Gregory XIII, a supporter of
Philip II and the Irish insurrectionists, is intended. "Turk" was synonymous with cruelty and savagery.
45. **paid:** killed; **made him sure:** rendered him harmless

PRINCE. He is indeed, and living to kill thee.
   I prithee lend me thy sword.
FALSTAFF. Nay, before God, Hal, if Percy be alive, thou get'st
   not my sword; but take my pistol, if thou wilt.
PRINCE. Give it me. What, is it in the case?   50
FALSTAFF. Ay, Hal. 'Tis hot, 'tis hot. There's that will sack a
   city.
        The PRINCE *draws it out and finds it to be a bottle of sack.*
PRINCE. What, is it a time to jest and dally now?
                            He throws the bottle at him. Exit.
FALSTAFF. Well, if Percy be alive, I'll pierce him. If he do come
   in my way, so; if he do not, if I come in his willingly, let him   55
   make a carbonado of me. I like not such grinning honor as
   Sir Walter hath. Give me life; which if I can save, so; if not,
   honor comes unlooked for, and there's an end.   [*Exit.*]

[SCENE IV. *Another part of the field.*]

Alarum. Excursions. Enter the KING, *the* PRINCE,
LORD JOHN OF LANCASTER, EARL OF WESTMORELAND.

KING. I prithee, Harry, withdraw thyself; thou bleedest too much.
   Lord John of Lancaster, go you with him.
JOHN. Not I, my lord, unless I did bleed too.
PRINCE. I [do] beseech your majesty make up,
   Lest your retirement do amaze your friends.   5
KING. I will do so.
   My Lord of Westmoreland, lead him to his tent.
WESTMORELAND. Come, my lord, I'll lead you to your tent.
PRINCE. Lead me, my lord? I do not need your help;
   And God forbid a shallow scratch should drive   10
   The Prince of Wales from such a field as this,
   Where stained nobility lies trodden on,
   And rebels' arms triumph in massacres!
JOHN. We breathe too long. Come, cousin Westmoreland,
   Our duty this way lies. For God's sake, come!   15
               [*Exeunt* PRINCE JOHN *and* WESTMORELAND.]

56. **carbonado:** meat cut crosswise and broiled
S.D. *Excursions:* sorties
4. **make up:** bring up your forces
5. **amaze:** bewilder

PRINCE. By God, thou has deceived me, Lancaster!
  I did not think thee lord of such a spirit.
  Before, I loved thee as a brother, John;
  But now, I do respect thee as my soul.
KING. I saw him hold Lord Percy at the point   20
  With lustier maintenance than I did look for
  Of such an ungrown warrior.
PRINCE.   O, this boy
  Lends mettle to us all!   *Exit.*

[Enter DOUGLAS.]

DOUGLAS. Another king? They grow like Hydra's heads.
  I am the Douglas, fatal to all those
  That wear those colors on them. What art thou 25
  That counterfeit'st the person of a king?
KING. The king himself, who, Douglas, grieves at heart
  So many of his shadows thou hast met,
  And not the very king. I have two boys
  Seek Percy and thyself about the field;   30
  But seeing thou fall'st on me so luckily,
  I will assay thee. So defend thyself.
DOUGLAS. I fear thou art another counterfeit;
  And yet, in faith, thou bearest thee like a king. 35
  But mine I am sure thou art, whoe'er thou be,
  And thus I win thee.

They fight. The KING *being in danger, enter* PRINCE OF WALES.

PRINCE. Hold up thy head, vile Scot, or thou art like
  Never to hold it up again. The spirits
  Of valiant Shirley, Stafford, Blunt are in my arms.
  It is the Prince of Wales that threatens thee, 40
  Who never promiseth but he means to pay.
              They fight. DOUGLAS *flieth.*
  Cheerly, my lord, how fares your grace?

21. **lustier maintenance:** more vigorous conduct
24. **Hydra:** the nine-headed monster of Greek mythology which grew
two new heads for each one cut off
29. **shadows:** likenesses
33. **assay:** challenge
43. **Cheerly:** a cry of encouragement

Sir Nicholas Gawsey hath for succor sent,
And so hath Clifton. I'll to Clifton straight.   45
KING. Stay and breathe awhile.
  Thou hast redeemed thy lost opinion,
  And showed thou mak'st some tender of my life
  In this fair rescue thou hast brought to me.
PRINCE. O God, they did me too much injury   50
  That ever said I hearkened for your death.
  If it were so, I might have let alone
  The insulting hand of Douglas over you,
  Which would have been as speedy in your end
  As all the poisonous potions in the world,   55
  And saved the treacherous labor of your son.
KING. Make up to Clifton; I'll to Sir Nicholas Gawsey.

                                              Exit.

                    Enter HOTSPUR.

HOTSPUR. If I mistake not, thou art Harry Monmouth.
PRINCE. Thou speak'st as if I would deny my name.
HOTSPUR. My name is Harry Percy.
PRINCE.   Why, then I see   60
  A very valiant rebel of the name.
  I am the Prince of Wales, and think not, Percy,
  To share with me in glory any more.
  Two stars keep not their motion in one sphere,
  Nor can one England brook a double reign   65
  Of Harry Percy and the Prince of Wales.
HOTSPUR. Nor shall it, Harry, for the hour is come
  To end the one of us; and would to God
  Thy name in arms were now as great as mine!
PRINCE. I'll make it greater ere I part from thee,   70
  And all the budding honors on thy crest
  I'll crop to make a garland for my head.
HOTSPUR. I can no longer brook thy vanities.   *They fight.*

  47. **redeemed:** recovered; **opinion:** reputation
  48. **tender:** regard
  51. **hearkened for:** desired
  53. **insulting:** scornfully triumphing
  71. **budding . . . crest:** the plumes on his helmet
  73. **vanities:** idle statements

Enter FALSTAFF.

FALSTAFF. Well said, Hal! to it, Hal! Nay, you shall find no boy's
play here, I can tell you.   75

> *Enter* DOUGLAS. *He fighteth with* FALSTAFF, [*who*] *falls down*
> *as if he were dead.* [*Exit* DOUGLAS.] *The* PRINCE
> *killeth* PERCY.

HOTSPUR. O Harry, thou hast robbed me of my youth!
  I better brook the loss of brittle life
  Than those proud titles thou hast won of me.
  They wound my thoughts worse than thy sword my flesh.
  But thoughts the slaves of life, and life time's fool,   80
  And time, that takes survey of all the world,
  Must have a stop. O, I could prophesy,
  But that the earthy and cold hand of death
  Lies on my tongue. No, Percy, thou art dust,
  And food for—   [*Dies.*] 85
PRINCE. For worms, brave Percy. Fare thee well, great heart;
  Ill-weaved ambition, how much art thou shrunk!
  When that this body did contain a spirit,
  A kingdom for it was too small a bound;
  But now two paces of the vilest earth
  Is room enough. This earth that bears thee dead   90
  Bears not alive so stout a gentleman.
  If thou wert sensible of courtesy,
  I should not make so dear a show of zeal.
  But let my favors hide thy mangled face;   95
  And, even in thy behalf, I'll thank myself
  For doing these fair rites of tenderness.
  Adieu, and take thy praise with thee to heaven.
  Thy ignominy sleep with thee in the grave,
  But not rememb'red in thy epitaph.   100
                      He spieth FALSTAFF *on the ground.*
  What, old acquaintance? Could not all this flesh

80. **fool:** dupe
92. **stout:** valiant
94. **dear:** heartfelt
95. **favors:** plumes (see note to l. 71 above)

Keep in a little life? Poor Jack, farewell!
I could have better spared a better man.
O, I should have a heavy miss of thee
If I were much in love with vanity.   105
Death hath not struck so fat a deer to-day,
Though many dearer, in this bloody fray.
Embowelled will I see thee by and by;
Till then in blood by noble Percy lie.   *Exit.*

FALSTAFF *riseth up.*

FALSTAFF. Embowelled? If thou embowel me to-day, I'll give 110
you leave to powder me and eat me too to-morrow. 'Sblood,
'twas time to counterfeit, or that hot termagant Scot had paid
me scot and lot too. Counterfeit? I lie; I am no counterfeit.
To die is to be a counterfeit, for he is but the counterfeit of a
man who hath not the life of a man; but to counterfeit dying 115
when a man thereby liveth is to be no counterfeit, but the
true and perfect image of life indeed. The better part of valor
is discretion, in the which better part I have saved my life.
'Zounds, I am afraid of this gunpowder Percy, though he be
dead. How if he should counterfeit too and rise? By my faith, 120
I am afraid he would prove the better counterfeit. Therefore
I'll make him sure; yea, and I'll swear I killed him. Why may
not he rise as well as I? Nothing confutes me but eyes, and
nobody sees me. Therefore, sirrah [*stabbing him*], with a new
wound in your thigh, come you along with me.   125

He takes up HOTSPUR *on his back. Enter* PRINCE [*and*]
JOHN OF LANCASTER.

PRINCE. Come, brother John; full bravely hast thou fleshed
    Thy maiden sword.
JOHN.   But, soft! whom have we here?

104. have . . . miss: disadvantaged by Falstaff's loss (with a pun on
Sir John's heaviness)
105. vanity: foolishness
108. Embowelled: disembowelled
111. powder: salt
112. termagant: violent
113. scot and lot: thoroughly
126–27. fleshed . . . sword: used it for the first time in battle

Did you not tell me this fat man was dead?

PRINCE. I did; I saw him dead,
Breathless and bleeding on the ground. Art thou alive?   130
Or is it fantasy that plays upon our eyesight?
I prithee speak. We will not trust our eyes
Without our ears. Thou art not what thou seem'st.

FALSTAFF. No, that's certain, I am not a double man; but if I
be not Jack Falstaff, then am I a Jack. There is Percy [throw-   135
ing the body down]. If your father will do me any honor, so;
if not, let him kill the next Percy himself. I look to be either
earl or duke, I can assure you.

PRINCE. Why, Percy I killed myself, and saw thee dead!

FALSTAFF. Didst thou? Lord, Lord, how this world is given to   140
lying. I grant you I was down, and out of breath, and so was
he; but we rose both at an instant and fought a long hour by
Shrewsbury clock. If I may be believed, so; if not, let them
that should reward valor bear the sin upon their own heads.
I'll take it upon my death, I gave him this wound in the   145
thigh. If the man were alive and would deny it, 'zounds! I
would make him eat a piece of my sword.

JOHN. This is the strangest tale that ever I heard.

PRINCE. This is the strangest fellow, brother John.
Come, bring your luggage nobly on your back.   150
For my part, if a lie may do thee grace,
I'll gild it with the happiest terms I have.

A retreat is sounded.

The trumpet sounds retreat; the day is ours.
Come, brother, let's to the highest of the field,
To see what friends are living, who are dead.   155

Exeunt [PRINCE HENRY *and* PRINCE JOHN].

FALSTAFF. I'll follow, as they say, for reward. He that rewards
me, God reward him. If I do grow great, I'll grow less; for I'll
purge, and leave sack, and live cleanly, as a nobleman should
do.

Exit [dragging off the body].

134. **double man:** (1) an apparition (2) two men (i.e., with Hotspur
on his shoulder)
135. **Jack:** knave
151. **do . . . grace:** reflect credit on you

[SCENE v. *Another part of the field.*]

The trumpets sound. Enter the KING, PRINCE OF WALES,
LORD JOHN OF LANCASTER, EARL OF WESTMORELAND,
with WORCESTER *and* VERNON *prisoners.*

KING. Thus ever did rebellion find rebuke.
　Ill-spirited Worcester, did not we send grace,
　Pardon, and terms of love to all of you?
　And wouldst thou turn our offers contrary?
　Misuse the tenor of thy kinsman's trust?　　　　　　5
　Three knights upon our party slain to-day,
　A noble earl, and many a creature else
　Had been alive this hour,
　If like a Christian thou hadst truly borne
　Betwixt our armies true intelligence.　　　　　　10

WORCESTER. What I have done my safety urged me to;
　And I embrace this fortune patiently,
　Since not to be avoided it falls on me.

KING. Bear Worcester to the death, and Vernon too;
　Other offenders we will pause upon.　　　　　　15

　　　　　　　　[*Exeunt* WORCESTER *and* VERNON, *guarded.*]

　How goes the field?

PRINCE. The noble Scot, Lord Douglas, when he saw
　The fortune of the day quite turned from him,
　The noble Percy slain, and all his men
　Upon the foot of fear, fled with the rest;　　　　　　20
　And falling from a hill, he was so bruised
　That the pursuers took him. At my tent
　The Douglas is, and I beseech your grace
　I may dispose of him.

KING.　　　　　　　　With all my heart.

PRINCE. Then, brother John of Lancaster, to you　　　　　　25
　This honorable bounty shall belong.
　Go to the Douglas and deliver him
　Up to his pleasure, ransomless and free.

2. **grace:** good will
5. **tenor:** tenure
15. **pause upon:** delay action on
26. **bounty:** act of generosity

His valors shown upon our crests to-day
Have taught us how to cherish such high deeds,   30
Even in the bosom of our adversaries.
JOHN. I thank your grace for this high courtesy,
Which I shall give away immediately.
KING. Then this remains, that we divide our power.
You, son John, and my cousin Westmoreland,   35
Towards York shall bend you with your dearest speed
To meet Northumberland and the prelate Scroop,
Who, as we hear, are busily in arms.
Myself and you, son Harry, will towards Wales
To fight with Glendower and the Earl of March.   40
Rebellion in this land shall lose his sway,
Meeting the check of such another day;
And since this business so fair is done,
Let us not leave till all our own be won.   *Exeunt.*

36. bend you: proceed

EXTRACTS FROM THE MAJOR SOURCES

This section contains selections from three of the works Shakespeare probably drew upon in writing *Henry IV, Part 1*. The first, Raphael Holinshed's *Chronicles of England*, provided the historical matter; the second, Samuel Daniel's *The Civil Wars*, a lengthy historical poem concerning the strife between the houses of Lancaster and York, suggested important elements in the characterization of the Prince and Hotspur; and the third, *The Famous Victories of Henry the Fifth*, a play entered in the *Stationers' Register* May 14, 1594, demonstrated the possibilities of the addition of certain comic scenes to the historical material.

Scholars have differed in their opinions, however, concerning the precise relationship between this last work and *Henry IV, Part 1*. Although some have maintained that Shakespeare actually used this play as a source, J. Dover Wilson and A. W. Pollard have argued that *The Famous Victories* is in reality an abridgement of two earlier plays, now lost, which Shakespeare made use of in writing *Henry IV, Part 1*. In their view, Shakespeare's play and *The Famous Victories* are related in that they derive from a common source.

The punctuation and spelling of the original works have been retained throughout, including certain typographical peculiarities (e.g., "i" for "j," "v" for initial "u," and "u" for medial "v").

I

RAPHAEL HOLINSHED

The Chronicles of England

[Anno 1402]: . . . Owen Glendouer, according to his accustomed manner, robbing and spoiling within the English borders, caused all the forces of the shire of Hereford to assemble togither against them, vnder the conduct of Edmund Mortimer earle of March. But coming to trie the matter by battell, whether by treason or otherwise, so it fortuned, that the English power was discomfited, the earle taken prisoner, and aboue a thousand of his people slaine in the place. The shamefull villainie vsed by the Welshwomen towards the dead carcasses, was such, as honest eares would be ashamed to heare, and continent toongs to speake thereof. The dead bodies might not be buried, without great summes of monie giuen for libertie to conueie them awaie.

The king was not hastie to purchase the deliuerance of the earle March, bicause his title to the crowne was well inough knowen, and therefore suffered him to remaine in miserable prison, wishing both the said earle, and all other of his linage out of this life, with God and his saincts in heauen, so they had beene out of the waie, for then all had beene well inough as he thought. . . . About mid of August, the king to chastise the presumptuous attempts of the Welshmen, went with a great power of men into Wales, to pursue the capteine of the Welsh rebell Owen Glendouer, but in effect he lost his labor; for Owen conueied himselfe out of the waie, into his knowen lurking places, and (as was thought) through art magike, he caused such foule weather of winds, tempest, raine, snow, and haile to be raised, for the annoiance of the kings armie, that the like had

From *The Chronicles of England, from William the Conqueror . . . Faithfullie gathered and compiled by Raphaell Holinshed* (Second edition, 1587), III, 520–524, 539. Reprinted from the copy in the Furness Memorial Library, University of Pennsylvania.

not beene heard of; in such sort, that the king was constreined to
returne home, hauing caused his people yet to spoile and burne first
a great part of the countrie. . . . The Scots vnder the leding of Pat-
rike Hepborne, of the Hales the yoonger, entring into England, were
ouerthrowen at Nesbit, in the marches, as in the Scotish chronicle
ye may find more at large. This battell was fought the two and
twentith of Iune, in this yeare of our Lord 1402.

Archembald earle Dowglas sore displeased in his mind for this
ouerthrow, procured a commission to inuade England, and that to
his cost, as ye may likewise read in the Scotish histories. For at a
place called Homildon, they were so fiercelie assailed by the Englishmen, vnder the leading of the lord Persie, surnamed Henrie Hotspur, and George earle of March, that with violence of the English
shot they were quite vanquished and put to flight, on the Rood
daie in haruest, with a great slaughter made by the Englishmen. . . .
There were slaine of men of estimation, sir Iohn Swinton, sir Adam
Gordon, sir Iohn Leuiston, sir Alexander Ramsie of Dalehousie, and
three and twentie knights, besides ten thousand of the commons:
and of prisoners among other were these, Mordacke earle of Fife,
son to the gouernour Archembald earle Dowglas, which in the fight
lost one of his eies, Thomas erle of Murrey, Robert earle of Angus,
and (as some writers haue) the earles of Atholl & Menteith, with
fiue hundred other of meaner degrees.

*   *   *   *   *

[Anno 1403] Edmund Mortimer earle of March, prisoner with
Owen Glendouer, whether for irkesomnesse of cruell captiuitie, or
feare of death, or for what other cause, it is vncerteine, agreed to
take part with Owen, against the king of England, and tooke to
wife the daughter of the said Owen.

Strange wonders happened (as men reported) at the natiuitie of
this man, for the same night he was borne, all his fathers horsses in
the stable were found to stand in bloud vp to the bellies. . . .

Henrie earle of Northumberland, with his brother Thomas earle
of Worcester, and his sonne the lord Henrie Persie, surnamed Hotspur, which were to king Henrie in the beginning of his reigne, both
faithfull freends, and earnest aiders, began now to enuie his wealth
and felicitie; and especiallie they were greeued, bicause the king demanded of the earle and his sonne such Scotish prisoners as were
taken at Homeldon and Nesbit: for of all the captiues which were

taken in the conflicts foughten in those two places, there was deliuered to the kings possession onelie Mordake earle of Fife, the
duke of Albanies sonne, though the king did diuers and sundrie
times require deliuerance of the residue, and that with great
threatnings: wherewith the Persies being sore offended, for that
they claimed them as their owne proper prisoners, and their peculiar
preies, by the counsell of the lord Thomas Persie earle of Worcester,
whose studie was euer (as some write) to procure malice, and set
things in a broile, came to the king vnto Windsore (vpon a purpose to prooue him) and there required of him, that either by
ransome or otherwise, he would cause to be deliuered out of prison
Edmund Mortimer earle of March, their cousine germane, whome
(as they reported) Owen Glendouer kept in filthie prison, shakled
with irons, onelie for that he tooke his part, and was to him faithfull
and true.

The king began not a little to muse at the request, and not
without cause: for in deed it touched him somewhat neere, sith
this Edmund was sonne to Roger earle of March, sonne to the ladie
Philip, daughter of Lionell duke of Clarence, the third sonne of
king Edward the third; which Edmund at king Richards going into
Ireland, was proclamed heire apparant to the crowne and realme,
whose aunt called Elianor, the lord Henrie Persie had married; and
therefore king Henrie could not well heare, that anie man should
be earnest about the aduancement of that linage. The king when he
had studied on the matter, made answer, that the earle of March
was not taken prisoner for his cause, nor in his seruice, but willinglie
suffered himselfe to be taken, bicause he would not withstand the
attempts of Owen Glendouer, and his complices, & therefore he
would neither ransome him, nor releeue him.

The Persies with this answer and fraudulent excuse were not a
little fumed, insomuch that Henrie Hotspur said openlie: Behold,
the heire of the relme is robbed of his right, and yet the robber with
his owne will not redeeme him. So in this furie the Persies departed, minding nothing more than to depose king Henrie from
the high type of his roialtie, and to place in his seat their cousine
Edmund earle of March, whom they did not onlie deliuer out of
captiuitie, but also (to the high displeasure of king Henrie) entered in league with the foresaid Owen Glendouer. Heerewith, they
by their deputies in the house of the archdeacon of Bangor, diuided
the realme amongst them, causing a tripartite indenture to be made

and sealed with their seales, by the couenants whereof, all England from Seuerne and Trent, south and eastward, was assigned to the earle of March: all Wales, & the lands beyond Seuerne westward, were appointed to Owen Glendouer: and all the remnant from Trent northward, to the lord Persie.

This was doone (as some haue said) through a foolish credit giuen to a vaine prophesie, as though king Henrie was the mold-warpe, curssed of Gods owne mouth, and they three were the dragon, the lion, and the woolfe, which should diuide this realme betweene them. Such is the deuiation (saith Hall) and not diuination of those blind and fantasticall dreames of the Welsh prophe-siers. King Henrie not knowing of this new confederacie, and noth-ing lesse minding than that which after happened, gathered a great armie to go againe into Wales, whereof the earle of Northumber-land and his sonne were aduertised by the earle of Worcester, and with all diligence raised all the power they could make, and sent to the Scots which before were taken prisoners at Homeldon, for aid of men, promising to the earle of Dowglas the towne of Berwike, and a part of Northumberland, and to other Scotish lords, great lordships and seigniories, if they obteined the vpper hand. The Scots in hope of gaine, and desirous to be reuenged of their old greefes, came to the earle with a great companie well appointed.

The Persies to make their part seeme good, deuised certeine ar-ticles, by the aduise of Richard Scroope, archbishop of Yorke, brother to the lord Scroope, whome king Henrie had caused to be beheaded at Bristow. These articles being shewed to diuerse noble-men, and other states of the realme, mooued them to fauour their purpose, in so much that manie of them did not onelie promise to the Persies aid and succour by words, but also by their writings and seales confirmed the same. Howbeit when the matter came to triall, the most part of the confederates abandoned them, and at the daie of the conflict left them alone. Thus after that the con-spirators had discouered themselues, the lord Henrie Persie desirous to proceed in the enterprise, vpon trust to be assisted by Owen Glendouer, the earle of March, & other, assembled an armie of men of armes and archers foorth of Cheshire and Wales. Incon-tinentlie his vncle Thomas Persie earle of Worcester, that had the gouernement of the prince of Wales, who as then laie at London in secret manner, conueied himselfe out of the princes house, and comming to Stafford (where he met his nephue) they increased their power by all waies and meanes they could deuise. The earle of Northumberland himselfe was not with them, but being sicke, had promised vpon his amendement to repaire vnto them (as some write) with all conuenient speed.

These noble men, to make their conspiracie to seeme excusable, besides the articles aboue mentioned, sent letters abroad, wherein was conteined, that their gathering of an armie tended to none other end, but onlie for the safegard of their owne persons, and to put some better gouernment in the commonwealth. For whereas taxes and tallages were dailie leuied, vnder pretense to be imploied in defense of the realme, the same were vainlie wasted, and vnprofit-ablie consumed: and where through the slanderous reports of their enimies, the king had taken a greeuous displeasure with them, they durst not appeare personallie in the kings presence, vntill the prelats and barons of the realme had obteined of the king licence for them to come and purge themselues before him, by lawfull triall of their peeres, whose iudgement (as they pretended) they would in no wise refuse. Manie that saw and heard these letters, did commend their diligence, and highlie praised their assured fidelitie and trustinesse towards the commonwealth.

But the king vnderstanding their cloaked drift, deuised (by what meanes he might) to quiet and appease the commons, and deface their contriued forgeries; and therefore he wrote an answer to their libels, that he maruelled much, sith the earle of Northumberland, and the lord Henrie Persie his sonne, had receiued the most part of the summes of monie granted to him by the cleargie and com-munaltie, for defense of the marches, as he could euidentlie prooue what should mooue them to complaine and raise such manifest slanders. And whereas he vnderstood, that the earles of Northumber-land and Worcester, and the lord Persie had by their letters signified to their freends abroad, that by reason of the slanderous reports of their enimies, they durst not appeare in his presence, without the mediation of the prelats and nobles of the realme, so as they re-quired pledges, whereby they might safelie come afore him, to de-clare and alledge what they had to saie in proofe of their innocencie, he protested by letters sent foorth vnder his seale, that they might safelie come and go, without all danger, or anie manner of in-damagement to be offered to their persons.

But this could not satisfie those men, but that resolued to go forwards with their enterprise, they marched towards Shrewesburie,

vpon hope to be aided (as men thought) by Owen Glendouer, and
his Welshmen, publishing abroad throughout the countries on
each side, that king Richard was aliue, whome if they wished to
see, they willed them to repaire in armour vnto the castell of Chester, where (without all doubt) he was at that present, and redie
to come forward. This tale being raised, though it were most vntrue,
yet it bred variable motions in mens minds, causing them to
wauer, so as they knew not to which part they should sticke; and
verelie, diuers were well affected towards king Richard, speciallie
such as had tasted of his princelie bountifulnes, of which there was
no small number. And to speake a truth, no maruell it was, if
manie enuied the prosperous state of king Henrie, sith it was euident
inough to the world, that he had with wrong vsurped the crowne,
and not onelie violentlie deposed king Richard, but also cruellie
procured his death, for the which vndoubtedlie, both he and his
posteritie tasted such troubles, as put them still in danger of their
states, till their direct succeeding line was quite rooted out by the
contrarie faction, as in Henrie the sixt and Edward the fourth it
may appeare.

But now to returne where we left King Henrie aduertised of the
proceedings of the Persies, foorthwith gathered about him such
power as he might make, and being earnestlie called vpon by the
Scot, the earle of March, to make hast and giue battell to his enimies, before their power by delaieng of time should still too much
increase, he passed forward with such speed, that he was in sight
of his enimies, lieng in campe neere to Shrewesburie, before they
were in doubt of anie such thing, for the Persies thought that he
would haue staied at Burton vpon Trent, till his councell had
come thither to him to giue their aduise what he were best to
doo. But herein the enimie was deceiued of his expectation, sith
the king had great regard of expedition and making speed for the
safetie of his owne person, whereunto the earle of March incited
him, considering that in delaie is danger, & losse in lingering. . . .

By reason of the kings sudden cōming in this sort, they staied
from assaulting the towne of Shrewesburie, which enterprise they
were readie at that instant to haue taken in hand, and foorthwith
the lord Persie (as a capteine of high courage) began to exhort the
capteines and souldiers to prepare themselues to battell, sith the
matter was growen to that point, that by no meanes it could be
auoided, so that (said he) this daie shall either bring vs all to

aduancement & honor, or else if it shall chance vs to be ouercome, shall delieuer vs from the kings spitefull malice and cruell disdaine: for plaieng the men (as we ought to doo) better it is to die in battell for the commonwealths cause, than through cowardlike feare to prolong life, which after shall be taken from vs, by sentence of the enimie.

Herevpon, the whole armie being in number about fourteene thousand chosen men, promised to stand with him so long as life lasted. There were with the Persies as chiefteines of this armie, the earle of Dowglas a Scotish man, the baron of Kinderton, sir Hugh Browne, and sir Richard Vernon knights, with diuerse other stout and right valiant capteins. Now when the two armies were incamped, the one against the other, the earle of Worcester and the lord Persie with their complices sent the articles (whereof I spake before) by Thomas Caiton, and Thomas Saluain esquiers to king Henrie, vnder their hands and seales, which articles in effect charged him with manifest periurie, in that (contrarie to his oth receiued vpon the euangelists at Doncaster, when he first entred the realme after his exile) he had taken vpon him the crowne and roiall dignitie, imprisoned king Richard, caused him to resigne his title, and finallie to be murthered. Diuerse other matters they laid to his charge, as leuieng of taxes and tallages, contrarie to his promise, infringing of lawes & customes of the realme, and suffering the earle of March to remaine in prison, without trauelling to haue him delieuered. All which things they as procurors & protectors of the common-wealth, tooke vpon them to prooue against him, as they protested vnto the whole world.

King Henrie after he had read their articles, with the defiance which they annexed to the same, answered the esquiers, that he was readie with dint of sword and fierce battell to prooue their quarrell false, and nothing else than a forged matter, not doubting, but that God would aid and assist him in his righteous cause, against the disloiall and false forsworne traitors. The next daie in the morning earlie, being the euen of Marie Magdalene, they set their battels in order on both sides, and now whilest the warriors looked when the token of battell should be giuen, the abbat of Shrewesburie, and one of the clearks of the priuie seale, were sent from the king vnto the Persies, to offer them pardon, if they would come to any reasonable agreement. By their persuasions, the lord **Henrie Persie began to giue eare vnto the kings offers, & so sent**

with them his vncle the earle of Worcester, to declare vnto the
king the causes of those troubles, and to require some effectuall
reformation in the same.

It was reported for a truth, that now when the king had con-
descended vnto all that was resonable at his hands to be required,
and seemed to humble himselfe more than was meet for his estate,
the earle of Worcester (vpon his returne to his nephue) made relation cleane contrarie to that the king had said, in such sort that he
set his nephues hart more in displeasure towards the king, than
euer it was before, driuing him by that meanes to fight whether he
would or not: then suddenlie blew the trumpets, the kings part
crieng S. George vpon them, the aduersaries cried *Esperance Persie*,
and so the two armies furiouslie ioned. The archers on both sides
shot for the best game, laieng on such load with arrowes, that manie
died, and were driuen downe that neuer rose againe.

The Scots (as some write) which had the fore ward on the
Persies side, intending to be reuenged of their old displeasures doone
to them by the English nation, set so fiercelie on the kings fore
ward, led by the earle of Stafford, that they made the same draw
backe, and had almost broken their aduersaries arraie. The Welshmen also which before had laine lurking in the woods, moun-
teines, and marishes, hearing of this battell toward, came to the aid
of the Persies, and refreshed the wearied people with new succours.
The king perceiuing that his men were thus put to distresse, what
with the violent impression of the Scots, and the tempestuous
stormes of arrowes, that his aduersaries discharged freely against
him and his people, it was no need to will him to stirre: for suddenlie with his fresh battell, he approched and relieued his men; so
that the battell began more fierce than before. Here the lord Henrie
Persie, and the earle Dowglas, a right stout and hardie capteine, not
regarding the shot of the kings battell, nor the close order of the
ranks, pressing forward togither bent their whole forces towards the
kings person, comming vpon him with speares and swords so fiercelie,
that the earle of March the Scot, perceiuing their purpose, with-
drew the king from that side of the field (as some write) for his
great benefit and safegard (as it appeared) for they gaue such a
violent onset vpon them that stood about the kings standard, that
slaieng his standard-bearer sir Walter Blunt, and ouerthrowing the
standard, they made slaughter of all those that stood about it, as
the earle of Stafford, that daie made by the king constable of the

realme, and diuerse other.

The prince that daie holpe his father like a lustie yoong gentle-man: for although he was hurt in the face with an arrow, so that diuerse noble men that were about him, would haue conueied him foorth of the field, yet he would not suffer them so to doo, least his departure from amongst his men might happilie haue striken some feare into their harts: and so without regard of his hurt, he continued with his men, & neuer ceassed, either to fight where the battell was most hot, or to incourage his men where it seemed most need. This battell lasted three long houres, with indifferent for-tune on both parts, till at length, the king crieng saint George vic-torie, brake the arraie of his enimies, and aduentured so farre, that (as some write) the earle Dowglas strake him downe, & at that instant slue sir Walter Blunt, and three other, apparelled in the kings sute and clothing, saieng: I maruell to see so many kings thus suddenlie arise one in the necke of an other. The king in deed was raised, & did that daie manie a noble feat of armes, for as it is written, he slue that daie with his owne hands six and thirtie persons of his enimies. The other on his part incouraged by his doings, fought valiantlie, and slue the lord Persie, called sir Henrie Hotspurre. To conclude, the kings enimies were vanquished, and put to flight, in which flight, the earle of Dowglas, for hast, falling from the crag of an hie mounteine, brake one of his cullions, and was taken, and for his valiantnesse, of the king frankelie and freelie deliuered.

There was also taken the earle of Worcester, the procurer and setter foorth of all this mischeefe, sir Richard Vernon, and the baron of Kinderton, with diuerse other. There were slaine vpon the kings part, beside the earle of Stafford, to the number of ten knights, sir Hugh Shorlie, sir Iohn Clifton, sir Iohn Cokaine, sir Nicholas Gausell, sir Walter Blunt, sir Iohn Caluerleie, sir Iohn Massie of Podington, sir Hugh Mortimer, and sir Robert Gausell, all the which receiued the same morning the order of knighthood: sir Thomas Wendesleie was wounded to death, and so passed out of this life shortlie after. There died in all vpon the kings side sixteene hundred, and foure thousand were greeuouslie wounded. On the contrarie side were slaine, besides the lord Persie, the most part of the knights and esquiers of the countie of Chester, to the number of two hundred, besides yeomen and footmen, in all there died of those that fought on the Persies side, about fiue thousand. This

battell was fought on Marie Magdalene euen, being saturdaie. Vpon
the mondaie folowing, the earle of Worcester, the baron of Kinderton, and sir Richard Vernon knights, were condemned and beheaded. The earles head was sent to London, there to be set on the
bridge.

*   *   *   *   *

[Anno 1412] . . . lord Henrie prince of Wales, eldest sonne to
king Henrie, got knowledge that certeine of his fathers seruants
were busie to giue informations against him, whereby discord might
arise betwixt him and his father: for they put into the kings head,
not onelie what euill rule (according to the course of youth) the
prince kept to the offense of manie: but also what great resort of
people came to his house, so that the court was nothing furnished
with such a traine as dailie followed the prince. These tales brought
no small suspicion into the kings head, least his sonne would presume to vsurpe the crowne, he being yet aliue, through which suspicious gelousie, it was perceiued that he fauoured not his sonne,
as in times past he had doone.

The Prince sore offended with such persons, as by slanderous reports, sought not onelie to spot his good name abrode in the realme,
but to sowe discord also betwixt him and his father, wrote his letters into euerie part of the realme, to reproue all such slanderous
deuises of those that sought his discredit. And to cleare himselfe
the better, that the world might vnderstand what wrong he had
to be slandered in such wise: about the feast of Peter and Paule,
to wit, the nine and twentith daie of Iune, he came to the court with
such a number of noble men and other his freends that wished him
well, as the like traine had beene sildome seene repairing to the court
at any one time in those daies. He was apparelled in a gowne of
blew satten, full of small oilet holes, at euerie hole the needle hanging by a silke thred with which it was sewed. About his arme he
ware an hounds collar set full of SS of gold, and the tirets likewise
being of the same metall.

The court was then at Westminster, where he being entred into
the hall, not one of his companie durst once aduance himselfe
further than the fire in the same hall, notwithstanding they were
earnestlie requested by the lords to come higher: but they regarding what they had in commandement of the prince, would not
presume to doo in any thing contrarie therevnto. He himselfe onelie

accompanied with those of the kings house, was streight admitted to the presence of the king his father, who being at that time greeuouslie diseased, yet caused himselfe in his chaire to be borne into his priuie chamber, where in the presence of three or foure persons, in whome he had most confidence, he commanded the prince to shew what he had to saie concerning the cause of his comming.

The prince kneeling downe before his father said: "Most redoubted and souereigne lord and father, I am at this time come to your presence as your liege man, and as your naturall sonne, in all things to be at your commandement. And where I vnderstand you haue in suspicion my demeanour against your grace, you know verie well, that if I knew any man within this realme, of whome you should stand in feare, my duetie were to punish that person, thereby to remooue that greefe from your heart. Then how much more ought I to suffer death, to ease your grace of that greefe which you haue of me, being your naturall sonne and liege man: and to that end I haue this daie made my selfe readie by confession and receiuing of the sacrament. And therefore I beseech you most redoubted lord and deare father, for the honour of God, to ease your heart of all such suspicion as you haue of me, and to dispatch me heere before your knees, with this same dagger [and withall he deliuered vnto the king his dagger, in all humble reuerence; adding further, that his life was not so deare to him, that he wished to liue one daie with his displeasure] and therefore in thus ridding me out of life, and your selfe from all suspicion, here in presence of these lords, and before God at the daie of the generall iudgement, I faithfullie protest clearlie to forgiue you."

The king mooued herewith, cast from him the dagger, and imbracing the prince kissed him, and with shedding teares confessed, that in deed he had him partlie in suspicion, though now (as he perceiued) not with iust cause, and therefore from thenceforth no misreport should cause him to haue him in mistrust, and this he promised of his honour. So by his great wisedome was the wrongfull suspicion which his father had conceiued against him remooued, and he restored to his fauour. And further, where he could not but greeuouslie complaine of them that had slandered him so greatlie, to the defacing not onelie of his honor, but also putting him in danger of his life, he humblie besought the king that they might answer their vniust accusation; and in case they were found to haue forged such matters vpon a malicious purpose, that then they might suffer some punishment for their faults, though not to the full of that they had deserued. The king seeming to grant his resonable desire, yet told him that he must tarrie a parlement, that such offendors might be punished by iudgement of their peeres: and so for that time he was dismissed, with great loue and signes of fatherlie affection.

Thus were the father and the sonne reconciled, betwixt whom the said pickthanks had sowne diuision, insomuch that the sonne vpon a vehement conceit of vnkindnesse sproong in the father, was in the waie to be worne out of fauour. Which was the more likelie to come to passe, by their informations that priuilie charged him with riot and other vnciuill demeanor vnseemelie for a prince. Indeed he was youthfullie giuen, growne to audacitie, and had chosen him companions agreeable to his age; with whome he spent the time in such recreations, exercises, and delights as he fansied. But yet (it should seeme by the report of some writers) that his behauiour was not offensiue or at least tending to the damage of anie bodie; sith he had a care to auoid dooing of wrong, and to tedder his affections within the tract of vertue, whereby he opened vnto himselfe a redie passage of good liking among the prudent sort, and was beloued of such as could discerne his disposition, which was in no degree so excessiue, as that he deserued in such vehement maner to be suspected. In whose dispraise I find little, but to his praise verie much. . . .

SAMUEL DANIEL

The Civil Wars

<BOOK III>

<86>

And yet new *Hydraes* lo, new heades appeare
T'afflict that peace reputed then so sure,
And gaue him much to do, and much to feare,
And long and daungerous tumults did procure,
And those euen of his chiefest followers were
Of whom he might presume him most secure,
Who whether not so grac'd or so preferd
As they expected, these new factions stird.

<87>

The *Percyes* were the men, men of great might,
Strong in alliance, and in courage strong
That thus conspire, vnder pretence to right
The crooked courses they had suffered long:
Whether their conscience vrgd them or despight,
Or that they saw the part they tooke was wrong,
Or that ambition hereto did them call,
Or others enuide grace, or rather all.

<88>

What cause soeuer were, strong was their plot,
Their parties great, meanes good, th'occasion fit:
Their practice close, their faith suspected not,
Their states far off and they of wary wit:

From *The First Fowre Bookes of the Ciuile Wars Between the Two Houses of Lancaster and Yorke* (1595) as reprinted by Samuel B. Hemingway in the Variorum edition of *Henry IV, Part 1* (Philadelphia, 1936), pp. 365–371.

Who with large promises draw in the Scot
To ayde their cause, he likes, and yeeldes to it,
Not for the loue of them or for their good,
But glad hereby of meanes to shed our bloud.

<89>

Then ioyne they with the *Welsh*, who fitly traind
And all in armes vnder a mightie head
Great *Glendowr*, who long warr'd, and much attaind,
Sharp conflicts made, and many vanquished:
With whom was *Edmond Earle* of *March* retaind
Being first his prisoner, now confedered,
A man the king much fear'd, and well he might
Least he should looke whether his Crown stood right.

<90>

For *Richard*, for the quiet of the state,
Before he tooke those *Irish* warres in hand
About succession doth deliberate,
And finding how the certaine right did stand,
With full consent this man did ordinate
The heyre apparent in the crowne and land:
Then iudge if this the king might nerely touch,
Although his might were smal, his right being much.

<91>

With these the *Percyes* them confederate,
And as three heades they league in one intent,
And instituting a Triumuirate
Do part the land in triple gouerment:
Deuiding thus among themselues the state,
The *Percyes* should rule all the *North* from *Trent*
And *Glendowr Wales*: the *Earle* of *March* should bee
Lord of the *South* from *Trent*; and thus they gree.

<92>

Then those two helpes which still such actors find
Pretence of common good, the kings disgrace
Doth fit their course, and draw the vulgar mind
To further them and aide them in this case:

The king they accusd for cruell, and vnkind
That did the state, and crowne, and all deface;
A periurde man that held all faith in skorne,
Whose trusted othes had others made forsworne.

<93>

Besides the odious detestable act
Of that late murdered king they aggrauate,
Making it his that so had will'd the fact
That he the doers did remunerate:
And then such taxes daily doth exact
That were against the orders of the state,
And with all these or worse they him assaild
Who late of others with the like preuaild.

<94>

Thus doth contentious proud mortality
Afflict each other and itselfe torment:
And thus o thou mind-tortring misery
Restles ambition, borne in discontent,
Turn'st and retossest with iniquity
The vnconstant courses frailty did inuent:
And fowlst faire order and defilst the earth
Fostring vp warre, father of bloud and dearth.

<95>

Great seemd the cause, and greatly to, did ad
The peoples loue thereto these crimes rehearst,
That manie gathered to the troupes they had
And many more do flocke from costs disperst:
But when the king had heard these newes so bad,
Th'vnlookt for dangerous toyle more nearly perst;
For bēt t'wards *Wales* t'appease those tumults there,
H'is for'st diuert his course, and them forbeare.

<96>

Not to giue time vnto th'increasing rage
And gathering fury, forth he hastes with speed,
Lest more delay or giuing longer age
To th'euill growne, it might the cure exceed:

All his best men at armes, and leaders sage
All he prepard he could, and all did need;
For to a mighty worke thou goest ô king,
To such a field that power to power shall bring.

<97>

There shall young *Hotespur* with a fury lead
Meete with thy forward sonne as fierce as he:
There warlike *Worster* long experienced
In forraine armes, shall come t'incounter thee:
There *Dowglas* to thy *Stafford* shall make head:
There *Vernon* for thy valiant *Blunt* shalbe:
There shalt thou find a doubtfull bloudy day,
Though sicknesse keepe *Northumberland* away.

<98>

Who yet reseru'd, though after quit for this,
Another tempest on thy head to raise,
As if still wrong reuenging *Nemesis*
Did meane t'afflict all thy continuall dayes:
And yet this field he happely might misse
For thy great good, and therefore well he staies:
What might his force haue done being ioynd thereto
When that already gaue so much to do?

<99>

The swift approch and vnexpected speed
The king had made vpon this new-raisd force
In th' vnconfirmed troupes much feare did breed,
Vntimely hindring their intended course;
The ioyning with the *Welsh* they had decreed
Was hereby stopt, which made their part the worse,
Northumberland with forces from the *North*
Expected to be there, was not set forth.

<100>

And yet vndaunted *Hotspur* seeing the king
So nere approch'd, leauing the worke in hand
With forward speed his forces marshalling,
Sets forth his farther comming to withstand:

And with a cheerfull voice incouraging
By his great spirit his well imboldened band,
Bringes a strong host of firme resolued might,
And plac'd his troupes before the king in sight.

<101>

This day (saith he) ô faithfull valiaunt frendes,
What euer it doth giue, shall glorie giue:
This day with honor frees our state, or endes
Our misery with fame, that still shall liue,
And do but thinke how well this day he spendes
That spendes his bloud his countrey to relieue:
Our holie cause, our freedome, and our right,
Sufficient are to moue good mindes to fight.

<102>

Besides th' assured hope of victory
That wee may euen promise on our side
Against this weake-constrained companie,
Whom force & feare, not will, and loue doth guide
Against a prince whose foule impiety
The heauens do hate, the earth cannot abide,
Our number being no lesse, our courage more,
What need we doubt if we but worke therefore.

<103>

This said, and thus resolu'd euen bent to charge
Vpon the king, who well their order viewd
And carefull noted all the forme at large
Of their proceeding, and their multitude:
And deeming better if he could discharge
The day with safetie, and some peace conclude,
Great proffers sendes of pardon, and of grace
If they would yeeld, and quietnes imbrace.

<104>

But this refusd, the king with wrath incensd
Rage against fury doth with speed prepare:
And ô saith he, though I could haue dispensd
With this daies bloud, which I haue sought to spare

That greater glory might haue recompensd
The forward worth of these that so much dare,
That we might honor had by th' ouerthrown
That th' wounds we make, might not haue bin our own.

<105>

Yet since that other mens iniquity
Calles on the sword of wrath against my will,
And that themselues exact this cruelty,
And I constrained am this bloud to spill:
Then on my maisters, on couragiously
True-harted subiects against traitors ill,
And spare them not who seeke to spoile vs all,
Whose fowle confused end soone see you shall.

<106>

Straight moues with equall motion equall rage
The like incensed armies vnto bloud,
One to defend, another side to wage
Foule ciuill war, both vowes their quarrell good:
Ah too much heate to bloud doth nowe inrage
Both who the deed prouokes and who withstood,
That valor here is vice, here manhood sin,
The forward'st hands doth ô least honor win.

<107>

But now begin these fury-mouing soundes
The notes of wrath that musicke brought from hell,
The ratling drums which trumpets voice côfounds,
The cryes, th' incouragements, the shouting shrell:
That all about the beaten ayre reboundes,
Thundring confused, murmurs horrible,
To rob all sence except the sence to fight,
Well handes may worke, the mind hath lost his sight.

<108>

O war! begot in pride and luxury,
The child of wrath and of dissention,
Horrible good; mischiefe necessarie,
The fowle reformer of confusion,

Vniust-iust scourge of our iniquitie,
Cruell recurer of corruption:
O that these sin-sicke states in need should stand
To be let bloud with such a boystrous hand!

<109>

And ô how well thou hadst been spar'd this day
Had not wrong counsaild *Percy* bene peruers,
Whose yong vndanger'd hand now rash makes way
Vpon the sharpest fronts of the most fierce:
Where now an equall fury thrusts to stay
And rebeat-backe that force and his disperse,
Then these assaile, then those chace backe againe,
Till staid with new-made hils of bodies slaine.

<110>

There lo that new-appearing glorious starre
Wonder of Armes, the terror of the field
Young *Henrie*, laboring where the stoutest are,
And euen the stoutest forces backe to yeild,
There is that hand boldned to bloud and warre
That must the sword in woundrous actions weild:
But better hadst thou learnd with others bloud
A lesse expence to vs, to thee more good.

<111>

Hadst thou not there lent present speedy ayd
To thy indaungerde father nerely tyrde,
Whom fierce incountring *Dowglas* ouerlaid,
That day had there his troublous life expirde:
Heroycall Couragious *Blunt* araid
In habite like as was the king attirde
And deemd for him, excusd that fate with his,
For he had what his Lord did hardly misse.

<112>

For thought a king he would not now disgrace
The person then supposd, but princelike shewes
Glorious effects of worth that fit his place,
And fighting dyes, and dying ouerthrowes:

Another of that forward name and race
In that hotte worke his valiant life bestowes,
Who bare the standard of the king that day,
Whose colours ouerthrowne did much dismaie.

<113>

And deare it cost, and ô much bloud is shed
To purchase thee this loosing victory
O trauayld king: yet hast thou conquered
A doubtfull day, a mightie enemy:
But ô what woundes, what famous worth lyes dead!
That makes the winner looke with sorrowing eye,
Magnanimous *Stafford* lost that much had wrought,
And valiant *Shorly* who great glory gote.

<114>

Such wracke of others bloud thou didst behold
O furious *Hotspur*, ere thou lost thine owne!
Which now once lost that heate in thine waxt cold,
And soone became thy Armie ouerthrowne;
And ô that this great spirit, this courage bold,
Had in some good cause bene rightly showne!
So had not we thus violently then
Haue termd that rage, which valor should haue ben.

The   Famous Victories of Henry the Fifth

Enter the yoong PRINCE, NED, *and* TOM.
HENRY THE FIFTH.

COME away *Ned* and *Tom.*

BOTH. Here my Lord.

HENR. 5. Come away my Lads:
Tell me sirs, how much gold haue you got?

NED. Faith my Lord, I haue got fiue hundred pound.

HEN. 5. But tell me *Tom*, how much hast thou got?

TOM. Faith my Lord, some foure hundred pound.

HEN. 5. Foure hundred pounds, brauely spoken Lads.
But tell me sirs, thinke you not that it was a villainous part of
   me to rob my fathers Receiuers?

NED. Why no my Lord, it was but a tricke of youth.

HEN. 5. Faith *Ned* thou sayest true.
But tell me sirs, whereabouts are we?

TOM. My Lord, we are now about a mile off *London.*

HEN. 5. But sirs, I maruell that sir *Iohn Old-castle*
Comes not away: Sounds see where he comes.

Enters IOCKEY.

How now *Iockey*, what newes with thee?

IOCKEY. Faith my Lord, such newes as passeth,
For the Towne of *Detfort* is risen,
With hue and crie after your man,
Which parted from vs the last night,
And has set vpon, and hath robd a poore Carrier.

HEN. 5. Sownes, the vilaine that was wont to spie
Out our booties.

IOCK. I my Lord, euen the very same.

HEN. 5. Now base minded rascal to rob a poore carrier,
Wel it skils not, ile saue the base vilaines life:

From *The Famovs Victories of Henry the fifth: Containing the Honourable Battell of Agin-court: As it was plaide by the Queenes Maiesties
Players* (1598). Reprinted from the Bodleian Library copy of the 1598
quarto edition as reproduced in the facsimile published by C. Praetorius
(Shakespere Quarto Facsimiles, No. 39, ed. P. A. Daniel, 1887).

I, I may: but tel me *Iockey*, whereabout be the Receiuers?

IOC. Faith my Lord, they are hard by,
But the best is, we are a horse backe and they be a foote,
So we may escape them.

HEN. 5. Wel, I[f] the vilaines come, let me alone with them.
But tel me *Iockey*, how much gots thou from the knaues?
For I am sure I got something, for one of the vilaines
So belamd me about the shoulders,
As I shal feele it this moneth.

IOCK. Faith my Lord, I haue got a hundred pound.

HEN. 5. A hundred pound, now brauely spoken *Iockey*:
But come sirs, laie al your money before me,
Now by heauen here is a braue shewe:
But as I am true Gentleman, I wil haue the halfe
Of this spent to night, but sirs take vp your bags,
Here comes the Receiuers, let me alone.

Enters two Receiuers.

ONE. Alas good fellow, what shal we do?
I dare neuer go home to the Court, for I shall be hangd.
But looke, here is the yong Prince, what shal we doo?

HEN. 5. How now you vilaines, what are you?

ONE RECEI. Speake you to him.

OTHER. No I pray, speake you to him.

HEN. 5. Why how now you rascals, why speak you not?

ONE. Forsooth we be. Pray speake you to him.

HEN. 5. Sowns, vilains speak, or ile cut off your heads.

OTHER. Forsooth he can tel the tale better then I.

ONE. Forsooth we be your fathers Receiuers.

HEN. 5. Are you my fathers Receiuers?
Then I hope ye haue brought me some money.

ONE. Money, Alas sir we be robd.

HEN. 5. Robd, how many were there of them?

ONE. Marry sir, there were foure of them:
And one of them had sir *Iohn Old-Castles* bay Hobbie,
And your blacke Nag.

HEN. 5. Gogs wounds how like you this *Iockey*?
Blood you vilaines: my father robd of his money abroad,
And we robd in our stables.
But tell me, how many were of them?

ONE RECEI. If it please you, there were foure of them,
    And there was one about the bignesse of you:
    But I am sure I so belambd him about the shoulders,
    That he wil feele it this month.
HEN. 5. Gogs wounds you lamd them faierly,
    So that they haue carried away your money.
    But come sirs, what shall we do with the vilaines?
BOTH RECEI. I beseech your grace, be good to vs.
NED. I pray you my Lord forgiue them this once.
[HEN. 5.] Well stand vp and get you gone,
    And looke that you speake not a word of it,
    For if there be, sownes ile hang you and all your kin.

                                    Exit Purseuant[s].

HEN. 5. Now sirs, how like you this?
    Was not this brauely done?
    For now the vilaines dare not speake a word of it,
    I haue so feared them with words.
    Now whither shall we goe?
ALL. Why my Lord, you know our old hostes
    At *Feuersham*.
HEN. 5. Our hostes at *Feuersham*, blood what shal we do there?
    We haue a thousand pound about vs,
    And we shall go to a pettie Ale-house.
    No, no: you know the olde Tauerne in Eastcheape,
    There is good wine: besides, there is a pretie wench
    That can talke well, for I delight as much in their toongs,
    As any part about them.
ALL. We are readie to waite vpon your grace.
HEN. 5. Gogs wounds wait, we will go altogither,
    We are all fellowes, I tell you sirs, and the King
    My father were dead, we would be all Kings,
    Therefore come away.
NED. Gogs wounds, brauely spoken *Harry*.

                    [*Exeunt omnes.*]

[In the scene which follows, the night-watch, John Cobler, Robin
Pewterer, and Lawrence Costermonger, assisted by Dericke, a clown,
apprehend a "Theefe" (Gadshill), who had taken part in the robbery of the carriers. A "Vintners boy" closes the scene with a report on a tavern escapade of the Prince.]

BOY. How now good man Cobler?

COB. How now *Robin*, what makes thou abroad
At this time of night?

BOY. Marrie I haue beene at the Counter,
I can tell such newes as neuer you haue heard the like.

COBLER. What is that *Robin*, what is the matter?

BOY. Why this night about two houres ago, there came the young
Prince, and three or foure more of his companions, and called
for wine good store, and then they sent for a noyse of Musitians,
and were very merry for the space of an houre, then whether
their Musicke liked them not, or whether they had drunke too
much Wine or no, I cannot tell, but our pots flue against the
wals, and then they drew their swordes, and went into the streete
and fought, and some tooke one part, & some tooke another, but
for the space of halfe an houre, there was such a bloodie fray as
passeth, and none coulde part them vntill such time as the Maior
and Sheriffe were sent for, and then at the last with much adoo,
they tooke them, and so the yong Prince was carried to the Counter, and then about one houre after, there came a Messenger
from the Court in all haste from the King, for my Lord Maior
and the Sheriffe, but for what cause I know not.

[Gadshill is then taken to Newgate Prison to await his appearance
before the Lord Chief Justice. In the following scene Henry IV receives an account from the Lord Mayor of London of his imprisoning the young Prince. Henry IV replies:]

HEN. 4. Stand aside vntill we haue further deliberated on your an-
swere.

Exit Maior.

HEN. 4. Ah *Harry*, *Harry*, now thrice accursed *Harry*,
That hath gotten a sonne, which with greefe
Will end his fathers dayes.
Oh my sonne, a Prince thou art, I a Prince indeed,
And to deserue imprisonment,
And well haue they done, and like faithfull subiects:
Discharge them and let them go.

[The next episode is the trial of Gadshill before the Lord Chief
Justice. The Prince appears and demands custody of Gadshill. When
the Chief Justice refuses, the Prince "giueth him a boxe on the

eare." The Chief Justice then commits the Prince to the Fleet.
There follows a "play extempore" between Dericke and John Cobler.]

DER. Sownds maisters, heres adoo,
     When Princes must go to prison:
     Why *Iohn*, didst euer see the like?
IOHN. O *Dericke*, trust me, I neuer saw the like.
DER. Why *Iohn* thou maist see what princes be in choller,
     A Iudge a boxe on the eare, Ile tel thee *Iohn*, O *Iohn*,
     I would not haue done it for twentie shillings.
IOHN. No nor I, there had bene no way but one with vs,
     We should haue bene hangde.
DER. Faith *Iohn*, Ile tel thee what, thou shalt be my
     Lord chiefe Iustice, and thou shalt sit in the chaire,
     And ile be the yong prince, and hit thee a boxe on the eare,
     And then thou shalt say, to teach you what prerogatiues
     Meane, I commit you to the Fleete.
IOHN. Come on, Ile be your iudge,
     But thou shalt not hit me hard.
DER. No, no.
IOHN. What hath he done?
DER. Marry he hath robd *Dericke*.
IOHN. Why then I cannot let him go.
DER. I must needs haue my man.
IOHN. You shall not haue him.
DER. Shall I not haue my man, say no and you dare:
     How say you, shall I not haue my man?
IOHN. No marry shall you not.
DER. Shall I not *Iohn*?
IOHN. No *Dericke*.
DER. Why then take you that till more come,
     Sownes, shall I not haue him?
IOHN. Well I am content to take this at your hand,
     But I pray you, who am I?
DER. Who art thou, Sownds, doost not know thy self?
IOHN. No.
DER. Now away simple fellow,
     Why man, thou art *Iohn* the Cobler.
IOHN. No, I am my Lord chiefe Iustice of England.

DER. Oh *Iohn*, Masse thou saist true, thou art indeed.

IOHN. Why then to teach you what prerogatiues mean
  I commit you to the Fleete.

DER. Wel I will go, but yfaith you gray beard knaue,
  Ile course you.

*   *   *   *   *

Enter the yoong PRINCE, with NED and TOM.

HEN. 5. Come away sirs, Gogs wounds *Ned*,
  Didst thou not see what a boxe on the eare
  I tooke my Lord chiefe Iustice?

TOM. By gogs blood it did me good to see it,
  It made his teeth iarre in his head.

Enter sir Iohn Old-Castle.

HEN. 5. How now sir *Iohn Old-Castle*,
  What newes with you?

IOH. OLD. I am glad to see your grace at libertie,
  I was come I, to visit you in prison.

HEN. 5. To visit me, didst thou not know that I am a Princes son,
  why tis inough for me to looke into a prison, though I come not
  in my selfe, but heres such adoo now adayes, heres prisoning,
  heres hanging, whipping, and the diuel and all: but I tel you
  sirs, when I am King, we will haue no such things, but my lads,
  if the old king my father were dead, we would be all kings.

IOH. OLD. Hee is a good olde man, God take him to his mercy the
  sooner.

HEN. 5. But *Ned*, so soone as I am King, the first thing
  I wil do, shal be to put my Lord chief Iustice out of office,
  And thou shalt be my Lord chiefe Iustice of England.

NED. Shall I be Lord chiefe Iustice?
  By gogs wounds, ile be the brauest Lord chiefe Iustice
  That euer was in England.

HEN. 5. Then *Ned*, ile turne all these prisons into fence Schooles,
  and I will endue thee with them, with landes to maintaine them
  withall: then I wil haue a bout with my Lord chiefe Iustice, thou
  shalt hang none but picke purses and horse stealers, and such
  base binded villaines, but that fellow that will stand by the high

way side couragiously with his sword and buckler and take a
purse, that fellow giue him commendations, beside that, send
him to me and I will giue him an anuall pension out of my
Exchequer, to maintaine him all the dayes of his life.

IOH. Nobly spoken *Harry*, we shall neuer haue a mery world til the
old king be dead.

NED. But whither are ye going now?

HEN. 5. To the Court, for I heare say, my father lies verie sicke.

TOM. But I doubt he wil not die.

HEN. 5. Yet will I goe thither, for the breath shal be no sooner out
of his mouth, but I wil clap the Crowne on my head.

IOCKEY. Wil you goe to the Court with that cloake so full of needles?

HEN. 5. Cloake, ilat-holes, needles, and all was of mine owne deuis-
ing, and therefore I wil weare it.

TOM. I pray you my Lord, what may be the meaning thereof?

HEN. 5. Why man, tis a signe that I stand vpon thorns, til the
Crowne be on my head.

IOC. Or that euery needle might be a prick to their harts that re-
pine at your doings.

HEN. 5. Thou saist true *Iockey*, but thers some wil say, the yoong
Prince will be a well toward yoong man and all this geare, that
I had as leeue they would breake my head with a pot, as to say
any such thing, but we stand prating here too long, I must needs
speake with my father, therefore come away.

*   *   *   *   *

Enter the KING, *with the* LORD OF EXETER.

HEN. 4. And is it true my Lord, that my sonne is alreadie sent to
the Fleete? now truly that man is more fitter to rule the Realme
then I, for by no meanes could I rule my sonne, and he by one
word hath caused him to be ruled. Oh my sonne, my sonne, no
sooner out of one prison, but into an other, I had thought once
whiles I had liued, to haue seene this noble Realme of England
flourish by thee my sonne, but now I see it goes to ruine and
decaie.

He wepeth.

Enters LORD OF OXFORD

ox. And please your grace, here is my Lord your sonne,
    That commeth to speake with you,
    He saith, he must and wil speake with you.
HEN. 4. Who my sonne *Harry?*
OXF. I and please your Maiestie.
HEN. 4. I know wherefore he commeth,
    But looke that none come with him.
OXF. A verie disordered company, and such as make
    Verie ill rule in your Maiesties house.
HEN. 4. Well let him come,
    But looke that none come with him.

He goeth.

*   *   *   *   *

Enters the PRINCE *with a dagger in his hand.*

HEN. 4. Come my sonne, come on a Gods name,
    I know wherefore thy comming is,
    Oh my sonne, my sonne, what cause hath euer bene,
    That thou shouldst forsake me, and follow this vilde and
    Reprobate company, which abuseth youth so manifestly:
    Oh my sonne, thou knowest that these thy doings
    Wil end thy fathers dayes.

He weepes.

I so, so, my sonne, thou fearest not to approach the presence of
thy sick father, in that disguised sort, I tel thee my sonne, that
there is neuer a needle in thy cloke, but it is a prick to my heart,
& neuer an ilat-hole, but it is a hole to my soule: and wherefore
thou bringest that dagger in thy hande I know not, but by con-
iecture.

He weepes.

HEN. 5. My cōscience accuseth me, most soueraign Lord, and wel-
    beloued father, to answere first to the last point, That is, whereas
    you coniecture that this hand and this dagger shall be armde
    against your life: no, know my beloued father, far be the thoughts
    of your sonne, sonne said I, an vnworthie sonne for so good a fa-
    ther: but farre be the thoughts of any such pretended mischiefe:
    and I most humbly render it to your Maiesties hand, and liue

my Lord and soueraigne for euer: and with your dagger arme show
like vengeance vpon the bodie of that your sonne, I was about
[to] say and dare not, ah woe is me therefore, that your wilde
slaue, tis not the Crowne that I come for, sweete father, because
I am vnworthie, and those vilde & reprobate company I abandon,
& vtterly abolish their company for euer. Pardon sweete father,
pardon: the least thing and most desire: and this ruffianly cloake,
I here teare from my backe, and sacrifice it to the diuel, which
is maister of al mischiefe: Pardō me, sweet father, pardon me:
good my Lord of *Exeter* speak for me: pardon me, pardō good
father, not a word: ah he wil not speak one word: A *Harry*, now
thrice vnhappie *Harry*. But what shal I do? I wil go take me into
some solitarie place, and there lament my sinfull life, and when
I haue done, I wil laie me downe and die.

Exit.

HEN. 4. Call him againe, call my sonne againe.
HEN. 5. And doth my father call me again? now *Harry*,
    Happie be the time that thy father calleth thee againe.
HEN. 4. Stand vp my son, and do not think thy father,
    But at the request of thee my sonne I wil pardon thee,
    And God blesse thee, and make thee his seruant.
HEN. 5. Thanks good my Lord, & no doubt but this day,
    Euen this day, I am borne new againe.
HEN. 4. Come my son and Lords, take me by the hands.

Exeunt omnes.

[The remaining two-thirds of the play is chiefly concerned with
Henry the Fifth's victory at Agincourt and his winning the hand
of Katharine, daughter of Charles VI of France.]

ESSAYS IN CRITICISM

The greatest success in "history" that Shakespeare attained was in *I Henry IV*. Here is to be found his liveliest and most richly-colored picture of tavern and country; here is to be found Falstaff, and Falstaff at his best; and here, in Hotspur, and in young Harry roused to emulation, are to be found a pair of Shakespeare's most radiant figures of English youth and chivalry.

E. E. Stoll, *Poets and Playwrights.*

FALSTAFF. . . . . . I am not only witty in myself, but the cause that wit is in other men.

2 Henry IV, I.ii.

The essays which follow are divided into two parts. Those in part I, for the most part complete essays, offer interpretations of the theme of the play, analyses of its major characters, considerations of its dramatic structure, and discussions of its style. Those in part II are excerpts illustrating, in a kind of historical survey in brief, significant interpretations of Falstaff and modes of critical approach in studying this figure.

In several of the critical articles, the present editor has altered the line number citations to agree with the text of the play as given in the present volume; these alterations occur in the essays by L. C. Knights, Cleanth Brooks and Robert B. Heilman, J. Dover Wilson, Arthur C. Sprague, M. A. Shaaber, Madeleine Doran, Milton Crane, and E. E. Stoll.

D. A. TRAVERSI

Henry IV, Part I: History and the Artist's Vision

The increased volume of work which has recently been devoted to Shakespeare's series of English historical plays has not been without its uses. In particular it has served to bring these works decisively out of the sphere of patriotic commonplace to which they had often been consigned by relating them firmly to the political conceptions of the Elizabethan period. The work, however, is not without dangers of its own. There is a very real risk that erudition, in its efforts to relate the plays to their period, may end by obscuring the personal contribution that makes them most valuable as works of art. For these plays—and more especially those dealing with the reign of Henry IV and his son—contain something of far deeper and more permanent significance than the social and political commonplaces of a departed age; they illuminate these commonplaces by the same profoundly personal vision which, at a more mature stage, developed further to produce Shakespeare's greatest plays. The true artist, when circumstances induce him to approach political problems, brings with him a concern for permanent human values which, while never limited to the momentary issue, may be none the less profoundly illuminating to those who can combine a serious interest in contemporary developments with the preservation, often equally necessary, of a proper detachment. To bear this truth in mind and to trace in detail the unfolding of a personal interpretation of his inherited theme is to throw light upon an important stage in the development of Shakespeare's art.

The broad conception of the whole trilogy, initially accepted by

Reprinted from "Henry IV—Part I," *Scrutiny*, XV (December 1947), 24–35, by permission of the author. The essay has been revised in minor details by the author for its appearance here. Title added by Ed.

Shakespeare as his starting-point, is clear enough. It emerges generally speaking from historical and dramatic works previously in existence and fits in with the current conceptions of the age. The three plays, as well as *Richard II* which preceded them, are evidently conceived as studies in kingship. The royal office is plainly regarded throughout as basing its claims to obedience upon divine ordination. The power of the King, a power conveyed upon him by God, is conferred as a guarantee of social order and of that acceptance of "degree" which cannot be denied without plunging society into anarchy and chaos. This conception is already clearly present in the opening scene of the first part of *Henry IV*. Bolingbroke, newly come to the throne, is weighed down from the first by recent memories of feudal anarchy and internal war. His opening speech has for its background the bitter memory of "civil butchery," of strife between armies "All of one nature, of one substance bred," clashes within the body politic that can only serve to wound and destroy it. Finding his country still "shaken" and made "wan with care" by these civil disasters, it is his desire and duty to propose a higher aim in the following of which the factions so recently at one another's throats may find a common unity. It is for this reason and in this spirit that Henry calls his barons, united under the "blessed Cross," to the liberation of the sepulchre of Christ. The crusade will serve both to calm the political passions which Henry himself exploited to reach the throne and to provide a foundation for the national unity which he now as King sincerely desires.

It is at this point that Shakespeare, though still using traditional conceptions, begins to unfold a personal interpretation of his historical material. In calling for a crusade Henry is moved by motives in which selfish calculation are oddly mixed with a true desire for the general good. As crowned King he genuinely wishes to follow his vocation by uniting his subjects in a worthy and religious enterprise; but as usurper he hopes that his proposal will "busy giddy minds with foreign quarrels" (*Part II*, IV, v) and so distract attention from the way in which he himself came to the throne. In other words—and here Shakespeare's thought is clearly working on traditional lines—Henry's desire to play properly the part of a King is hindered past mending by a flaw in the way in which he came to the throne. His overthrow and murder of Richard II, a crime not only against common humanity but still more against the divine foundation of order centred on the crown, fatally produces the very strife and division which he now aims at ending. No sooner has he stated his purpose than "heavy news" comes "all athwart" from Wales to force for the first time what will turn out to be a life-long postponement of Henry's project. The reign which opens with the call to a crusade ends, after years of weariness and disillusion with death in a room "called Jerusalem" which is fated to be his nearest approach to the Holy Land; and in between it has seen little but rebellion, plot and counterplot, and battles where victory serves only to sow the seed of further domestic strife.

If the whole conception of these plays could be summed up in this way their interest would lie only in the skill with which Shakespeare had unfolded what was, after all, a completely traditional scheme. The fact is, however, that his real conception, far from ending here, has its true beginning at this point. Its true originality begins to appear when the political is over-shadowed by the personal interest. Henry IV is punished for his past sins not only as King in the weariness which increasingly overtakes him and in the growing sense of impotence which sometimes raises him to moments of tragic intensity, but as father in the most intimate concerns of his life. It is here that Shakespeare, still using inherited and familiar material, shows the true originality of his conception. For Prince Hal who is destined to become the incarnation of political competence and to achieve all his father's desires, is at the same time "a scourge" in the hands of God, a continual reminder to Henry of his "displeasing service" in the past. This disappointment, which accompanies the father through his own life and is not wholly dispelled by his apparent transformation at Shrewsbury, is related ultimately to unresolved contradictions in the family character. Henry's first speech to his son (III, ii) is most revealing in its remarkable blend of true personal pathos and political calculation. The former shades indeed almost insensibly into the latter. That the father is genuinely wounded by his son's behaviour, that he is moved with "tenderness," that he "hath desired to see" him more often, is certain; but as we read the long speech we cannot help suspecting that the speaker's only true *moral* criterion is *political* success. To say this is to put one's finger upon the motive that impels the House of Lancaster all through these plays. Henry's criticism of the prodigality of Richard, "the skipping king," is expressed with a linguistic freshness that draws freely upon the vernacular—"*carded* his state," "*capering* wits," "glutted, gorged, and full"—and reflects the keenness of his interest in the intricacies of political behaviour. That interest is a constant feature of the family. Behind it, however, Shakespeare is careful to convey a significant note of falseness and moral deficiency. Bolingbroke, in his own words, "*stole* all courtesy from heaven," "dressed" himself in a humility which is clearly less a moral virtue than the conscious device of policy. For Henry the criterion of morality tends always to be success; and that being so, it is not surprising that his son should have learned from the first to separate the promptings of humanity from the necessities of political behaviour and that filial tenderness in him should exist side by side with a readiness to subject all personal considerations to public achievement. In the realization, born of bitter experience, that the quest for this achievement can be an illusion lies the secret of the tragic note which dominates the father's later years.

These considerations illuminate considerably Shakespeare's conception of Prince Hal and show that the developments later revealed in *Henry V* [1] are already substantially present in his father. It might almost be said, indeed, that the motives which underlie the behaviour of the family throughout the trilogy are revealed in the Prince's opening soliloquy (I, ii). These motives in turn spring at least in part from the nature of the material which the dramatist inherited. In writing his play Shakespeare's freedom of conception was faced by what might have seemed at first sight a grave limitation: the necessity of squaring his account of the Prince's character with a traditional story as naïve in its moral values as it was familiar in all its details. The Prince, as Shakespeare found him in the popular account on which he based his play, was an outstanding example of the familiar story of the dissolute young man who underwent a kind of moral conversion when faced by grave responsibilities and finally made good in the great sphere of political action to which he was called. The story, conceived in these terms, was too familiar and too popular to be ignored by a practical dramatist; on the other hand its conception of human character and motive was too naïvely optimistic to appeal to a Shakespeare moving at this stage towards the mood that was shortly to produce *Hamlet*. Faced with this dilemma Shakespeare

[1] I have tried to interpret the spirit of this play in a previous article in *Scrutiny*, March 1941.

chose to accept the very improbability of the story and to turn it to account. The Prince, from his very first appearance, looks forward to a reformation which, just because it is too good to be true, is seen to be moved by a political calculation which clearly reflects the character of his father. If his character is to change, as he announces in his very first soliloquy, it is because a transformation of this kind will attract popularity: for "nothing pleaseth but rare accidents." The whole process of "reformation," as the Prince himself describes it, has a surface quality which Shakespeare is clearly concerned to emphasize. It is seen "glittering" with metallic speciousness over previous faults, "like bright metal on a sullen ground"; and its purpose, above all, is to "*show* more goodly" and "attract more eyes." The conversion, thus transformed from an edifying example to an instrument of political success, enters fully into the permanent characteristics of the House of Lancaster. The future Henry V, already regarded as an example of the perfect political figure, begins by consciously abstaining from the finer aspects of human nature; for behind Shakespeare's acceptance of a traditional story lies the conviction that success in politics implies a spiritual loss, commonly involves the sacrifice of more attractive qualities which are distinctively personal.

The character of the Prince as it is developed through the play brings home this conception with a variety of detail. It is the character of a man whose keen if limited intelligence is placed consistently at the service of his political interests. If the politician is not so much a man of intellectual subtlety and spiritual discernment as one who can envisage with clarity the practical end of his activities and devote all his faculties without division to its attainment then the Prince is a complete example of the type. His intelligence is of the kind that, operating entirely in the practical order, sees through all pretences and evasions to the concrete issues that underlie them. Hotspur's reputation does not blind him to his failings, and when he now describes him he at once conforms to his own assumption of a cynical tone—appropriate to the "humours" of his tavern associates—and stresses the lack of imagination which we have just witnessed in his rival's attitude to his wife. Hotspur is the man who "kills me six or seven dozens of Scots at a breakfast" and then complains of his quiet life, like Douglas whose prowess in battle is filled out, in the popular imagination, with adornments which strike Hal, in his ironical detachment, as simply absurd:

> PRINCE. He that rides at high speed and with his pistol kills a
> sparrow flying.
> FALSTAFF. You have hit it.
> PRINCE. So did he never the sparrow. (II, iv).

For the Prince Douglas is an enemy, but his attitude would not
have been different had he been an ally. In either case the firm if
limited judgment would be based on the same clear narrow principles of expedience. His intelligence is of the kind that judges all
men by their value in relation to a coldly conceived political scheme;
that is the reason both for his success and his inhumanity.

This detachment in the Prince's attitude towards friend and foe
is based in turn upon a series of moral deficiencies which Shakespeare is concerned to stress from the first moment. His relationship
to those around him, invalidated by the peculiar mental reservation
which invariably accompanies it, is necessarily unsatisfactory. The
Prince is to all appearances capable of sinking himself into his sur-
roundings and meeting his "low" associates on their own level; but
his attitude to them, when he is alone and expresses his inmost
feelings, shows a certain false humility that is most revealing: "I
have sounded the very base-string of humility. Sirrah, I am sworn
brother to a leash of drawers; and can call them all by their christen
names, as Tom, Dick, and Francis" (II, iv). The confidence with
which he moves among the "lower orders"—I choose the phrase,
with all its implications of set purpose—expresses itself, moreover,
in a peculiar and typical tone. The quality of many of his observations upon those whom he encourages to regard themselves as his
friends reflects a coarseness which is, in the true sense of the word,
vulgar and thoroughly characteristic of his entirely amoral personality. Shakespeare brings this home to us in numerous apparently
petty turns of phrase: "If there come a hot June and this civil
buffeting hold, we shall buy maidenheads as they buy hob-nails,
by the hundreds" (II, iv). Spoken of itself in one of the tavern
scenes of this play we might pass over phrasing of this type; but
Shakespeare brings us into contact with the kind of feeling that
prompted it too often for us to ignore it in the long run. Falstaff,
whose relationship to the Prince lies at the heart of the whole play, is
the particular butt of a kind of intensity in grossness which is surely
revealing. After the trick played on him at Eastcheap, he "*lards* the
lean earth as he walks along" (II, ii); and in the great parody of

the relationship between the King and his son the Prince heaps upon him such a list of epithets as "bolting-hutch of beastliness," "swollen parcel of dropsies," "huge bombard of sack" and "stuffed cloak-bag of guts" (II, iv). The insistence upon this type of imagery, so lacking in the spontaneous imaginative warmth that character- izes Falstaff's fleshliness, is certainly intentional. It is as though the Prince, whose every action is based on calculation, felt for Falstaff, who represents in himself the vitality and the weakness of human flesh, the semi-conscious repulsion felt by the cold practical in- tellect for something which it can neither understand, ignore, nor, in the last resort, use. The Prince, echoing Falstaff's idiom, brings to it a cold, efficient intensity that points to an underlying aversion. The flesh, with which the finished politician needs to reckon, is nevertheless an object of repulsion to him. Beneath the burlesque and the rowdiness we may already look forward to the ultimate rejection of Falstaff. That rejection indeed is actually anticipated in the same scene. Falstaff, in a plea that is not less pathetic for being a parody based on monstrous presumption, concludes by begging the Prince not to banish him: "banish plump Jack and banish all the world" (II, iv). Banish Falstaff, in other words, and banish everything that cannot be reduced to an instrument of policy in the quest for empty success. It is true to the Prince's character and to the tragedy of his family that he already replies without hesitation "I do, I will."

The tracing of a common destiny working itself out through character in the actions of the family of Lancaster is, then, an es- sential part of Shakespeare's conception. It is not, however, the whole. In many of the political plays written by Shakespeare at this period we are aware that the individuals whose actions are repre- sented are in fact bound together in character as different aspects of an embracing whole; their virtues and their faults, their suc- cesses and failures are inter-dependent parts of a world whose unity is to be sought in the author's experience projected into the com- plete conception of the play. In *Troilus and Cressida*, as I have tried to show elsewhere,[2] this unity of characters connected by complementary qualities and related imagery is obviously of funda- mental importance; but it exists already in the Second Part of *Henry IV* and is at least foreshadowed in the first. For the rebel leaders in this play, when they attempt to translate their aspira-

[2] *Scrutiny*, December 1938.

tions into action, are affected by a flaw not fundamentally dis-similar from that which dominates the royal camp. If Henry IV's kingship is rendered sterile in its higher aspirations by the fact that his seizure of the crown involved the murder of his predecessor and was prompted by egoism the same is true of those who, having helped to bring him to the throne, now wish to see his power curbed or destroyed. The part played by the rebels in Henry's rise to power is stressed from the very beginning. It is, indeed, a chief point in the presentation of their case. Worcester, whose first ap-pearance involves a clash with the King, refers in his very first speech to:

> that same greatness too which our own hands
> Hath holp to make so portly. (I, iii).

A little later in the same scene Hotspur puts the relationship in less flattering terms. He describes his associates as the "base second means," "the cords, the ladder, or the hangman" involved in Rich-ard's murder and is at pains to emphasize that what they have done is criminal, committed in "an unjust behalf." The fact is that it was desire for power which prompted the rebel leaders to crime, and now it is mutual fear, itself the consequence of crime, that makes their clash inevitable. Henry, conscious that his own power was criminally obtained, cannot help suspecting that those who once followed their own interest in dethroning a king may do so again; and the rebels (or the more reflective of them) understand that the King must think in this way and that they themselves can therefore never be safe. The result is an endless mistrust, the con-sequences of which continue until they fatally conclude at Shrews-bury. The preliminaries of that battle are in themselves highly sig-nificant. Both sides at heart desire peace, the rebels because they know they are not strong enough to win, the King because he real-izes in the light of experience that the disunity in his kingdom is not one which battle, however victorious, can resolve. Reason, in-deed, demands peace and unity; but the consequences of the original crime against order and therefore against reason are still there and need to work themselves out in blood. The King makes Worcester and Vernon a generous offer of peace, seeing in peace a restoration of natural order based on the free recognition of just and beneficent authority. His behaviour in doing so is that proper to a King. He uses the familiar image of the planets to drive home his contrast between selfish anarchy and ordered peace:

> will you again unknit
> This churlish knot of all-abhorred war?
> And move in that obedient orb again
> Where you did give a fair and natural light.
> And be no more an exhaled meteor,
> A prodigy of fear, and a portent
> Of broached mischief to the unborn times? (V, i).

Henry speaks here as he had spoken at the opening of the Crusade, as a King fulfilling the terms of his vocation. He calls for unity, using the accepted imagery; but the origins of his power, which he would now wish to forget, make themselves felt in their endless consequences to frustrate the lawfulness of his intentions.

Worcester's reaction to the offer serves to bring out a parallel weakness in the rebel camp. In the figure of Worcester Shakespeare sought to study the type of the political courtier. Persuasiveness and reason, born of cunning and experience, are his gods; in the early scenes we see him restraining the impetuosity of Hotspur basing his argument on the very appeal to expediency that Henry himself uses to his son; for Hotspur's impatience, he tells him, is such that it "loseth men's hearts" (III, i) and compromises their chances of success. Yet Worcester, all reason and moderation as he appears, is a rebel and, being a rebel in the name of interest, he is driven to exclude the operation of reason as the most dangerous enemy of his projects. For reason, according to the original conception, is necessarily on the side of order, of kingship, and rebellion owes its origin to the promptings of selfish passion against rational restraint. Worcester stresses this flaw in their position to his fellow-conspirators:

> For well you know we of the offering side
> Must keep aloof from strict arbitrement,
> And stop all sight-holes, every loop from whence
> The eye of reason may pry in upon us. (IV, i).

Rebellion, according to the convention which Shakespeare accepted as the starting-point of his political plays, is based upon the exclusion of reason, though it takes a rebel as rational as Worcester so to define it. Priding himself on his realistic attitude to political events, he is yet driven first to shut out reason and then to conceal the fact that peace has been offered by the King and that the battle itself has become unnecessary. The reasons he gives to Vernon are highly significant:

> It is not possible, it cannot be,
> The king should keep his word in loving us;
> He will suspect us still, and find a time
> To punish this offence in other faults . . . .
>   . . . treason is but trusted like the fox
> Who, ne'er so tame, so cherish'd and lock'd up,
> Will have a wild trick of his ancestors. (V, ii).

Worcester's distrust, like Henry's tragedy, has its roots far in the past. It owes its existence to the original crime against Richard by which the bond of freely accepted rule once broken, the seeds of disorder and suspicion are sown to work themselves out on both sides in mutual destruction. The combatants in either camp at Shrewsbury invoke "honour" and other lofty sanctions to justify their cause; but the reality is that crime born of self-interest on either side has born fruit in unnecessary bloodshed.

Shakespeare's treatment of the rebel leaders is designed to drive home these points as they reveal themselves in the details of character expressed in action. If their handling of the campaign is futile and their motives based on an unhappy mixture of fear and self-seeking the divisions that make their common action impossible spring from the dubious foundations of a cause conceived in egoism and executed without conviction. Of their moral and intellectual qualities we are left in no doubt. Glendower is a mixture of superstition, vanity and incompetence whose self-regard prompts him to look everywhere for insults and makes it impossible for him to collaborate honestly with his fellow-conspirators; Douglas is as the Prince has described him, a brainless butcher as contemptuous of the reasoning of others as he is himself incapable of rational thought. Throughout the rebel camp before the battle there exists the familiar division between the counsels of reason, which cannot see beyond timidity and selfish fear, and those of passion which drive those possessed by them to actions which cannot be justified upon the slightest reflection. Reason prompts Northumberland and

Glendower to withhold their forces in order not to commit themselves to the common cause at the decisive moment, just as it has
caused Vernon and Worcester to conceal the King's offer of peace;
passion drives Hotspur and Douglas to accept battle against better
advice on hopeless terms and to despise the reasonable counsels of
strategy as inspired by "fear and cold heart." In this world of political sordidness and folly Hotspur stands out as a figure relatively
attractive. That he is not without a critical eye is proved by his
understanding of the nature of Glendower (III, i) and by his in-
cisive description of the courtly popinjay who brought him the
King's demand for his prisoners after his victory at Holmedon (I,
iii). In both cases the justice of his comment is reflected in a vivid
vernacular phrasing that guarantees its genuineness. Yet, in spite
of these qualities, Hotspur remains a rebel and time shows him to
be the instrument of politicians more calculating than himself. A
warrior and man of action, the cause for which he fights is one
whose moral basis cannot be reasonably sustained; so that his motives, far from being adequate, reduce themselves to an acceptance
of the rhetorical idea of honour which prompts him, whenever it
is mentioned, to emotional outbursts which contrast completely
with Worcester's tight-lipped calls to reason and calculation. We
are reminded of the Trojans in *Troilus and Cressida* with their facile
surrenders to emotion leading to the acceptance of a cause indefensible in reason. At Shrewsbury Hotspur falls on behalf of policies
less creditable than those his own nature should have been capable
of accepting. His death leaves us with a sensation somewhere between the tragic and the ironic, adequately summed up in the contrasted attitude contained in his conqueror's brief words—"For
worms, brave Percy" (V, iv). It is simply one aspect of the futility
which is the real meaning of the battle of Shrewsbury, in which the
rebels fail to achieve their end and at the same time prevent the
King from obtaining the unity for which he is *now*, but too late,
genuinely striving.

So far we might call the First Part of *Henry IV* an acute political
study based on a personal elaboration of ideas rooted in traditional
thought. But Shakespeare's most individual contribution to his
material lies in the figure of Falstaff. Falstaff is given in the play
a position of peculiar significance which enables him to transcend
the political action in which he moves and to provide a sufficient
comment on it. He serves, in a sense, as a connecting-link between

two worlds, the tavern world of comic incident and broad humanity in which he is at home and the world of court rhetoric and political intrigue to which he also has access. So situated in two worlds and limited by neither, Falstaff is thus used as a commentator who passes judgment on the events represented in the play in the light of his own superabundant comic vitality. Working sometimes through open comment, sometimes even through open parody, his is a voice that lies outside the prevailing political spirit of the play, that draws its cogency from the author's own insight expressing itself in a flow of comic vitality. He represents, we might say, all the humanity which it seems that the politician bent on the attainment of success must necessarily exclude. That humanity, as it manifests itself in the tavern scenes, is full of obvious and gross imperfections; but the Falstaff of the play, whilst he shares these imperfections, is not altogether limited by them. His keen intelligence, his real human understanding, his refusal to be fobbed off by empty or hypocritical phrases—all these are characteristics that enable him to transcend his world and to become the individual expression of the conscience of a great and completely serious artist. In the elaboration of this point we approach the very heart of Shakespeare's conception in this play.

The true nature of Falstaff becomes most apparent when we realize that he comes to be in this series of plays a complete and significant contrast to the figure of the Prince. The full force of this contrast probably only became apparent to Shakespeare as he proceeded with his trilogy; but something of it is present from the first. It becomes fully clear for the first time in the scene of tavern parody when the two men caricature the relationship of Henry IV and his son (II, iv). Falstaff's behaviour after ascending his mock throne at Eastcheap in a scene which parodies by anticipation the real one shortly to take place (III, ii) envelops that relationship at once in the atmosphere of the popular stage, of the "harlotry players," to use the Hostess' own words, and provides us with a new standpoint from which to consider the central political theme. The description he gives of the Prince, using his father's supposed words, is in itself a criticism, realistic and sardonic, of the whole family: "That thou art my son, I have partly thy mother's word, partly my own opinion, but chiefly a villanous trick of thine eye, and a foolish hanging of thy nether lip, that doth warrant me." It is not thus that Henry does actually speak to his son, nor is it true to say that the relationship between them is of this kind. That relationship is on the contrary truly tragic, and becomes more so as the father grows older and more conscious of the weariness that besets him through life; but the disillusioned clarity, even the coarseness, of Falstaff's description corresponds to something really present, that makes itself felt time and again in the Prince's attitude towards his life in the taverns and is a symptom of the detached inhumanity which is one ingredient of his political sense. This is not the Prince as he is, but it is one true aspect of him as seen by an eye clear and unfailing in its realism in the world in which this aspect is most in evidence. To bring out that aspect in those who surround him is the first of Falstaff's functions in the play.

The second is to provide on the basis of this clarity of vision a criticism of the whole political action, both on the loyalist and rebel side, which leads up to the dubious battle in which it concludes. In this action, and especially in its warlike phases, Falstaff is involved without being of it or subdued to the spirit, now cynical, now wordily "honourable," in which it is habitually conceived. His comments on the motives of the rebels are characteristically clearheaded; his reaction to Worcester's disclaimer of responsibility for the rising is summed up in the phrase "Rebellion lay in his way, and he found it" (V, i). More revealing still, because based on sentiments more deeply human beneath the comic vision, is his attitude towards the pressed troops placed under his command to lead into battle. He has, as always, no particular illusion about the nature and the origins of this human material, "the cankers of a calm world and a long peace" (IV, ii); but his very account of them in the same speech as "discarded unjust serving-men, younger sons to younger brothers, revolted tapsters, and ostlers tradefallen," together with many other references, implies an awareness of social issues possessed by no other character in the play. This awareness is based in its turn upon Falstaff's outstanding quality, the capacity for human sympathy which marks him out in a world of calculation and inspires the respect for human life implied in his magnificent ironic reply to the Prince when the latter sums up his contingent as so many "pitiful rascals"—"Tut, tut; good enough to toss; food for powder, food for powder; they'll fill a pit as well as better; tush, man, mortal men, mortal men" (IV, ii). For the Prince as for all his world, soldiers are mere pawns, the wretched instruments of political calculation to be considered from the point of view of their possible efficiency in the tasks imposed upon them by their leaders; for Falstaff alone they are human victims, individuals exposed to the manipulations of discreditable interests, "mortal men" and as such to be respected after detached and unsentimental scrutiny in the very sordidness of their tragedy. It is his sense of humanity in its weakness and its irreducibility that prompts Falstaff's behaviour in the battle. Precisely because he is so human himself in his very irony he has no desire to die, to pay the debt of death "before his day" (V, i); and precisely because he can realize in others the human desire to survive which he feels so strongly in himself he is keenly aware that "honour" in the mouths of politicians who have been brought to battle by a combination of past selfishness and present refusal to face their responsibilities is an empty word and a delusion. "I like not such grinning honour as Sir Walter hath" (V, iii) is his final comment, at once human and dispassionate, on the waste implied in a battle based on causes so suspect; and inspired by its spirit he moves through the conflict without being subdued to its tone, viewing it and himself with characteristic frankness and dominating it, when all is said and done, by the very force of his vitality.

These observations bring us to a third characteristic of Falstaff, the one which is perhaps the ultimate source of his strength and the key to Shakespeare's deepest conception in this play. There is in Falstaff a true and rare combination of the warm, alert humanity we have already noted with a background, sometimes accepted and sometimes rebelled against, but continually present, of inherited Christian tradition. It is reasonable to suppose that the latter element makes itself felt in a spontaneous acceptance of the inheritance, still not so distant from Shakespeare, of the mediaeval religious theatre. We may sense the presence of this inheritance in the readiness with which Falstaff in his phrasing draws upon images and ideas which derive their force from their relation to crucial moments in the familiar Christian drama. When he calls upon his tavern companions to "watch to-night, pray to-morrow" (II, iv) the effect of the phrase depends largely upon its relation to the originally Christian ethic; when in the same scene he greets the news of the arrival of the King's messenger with "What doth gravity out of his bed at midnight?" it is not fanciful to seek in "gravity" a personification of the kind familiar in the bearded, solemn figures of the old morality plays. Falstaff's utterances, indeed, are steeped in tradition, at once religious and theatrical, of this kind. He shares with his audience a whole world of imagery, drawn upon in such phrases as that in which his troops are described as "slaves as ragged as Lazarus in the painted cloth, where the glutton's dogs licked his sores" (IV, ii). This common inheritance itself gives him reality by contrast with the orators and politicians of the verse scenes of this play. The ease with which the theatrical passes into the religious reference is clearly seen in his comment on Bardolph's nose (III, iii), to which he refers as "a Death's head or a *memento mori*"— "I never see thy face but I think upon hell-fire and Dives that lived in purple." In such phrases we feel what the strength of a still living popular tradition could offer to the dramatist. Assimilated into his utterances it enables Falstaff to bring to his criticism of the political action around him a realism that, in its profounder moments, is neither self-regarding nor cynical, but that derives from a balanced view of man's destiny and in particular of the peculiar complexity of spiritual motives. At his best Falstaff, recognizing his own faults, gives them a taste of tragic significance by relating them to the familiar but profound spiritual drama of mankind worked out in the individual between birth and death, in mankind between the Creation and the Last Judgment: "Thou knowest in the state of innocency Adam fell; and what should poor Jack Falstaff do in the days of villainy? Thou seest I have more flesh than another man, and therefore more frailty" (III, iii). To take this too seriously would be as naïve as it would be short-sighted to deny it all seriousness. Falstaff's tone is in part ironical, mocking as usual; but the reference to the physical flesh here is subsidiary to the spiritual meaning of the word sanctioned by Christian theology, and it is in the sense of the relationship between the two, a relationship comprehending dependence and separation in a single unity, that Falstaff acquires his full stature. Such were the advantages for Shakespeare of inheriting—I say inheriting because the question of personal belief need not arise—a set of spiritual conceptions at once simple enough to be popular and sufficiently profound to cover the wealth of human experience. We need not say—should not say—that Falstaff simply accepts the Christian tradition. Part of him, what we may call the flesh, clearly does not;

but the tradition is there, alive in his utterances and giving him even in his refusal to conform a vitality that enables him to dominate the play. We shall see this Christian background deepened and developed in the Second Part of the play.

L. C. KNIGHTS

Henry IV *as Satire*

Henry IV does not fit easily into any of the critical schemata,* though "incongruity" has served the critics in good stead. But, at any rate, since the time of Morgann, Falstaff has received a degree of sympathetic attention (how we love the fat rascal!) that distorts Shakespeare's intention in writing the two plays. We regard them as a sandwich—so much dry bread to be bitten through before we come to the meaty Falstaff, although we try to believe that "the heroic and serious part is not inferior to the comic and farcical." Actually each play is a unity, sub-plot and main plot cooperating to express the vision which is projected into the form of the play. And this vision, like that of all the great writers of comedy, is pre-eminently serious. It is symptomatic that Hazlitt, defending Shakespeare's tragedies against the comedies, said, "He was greatest in what was greatest; and his *forte* was not trifling."

The first speech of the King deserves careful attention. The brittle verse suggests the precarious poise of the usurper:

> So shaken as we are, so wan with care,
> Find we a time for frighted peace to pant,
> And breathe short-winded accents of new broils
> To be commenced in stronds afar remote.

Pt. II of "Notes on Comedy" from *The Importance of Scrutiny,* ed. Eric Bentley (New York, 1948). Reprinted by permission of the author and the publisher, George W. Stewart, Inc. Title added by Ed. The essay first appeared in *Scrutiny,* I (March 1933), 356–367.

* That is, the various theories about comedy discussed by Professor Knights earlier in his essay. Ed.

The violence of the negative which follows suggests its opposite:

> No more the thirsty entrance of this soil
> Shall daub her lips with her own children's blood:
> No more shall trenching war channel her fields,
> Nor bruise her flowerets with the armed hoofs
> Of hostile paces.

"Thirsty" contains the implication that the earth is eager for more blood; and when the prophecy of peace ends with the lisping line, "Shall now, in mutual well-beseeming ranks," we do not need a previous knowledge of the plot or of history to realize that Henry is actually describing what is to come. The account of the proposed crusade is satiric:

> But this our purpose is a twelvemonth old, . . .
> Therefore we meet not now.

Throughout we are never allowed to forget that Henry is a usurper. We are given four separate accounts of how he gained the throne—by Hotspur (I, iii, 160–186), by Henry himself (III, ii, 39–84), by Hotspur again (IV, iii, 52–92), and by Worcester (V, i, 32–71). He gained it by "murd'rous subornation," by hypocrisy, his "seeming brow of justice," by "violation of all faith and troth." Words expressing underhand dealing occur even in the king's account to his son:

> And then I stole all courtesy from Heaven,
> And dress'd myself in such humility
> That I did pluck allegiance from men's hearts.

There is irony in the couplet that concludes the play:

> And since this business *so fair* is done,
> Let us not leave till all *our own* be won.

The rebels, of course, are no better. The hilarious scene in which the plot is hatched (I, iii, 187–299) does not engage much sympathy for the plotters, who later squabble over the expected booty like any long-staff sixpenny strikers. Their cause does not bear prying into by "the eye of reason" (IV, i, 69–72), and Worcester, for his own purposes, conceals "the liberal kind offer of the King" (V, ii, 1–25). But this is relatively unimportant; there is no need to take sides and "like Hotspur somewhat better than the Prince because he is unfortunate." The satire is general, directed against statecraft and warfare. Hotspur is the chief representative of chivalry, and we have only to read his speeches to understand Shakespeare's attitude towards "honour"; there is no need to turn to Falstaff's famous soliloquy. The description of the Mortimer-Glendower fight has just that degree of exaggeration which is necessary for not-too-obvious burlesque, though, oddly enough, it has been used to show that Hotspur "has the imagination of a poet." But if the image of the Severn—

> Who then, affrighted with their bloody looks,
> Ran fearfully among the trembling reeds,
> And hid his crisp head in the hollow bank—

is not sufficient indication, the rhyme announces the burlesque intention:

> He did confound the best part of an hour
> In changing hardiment with great Glendower.

There is the same exaggeration in later speeches of Worcester and Hotspur; Hotspur's "huffing part"—"by Heaven methinks it were an easy leap"—did not need Beaumont's satire.* In the battle scene the heroics of "Now, Esperance! Percy! and set on," the chivalric embrace and flourish of trumpets are immediately followed by the exposure of a military dodge for the preservation of the King's life. "The King hath many marching in his coats."—"Another King! They grow like Hydra's heads."

The reverberations of the sub-plot also help to determine our attitude towards the main action. The conspiracy of the Percys is sandwiched between the preparation for the Gadshill plot and counterplot and its execution. Poins has "lost much honour" that he did not see the "action" of the Prince with the drawers. When we see the court we remember Falstaff's joint-stool throne and his account of Henry's hanging lip. Hotspur's pride in himself and his associates ("Is there not my father, my uncle and myself?") is

* See the "Induction" to *The Knight of the Burning Pestle* by Francis Beaumont and John Fletcher. Ed.

parodied by Gadshill: "I am joined with no foot land-rakers, no long-staff sixpenny strikers . . . but with nobility and tranquility, burgomasters and great oneyers." The nobles, like the roarers, prey on the commonwealth, "for they ride up and down on her and make her their boots."

The Falstaff attitude is therefore in solution, as it were, throughout the play, even when he is not on the stage; but it takes explicit form in the person and speeches of Sir John. We see a heroic legend in process of growth in the account of his fight with the men in buckram. The satire in the description of his ragged regiment is pointed by a special emphasis on military terms—"soldiers," "captain," "lieutenant," "ancients, corporals . . . gentlemen of companies." His realism easily reduces honour to "a mere scutcheon.' Prince Henry's duel with Hotspur is accompanied by the mockery of the Douglas-Falstaff fight, which ends with the dead and the counterfeit dead lying side by side. If we can rid ourselves of our realistic illusions and their accompanying moral qualms we realize how appropriate it is that Falstaff should rise to stab Hotspur's body and carry him off as his luggage on his back.

The satire on warfare, the Falstaff attitude, implies an axis of reference, which is of course found in the gross and vigorous life of the body. We find throughout the play a peculiar insistence on imagery deriving from the body, on descriptions of death in its more gruesome forms, on stabbing, cutting, bruising, and the like. We expect to find references to blood and death in a play dealing with civil war, but such references in *Henry IV* are far more pervasive than in a war play such as *Henry V*. In the first scene we hear of the earth "daubing her lips with her own children's blood." War is "trenching"; it "channels" the fields and "bruises" the flowers. "The edge of war" is "like an ill-sheathed knife" which "cuts his master." Civil war is an "intestinal shock," and battles are "butchery." We learn that the defeated Scots lay "balk'd in their own blood," and that "beastly shameless transformation" was done by the Welsh upon the corpses of Mortimer's soldiers. Later Hotspur mentions the smell of "a slovenly unhandsome corpse," and we hear of Mortimer's "mouthed wounds." So throughout the play. The dead Blunt lies "grinning," Hotspur's face is "mangled," and Falstaff lies by him "in blood." Falstaff's "honour" soliloquy insists on surgery, on broken legs and arms.

To all this Falstaff, a walking symbol, is of course opposed. "To shed my dear blood drop by drop i' the dust" for the sake of honour appears an imbecile ambition. Falstaff will "fight no longer than he sees reason." His philosophy is summed up when he has escaped Douglas by counterfeiting death: "S'blood! 'twas time to counterfeit, or that hot termagant Scot had paid me scot and lot too. Counterfeit? I lie, I am no counterfeit: to die is to be a counterfeit; for he is but the counterfeit of a man who hath not the life of a man; but to counterfeit dying, when a man thereby liveth, is to be no counterfeit, but the true and perfect image of life indeed." The same thought is implicit in the honour soliloquy.

Once the play is read as a whole, the satire on war and policy is apparent. It is useful to compare the first part of *Henry IV* with *King John* in estimating the development of Shakespeare's dramatic power. *King John* turns on a single pivotal point—the Bastard's speech on commodity; * but the whole of the later play is impregnated with satire which crystallizes in Falstaff. Now, satire implies a standard, and in *Henry IV* the validity of the standard itself is questioned; hence the peculiar coherence and universality of the play. "Honour" and "state-craft" are set in opposition to the natural life of the body, but the chief body of the play is, explicitly, "a bolting-hutch of beastliness."—"A pox on this gout! or a gout on this pox, I should say." Other speeches reinforce the age-and-disease theme which, it has not been observed, is a significant part of the Falstaff theme. Hotspur pictures the earth as an "old beldam"

> pinch'd and vex'd
> By the imprisoning of unruly wind
> Within her womb.

Again, he says:

> The time of life is short;
> To spend that shortness basely were too long,
> If life did ride upon a dial's point,
> Still ending at the arrival of an hour.

The last two lines imply that no "if" is necessary; life does "ride upon a dial's point," and Hotspur's final speech takes up the theme of transitoriness:

* II, i, 561–598. Ed.

But thought's the slave of life, and life time's fool:
And time, that takes survey of all the world,
Must have a stop.

There is no need to emphasize the disease aspect of Falstaff (Bardolph's bad liver is not merely funny). He "owes God a death." He and his regiment are "mortal men." It is important to realize, however, that when Falstaff feigns death he is meant to appear actually as dead in the eyes of the audience; at least the idea of death is meant to be emphasized in connexion with the Falstaff-idea at this point. No answer is required to the Prince's rhetorical question,

What! old acquaintance! could not all this flesh
Keep in a little life? Poor Jack, farewell!

The stability of our attitude after a successful reading of the first part of *Henry IV* is due to the fact that the breaking-down process referred to above is not simple but complex; one set of impulses is released for the expression of the Falstaff-outlook; but a set of opposite complementary impulses is also brought into play, producing an effect analogous to that caused by the presence of comedy in *King Lear* [1] (compare the use of irony in *Madame Bovary*). *Lear* is secure against ironical assault because of the irony it contains; *Henry IV* will bear the most serious ethical scrutiny because in it the "serious" is a fundamental part of the "comic" effect of the play. (The second part of *Henry IV* is no less interesting. No one has yet pointed out that drunkenness, lechery, and senile depravity (in II, iv, for example) are *not* treated by Shakespeare with "good-natured tolerance." Shakespeare's attitude toward his characters in *2 Henry IV* at times approaches the attitude of Mr. Eliot towards Doris, Wauchope, etc., in *Sweeney Agonistes*. Northumberland's monody on death (I, i) needs to be studied in order to understand the tone of the play.)

[1] See the admirable essay on "Lear and the Comedy of the Grotesque" in *The Wheel of Fire*, by G. Wilson Knight.

CLEANTH BROOKS and ROBERT B. HEILMAN

Dramatic Balance in Henry IV, Part I

1. THE PROBLEM OF UNITY

The salient problem in this play must be the problem of unity. To most readers at least, the most important general question which presents itself is this: does the play achieve a real dramatic unity, or is it, after all, merely a not-too-interesting "history" play to which Shakespeare has added, in the interest of amusement, the Falstaff tavern scenes? To state the problem with special reference to Act V, does this last act really succeed in uniting the various threads of interest that run through the play?

The "history" plot is, of course, brought to a conclusion in this act with the decision gained in the Battle of Shrewsbury.[1] But what of the comic underplot? Does it come here into any organic relation with the other elements of the play, or does it remain isolated? What happens to Hotspur when he comes within the orbit of Falstaff? Or what, for that matter, happens to Falstaff when he comes between the "fell incensed points/ Of mighty opposites"? If he affords no more than comic relief, then we are perhaps justified in holding that as a character he is a lucky accident, a character who was, in Shakespeare's original plans, to have

From *Understanding Drama*, by Cleanth Brooks and Robert B. Heilman, pp. 376–387. Copyright © 1948 by Holt, Rinehart and Winston, Inc., New York. Reprinted by permission. Title added by Ed.

[1] To a temporary conclusion at least, for Shakespeare continued the story in *Henry IV, Part 2*, which the student should read. The two-part arrangement in itself raises the problem of unity in a special form. Suffice it to say here that, whatever the total unity which the two parts taken together may have, this first part has its own special unity which it is our immediate problem here to attempt to define.

Falstaff's death is mentioned in *Henry V*, and he is the central figure in *The Merry Wives of Windsor;* but in this latter play, most critics and scholars agree that he comes closer to the mere buffoon—that he lacks the special quality of character shown in the *Henry* plays.

figured as a sort of jester, but who became something richer and more imaginative than intended. As a matter of fact, one might, pushing this line of argument a step further, contend that Falstaff has actually so far outgrown the needs of the play, strictly considered, that he comes close to destroying it.

It is possible, however, to see Falstaff's role as a more positive one than that of merely diverting us *from* the more serious concerns of the play. It is possible that his function is to define—as well as enrich—the theme of the play. But to explore this possibility will involve a rather careful consideration of his relation to the other characters in the play and a further inquiry into the theme—the total "meaning" of the play.

2. THE SYSTEM OF CONTRASTS IN THE PLAY

If *Henry IV, Part I* does have a principle of unity, it is obviously one which allows for, and makes positive use of, an amazing amount of contrast. There is the contrast between the king's hopes for his son and the life which Prince Hal has actually been leading; the contrast between the pomp and state of the councils at court which are called to debate the state of the realm and those other councils at the Boar's Head which take measures for the better lifting of travelers' purses. Moreover, as we have remarked earlier, Prince Hal and Percy Hotspur are obvious foils for each other; they are specifically contrasted again and again throughout the play. But one of the most important contrasts developed in the play is that between Falstaff and Percy Hotspur.

On one level, it ought to be pretty obvious, the play involves a study in the nature of kingship—not an unduly solemn study, to be sure—but a study, nevertheless, of what makes a good king. In this study, of course, Prince Hal is the central figure, and the play becomes, then, the study of his development.

On this level of consideration, Percy Hotspur not only is Hal's rival but also furnishes an ideal of conduct toward which Hal might aspire (and toward which his father, the king, actually wishes him to aspire). Falstaff represents another ideal of conduct—and here, consequently, finds his foil in Hotspur. (If the pairing of Falstaff and Hotspur seems, at first glance, forced, nevertheless we shall presently see that there is abundant evidence that Shakespeare thought the contrast important and relevant to his purpose.)

Indeed, as Mr. R. P. Warren has pointed out, it is almost as if
Shakespeare were following, consciously or unconsciously, the
theme of Aristotle's Nichomachaean ethics: virtue as the mean between two extremes of conduct. This suggestion can be used to
throw a good deal of light on the relationship of the characters of
Falstaff, Prince Hal, and Hotspur to each other.

Consider the matter of honor. Hotspur represents one extreme,
Falstaff, the other. Hotspur declares characteristically

> By heaven, methinks it were an easy leap,
> To pluck bright honour from the pale-faced moon, . . .
> (I, iii, 201–202)

Falstaff speaks just as characteristically when he argues in his
famous speech on honor: "Well, 'tis no matter; honour pricks me
on. Yea, but how if honour prick me off when I come on? how
then? Can honour set to a leg? no: or an arm? no: or take away
the grief of a wound? no . . . (V. i)

Falstaff's common sense is devastating; but it is also crippling—
or would be to a prince or ruler. If it does not cripple Falstaff, it is
because Falstaff frankly refuses to accept the responsibilities of
leadership. Perhaps he chooses wisely in so refusing. By refusing
he achieves a vantage point from which he can perceive the folly
and pretentiousness which, to a degree, always tend to associate
themselves with authority of any kind.

But Hotspur's chivalry is crippling too. He wants to fight for
honor's sake: he will not wait for reinforcements because it will
beget more honor to fight without waiting for them; but, on the
other hand, he will not fight at all (Worcester fears) if he hears of
the king's mollifying offer, for then his pride will be saved, his
honor preserved, and the political aspects of the rebellion can go
hang; for Hotspur has little or no interest in them. Indeed, Hotspur can rely on the obvious fact that he is fighting merely for
honor to gain the forgiveness of the king, though Worcester fears
that the forgiveness extended to himself will be only a nominal
forgiveness and that the king will be on the lookout for later excuses to injure him.

If one assumes the necessity for leadership (and there is little
doubt that the Elizabethan audience and Shakespeare did), then
Hotspur points to an extreme which the truly courageous leader

must avoid quite as clearly as he must avoid the other extreme represented by Falstaff. True courage, we may say, has as one frontier an unthinking impetuousness like that of Hotspur: it has as its other frontier a kind of calculation, which, if not cowardice, at least results in actions which look very much like cowardice. Falstaff is too "practical"; Hotspur, not "practical" enough.

3. THE "IMMATURITY" OF FALSTAFF AND HOTSPUR

Yet Shakespeare does not give us an oversimplified picture of either extreme. Falstaff redeems himself for most of us by his humor, by his good nature, by his love of life, and perhaps, most of all, by a thoroughgoing intellectual honesty. Hotspur also has his attractive side. There is a kind of abandon, a kind of light-hearted gaiety—in his whole-souled commitment to the pursuit of honor, in his teasing of his wife, and in his laughing at the pompous mystery-mongering of Glendower—which puts him, like Falstaff, *above* the plots and counter-plots that fill up the play.

Yet—if we assume the necessity for leadership and authority— both Falstaff and Hotspur are *below* the serious concerns that fill the play. About both of them there is a childlike quality which relieves them of the responsibility of mature life, a frankness which is the opposite of the pretense and hypocrisy so apparent in the adult world.[2]

This suggestion that there is something childlike and immature about Falstaff and Hotspur must, of course, be heavily qualified. There is a sense in which Hotspur is the epitome of manliness and aggressive masculinity, and certainly he thinks of himself as anything but childish. Moreover, Falstaff, in spite of the war cry with which he sets upon the travelers, "They hate us youth: down with them; fleece them," is old in the ways of vice, and indeed possesses a kind of wisdom which makes the solemn concerns of Henry IV's court appear callow and naïve beside it.

And yet, even so, the pair do not stand quite on the level of the adult world where there are jobs to be done and duties to be performed. They are either below it or else they transcend it; and

[2] If the student, remembering, for example, how "damnably" Falstaff has "misused the king's press," feels disposed to challenge this observation, he should be reminded that the matter in question is not Falstaff's goodness but his frankness and irresponsibility. He has the child's honest selfishness and the child's lack of conscience as he frankly goes after his own ends.

Shakespeare is wise enough to let them—particularly Falstaff—do both. That is, they appear sometimes *childish* in their attitudes and sometimes *childlike*, for Shakespeare exploits both aspects of their characters in the play.

The childlike qualities, of course, are found predominantly in Falstaff—in his vitality and in his preservation of a kind of innocence. But Hotspur, too, has a kind of innocence which sets him apart from the more calculating of his fellow-conspirators. He is impulsive where they are Machiavellian; boyish, in his love of adventure, where they are playing coldly for high stakes. But the childlike innocence (or, if one prefers, the boyish impulsiveness) merges into childish foolhardiness when he insists on fighting the king at Shrewsbury before reinforcements can be brought up.

4. FALSTAFF AT THE BATTLE OF SHREWSBURY

Falstaff is, of course, a far more complex character than Hotspur, or, for that matter, than any other character in the play. But an examination of the childish-childlike aspects of his nature may, even if it will not wholly account for the richness of his personality, lead the student into a further knowledge of that richness. Certainly, it may give us one of the most important clues as to how his character is related to the central problems of the play.

Falstaff as Philosopher. Falstaff, we may say, is like the child in the story who alone was able to detect the fact that the emperor's new clothes were entirely imaginary. With a clarity of vision that is unclouded by reverence towards authority of any kind, the child sees that the emperor is naked, and says so. (Falstaff strips Henry IV quite naked in his famous parody of the king's speech in Act II, iv. King Henry's concern for his son's wicked ways, as we see in Act III, is more than half an extension of his own self-conceit. His son's reputation disturbs him because he regards it as a reflection upon himself.)

Falstaff's clarity of vision, however, is not an effect of cynicism. The spectacle of the world in its nakedness, stripped of its pretensions, does not move Falstaff to bitterness. He can laugh in thorough good humor. And Falstaff does laugh continually through the play as he sees through what is glibly called "honor," through self-righteousness, through the pretensions of royalty. In this sense, like the child, he is fundamentally a moral anarchist. But

Falstaff is—again like the child—not a missionary anarchist. He does not for a moment intend to convert others to his views; he is not the moralist, certainly, nor the inverted moralist, the cynic.

In short, in spite of the fact that he speaks merely to amuse himself and others, Falstaff supplies a brilliant and what is—up to a point—a perfectly true commentary upon the world about him. Falstaff is doubtless the last man in the world to set up for a philosopher; yet his humor, because it does have point and does make a rich commentary upon the world about him, does have a philosophical quality.

Falstaff as Man of Action.   But in Act V we see Falstaff as man of action, and this action tests him even as the world of action is tested by Falstaff's commentary. On a battlefield the committed man of action must be prepared to die, but Falstaff does not feel the need to die for any man. He frankly sees no point in dying by Douglas's sword for King Henry. King Henry himself, as Falstaff well knows, is scarcely likely to appreciate such a devotion on Falstaff's part. Hal himself will not lose or retain his chances for the crown by Falstaff's death alone; and the issue, when Douglas challenges him, is certainly death; for Falstaff, in spite of his playful boasting, has absolutely no illusions about his own prowess as a warrior.

Falstaff loses no time in resolving his problem: he contents himself with playing 'possum. From one point of view, this is simply cowardice; from another, Falstaff is being perfectly consistent, and, to be so, risking the imputation of cowardice. In the same situation Blunt declares heroically, "I was not born a yielder, thou proud Scot"; he believes in honor, and so he has his reward, even in death. Falstaff is equally consistent because he does not believe in honor; for him, heroics would be a pretense—phony honor.

The Parallelism of Falstaff and Hotspur.   If the student has had any difficulty in seeing and accepting the parallelism between Falstaff and Hotspur, he might reflect that in this last act of the play the author himself has taken some pains to point it up, and may be said to have allowed at least Prince Hal, among the characters, to see it. In this connection Hal's speech over the dead body of Hotspur and his remarks over Falstaff's "dead" body, which he discovers a moment later, are worth careful consideration.

William Empson has pointed out (in his *English Pastoral Po-*

etry) that Hal's remarks here involve a series of puns applying both to largeness of body and to greatness of spirit. Of Hotspur the prince says:

> When that this body did contain a spirit,
> A kingdom for it was too small a bound. . . .
> . . . . this earth that bears thee dead
> Bears not alive so stout a gentleman.

A few lines later, he is saying of Falstaff:

> What, old acquaintance! could not all this flesh
> Keep in a little life? Poor Jack, farewell!
> I could have better spared a better man:
> O, I should have a heavy miss of thee,
> If I were much in love with vanity!
> Death hath not struck so fat a deer to-day, . . .

Hotspur has had too much spirit for the flesh; Falstaff has had so much flesh that it is ironical that the spirit has escaped at all. (The irony is increased, of course, by our knowing that Prince Hal little realizes how truly he speaks: the flesh that Falstaff so comfortably hugs about himself has *not*, as a matter of fact, allowed the spirit to escape.)

Moreover, it is significant that the prince, although he thinks that Falstaff has died in battle, refers to him as a "deer," a hunted animal, who would not fight back but would try to escape from the pursuit of death. From the standpoint of the huntsman (death) he is a fine animal ("so fat a deer"), and to the prince a "heavy loss" (another pun) though "better men" have died for his cause that day.

Is the prince mocking and cold-hearted? Hardly; the jesting farewell is the sort which accords with the jesting and affectionate companionship of the two in the past. It conveys a depth of feeling that perhaps would not be conveyed by a more solemn tribute.

At least Falstaff, who of course hears the prince's tribute, suffers no hurt feelings from the nature of the tribute. He has no shame and no qualms. In fact, only the word "Embowelled" runs the shivers up and down his back. The idea of being embalmed and given a fine burial by the prince stirs no regrets in him that he did not stand his ground and die honorably. Falstaff values his bowels. He is far from done with his gorbelly. Hotspur may have the prince's compliment and the noble burial which, doubtless, the prince intends for him. Falstaff is perfectly satisfied to abide by the choice which he has made.

Falstaff's Failure. Still, from the point of view of the need for responsibility and authority, Falstaff's conduct is childishly frivolous, if not much worse—as is his conduct throughout the battle. On one level, it is very funny when Prince Hal reaches into Falstaff's holster and pulls out a bottle of sack; and the prince himself doubtless smiles as he delivers his reprimand. But the reprimand is deserved: Falstaff won't realize that the battlefield is no place for joking. Indeed, though Shakespeare allows Falstaff his due even here, he has made the case against Falstaff very plain.

Consider the incident in Act V, iv. An Elizabethan audience would not have missed the point when, just after Falstaff has stabbed the dead Hotspur, Prince Hal came on the scene with his younger brother, Prince John, and says to him

> Come, brother John; full bravely hast thou flesh'd
> Thy maiden sword.

The commendation of Prince John applies ironically to "Brother" John Falstaff—here in full view of the audience—whose sword is a "maiden" sword too, which he has just "flesh'd" safely in the dead Percy. The boy prince John has shown himself a man: Sir John Falstaff has shown himself a child.

5. FALSTAFF AND THE WORLD OF HISTORY

The student may possibly object to so heavy an emphasis upon the battlefield scenes: yet our search for the unity of the play demands that we consider carefully this one group of scenes in which all the characters come together. Besides bringing all the characters together, too, the battle scenes subordinate Falstaff, for all his delightfulness, to something larger (somewhat to the resentment of readers to whom Falstaff is a kind of demigod); and this subordination itself is a unifying process.

But the battle scenes do not cancel out the more widely discussed tavern scenes; they qualify the tavern scenes. We may now return to reconsider the tavern scenes in the light of these qualifications.

It is perhaps significant that Falstaff is introduced to us with the line: "Now, Hal, what time of day is it, lad?"—a question which the prince answers with a jest: ". . . What a devil hast thou to do with the time of the day? Unless hours were cups of sack and minutes capons and clocks the tongues of bawds and dials the signs of leaping-houses and the blessed sun himself a fair hot wench in flame-coloured taffeta, I see no reason why thou shouldst be so superfluous to demand the time of the day." The jesting in the prince's speech may not come quite up to the better efforts of Falstaff himself; but the speech, quite apart from the jesting, is perfectly true. It is true in a deeper sense than even the prince realizes.

It is indeed an absurdity for Falstaff to ask the time of day, for Falstaff has properly nothing to do with the world of time. He transcends the time-ridden world of important affairs—the world of appointments to be kept, of tasks to be performed, of responsibilities to be undertaken. Time does not exist in his world. This is not to say, of course, that Falstaff's world is one in which nothing ever happens. For Falstaff, that world is interesting and even exciting. But in it, one is not dogged by time just as the child is not dogged by time in his world.

Falstaff and the King. For Falstaff, each day is a new day, lived for itself. The future does not cast a cloud over the present. This characteristic Shakespeare has emphasized by pointing up a sharp contrast between Falstaff and the king. The king is bedeviled with insomnia; Falstaff is not. Even with the bailiff at the door looking for a "gross fat man" suspected of robbery, Falstaff behind the arras drops off to sleep as naturally as would an exhausted child. Falstaff has nothing to do with time; but Henry, the king, is obsessed with time. The king not only makes history—his life *is* history. In the great tavern scene (II, iv) in which Falstaff plays the part of the king, Falstaff . . . parodies the sententious Euphuistic style which was popular in the period. But the parody involves more than a mere topical allusion: Falstaff is using the parody of style as an instrument for a deeper parody. He is mocking at the kind of seriousness with which authority has to express—and *take* —itself: the carefully balanced antitheses, the allusions to natural history, the appeal to learned authorities, the labored truisms— e.g., "There is a thing, Harry, which thou hast often heard of, and it is known to many in our land by the name of pitch: this pitch, as ancient writers do report, doth defile; . . ." The fun is good-humored; but the criticism which it turns upon the institutions of authority is penetrating, and, as far as it goes, perfectly fair. Falstaff as "king" in the tavern is a delightful comedian *because* he is a recognizable monarch; that is, he does not use the pose of royalty merely for slap-stick effects.

But Shakespeare, whom we see constantly balancing scene against scene, has the king "counterfeited" once more in the play —on the battlefield, where knights and nobles wear the king's armor. Sir Walter Blunt, so dressed, is accosted by Douglas with "some tell me that thou art a king," and replies with the noble lie, "They tell thee true." He fights with Douglas and dies for the king—doubly. Falstaff appears on the scene immediately and, noticing Blunt's dead body, remarks "there's honour for you!" No aping of the king for him! The king's robes in the tavern play are one thing; the king's coat of arms on the battlefield, quite another.[3]

6. SHAKESPEARE'S ATTITUDE TOWARD FALSTAFF AND THE PRINCE

Here we come to the crucial problem of unity: what attitude, finally, are we to adopt toward Falstaff and the prince? Which is right? With which of the two are our sympathies finally to rest? Those readers who have felt the charm of Falstaff and who have sensed the fact that Shakespeare is not disposed to defend the duplicities of the king are surely right in refusing to dismiss Fal-

[3] There has been of late a tendency to defend Falstaff even here: to say that Falstaff in his debunking of honor is right after all; that Falstaff sees truly through the empty conventions of "honor"; that he refuses to be taken in by the vainglorious pretensions of the usurper, Henry Boling-broke, to "honor" and to a legitimacy which he does not deserve. Such critics go on to point out that the device of clothing a number of knights so as to counterfeit the king makes rather hollow all the talk about chivalry and honor that goes on with regard to the battle.

But to take this position is to read into the play far more than the play warrants. If the dynastic pretensions of various people in fifteenth-century England seem trivial enough to us, they did not seem so to Shakespeare's audience or to Shakespeare himself. There is nothing in the play to warrant the belief that Shakespeare is bitterly denying the reality of honor and chivalry. Falstaff never rises to a philosophic indictment which will issue in his calling down a "plague on both your houses."

staff as a coward or buffoon. Furthermore, they may be right in feeling that Shakespeare has even revealed in Prince Hal himself a certain cold-blooded calculation.

The probability is that we shall miss the play if we assume that Shakespeare is forcing upon us a choice of the *either-or* variety. Is it not possible that Shakespeare is not asking us to choose at all, but rather to contemplate, with understanding and some irony, a world very much like the world that we know, a world in which compromises have to be made, a world in which the virtues of Falstaff become, under changed conditions, vices, and the vices of the Prince Hal become, under certain conditions, necessary, and thus, in a sense, accommodated to virtue? (One might well reverse the form of this statement. From the point of view of an Elizabethan audience, one would almost certainly have to reverse it thus: Falstaff's vices partake of virtue and the virtues of the prince—an easy camaraderie, a genial understanding, an unwillingness to stand on a haughty dignity—are revealed to him ultimately as vices which must be put away.)

The Two Worlds of the Play. Human beings live in a world of time, and a world in which—except at rare heroic moments—compromises have to be made. Falstaff lives, as we have already suggested, in a world of the eternal present, a timeless world which stands apart from the time-harried world of adult concerns. Yet Shakespeare keeps the balance with complete fairness. Each world has its claims. For the prince to be able to retire for awhile into Falstaff's world is worth something to him. It testifies to his humanity, since Falstaff's world is a part of the human world. It probably makes him a better king than he would be if he followed his more calculating and limited father's wishes. Bathed in the light of Falstaff's world, the coldness, the pomposity, the pretentiousness of the world of high concerns is properly exposed. Yet, after all, men must act; responsibilities must be assumed. To remain in Falstaff's world is to deny the reality of the whole world of adult concerns.

It is ironic, of course, that the human being is thus divided between the claims of two aspects of life. It is ironic, from one point of view, that men must grow up at all—must grow away from the innocence of the timeless and amoral world of childhood into the adult world, where except when crises evoke extraordinary devotion and resolution, compromises and scheming are a regular, and perhaps inevitable, part of human experience. Prince Hal, for example, in entering into the world of affairs, loses something as well as gains something—a matter which the play (particularly in its second part) rather clearly indicates. Falstaff may belong to a world unshadowed by time, but it is not for nothing that Prince Hal appears in a "history" play. He belongs to history—to the world of time—and in the Battle of Shrewsbury he enters into history.

7. HENRY IV AS MATURE COMEDY

The problem of Shakespeare's attitude toward Hal and Falstaff has been argued for a long time, and doubtless will continue to be argued. At the end of *Henry IV, Part Two* the prince, on being crowned, publicly rejects Falstaff, and thus makes formal and explicit what is hinted at at the end of *Part One*. Having arrived at kingship with its serious duties, he can have no more time for such play as the Boar's-Head Tavern afforded. Delightful as Falstaff is, he must now be put by.

The Two Interpretations of Shakespeare's Attitude. With regard to Shakespeare's attitude toward this relationship there have been, in general, two courses taken. The first considers the two plays as constituting a study in the discipline of a young king, a king who was to be celebrated as the ideal king in Shakespeare's *Henry V.* According to this interpretation, the two plays present Falstaff as undergoing a gradual degeneration of character. Thus, it is argued, we lose some of our sympathy for him and are reconciled to the young king's rejection of him.

The second interpretation reverses the first. Here it is argued that Falstaff retains our sympathies to the end. Hal's conduct, on the other hand, is regarded as having, from the beginning, something of Machiavellian policy in it. Hal delights in Falstaff's company during his carefree youth but dashes the old man's hopes rather brutally at the end by publicly disowning him and reading him a rather smug sermon on the subject of good conduct.

Few critics have, of course, accepted either view without some reservations and qualifications, but it may make the issues clearer to state the views in extreme form as is here done. That the matter of our attitude toward the Falstaff-Hal relationship is important comes out clearly if we consult the most recent book on the subject, Dover Wilson's *Falstaff.* Wilson sees the plays as involving basically a study in kingship. Falstaff has to be rejected. Though, for Wilson, he remains brilliantly witty, even through the whole of *Henry IV, Part Two,* he becomes more boastful, with a correspondent weakening of our sympathy for him. And Wilson defends the terms of the rejection: Hal is not a "cad or a prig." Falstaff, after all, is not visited with a heavy punishment. The king sees to it that he, along with his other "wonted followers," is "very well provided for."

Shakespeare's Balance. To repeat, the present analysis agrees on the need of having the matter both ways. Surely, Wilson is at his soundest when he argues that Shakespeare keeps the balance most impartially between Hal and Falstaff; but perhaps he might, on the whole, have made out a more convincing case had he pressed this argument further still instead of trying to mitigate the terms of Falstaff's rejection or to argue that the later Falstaff becomes less attractive than the earlier Falstaff. Is not the real point this: that in Hal's rejection of Falstaff something is lost as well as gained —that a good king, one grants, must reject Falstaff, but that in the process by which a man becomes a good king, something else —something spontaneous, something in itself good and attractive —must be sacrificed; that growing up is something which man must do and yet that even in growing up he loses, necessarily, something that is valuable?

Shakespeare does not sentimentalize the situation. The rejection is necessary if Hal is to become the king that he ought to be and that England doubtless needs; and yet Falstaff's dashed hopes are presented with due pathos. The sentimentalist will doubtless need to blacken Falstaff's character a little—suppress his sympathy for him—in order to be able to accept his being turned off; or, if he is unable to do this, he will, in order to justify Falstaff's rejection, doubtless have to blacken the prince's character, reading into it more of the "vile politician Bolingbroke" than Shakespeare ever intended. The stern moralist (and he is nearer allied to the sentimentalist than is usually suspected) will do much the same: he will probably applaud the rejection of Falstaff whole-heartedly, or, just possibly and perversely, he will condemn the prince for his acceptance of pomp and power and for his cold heart.

Neither the sentimentalist nor the moralist, then, will be able to accept the play in its fullness. It is possible, of course, that even for the mature reader, the play finally lacks unity—that the balancing of attitudes which has been argued for in this analysis is something which perhaps Shakespeare should have attempted to accomplish but did not, for one reason or another, actually succeed in accomplishing. This, of course, each reader must decide for himself. For the reader who remains unconvinced of any totality of effect, the play will probably remain a collection of brilliant but ill-assorted fragments—the wonderful tavern scenes juxtaposed oddly with passages of dull and pawky history.

For the reader, however, for whom the play does achieve a significant unity it may well seem that here Shakespeare has given us one of the wisest and fullest commentaries on human action possible to the comic mode—a view which scants nothing, which covers up nothing, and which takes into account in making its affirmations the most searching criticism of that which is affirmed. For such a reader, Shakespeare has no easy moral to draw, no simple generalization to make.

Shakespeare's Irony. Moreover, it will be evident that Shakespeare's final attitude toward his characters (and toward the human predicament, generally) is one of a very complex irony, though it is an irony which will be either missed altogether, or easily misinterpreted as an indifferent relativism—that is, a mere balancing of two realms of conduct and a refusal to make any judgment between them. The world which Shakespeare portrays here is a world of contradictions and of mixtures of good and evil. His vision of that world is ultimately a comic vision—if not gaily comic, and surely not bitterly comic, yet informed with the insights of mature comedy, nonetheless. For the comic writer does not attempt to transcend the world of compromises, even though the more thoughtful writer of comedy, as here, may be fully aware of the seriousness of the issues. Comedy, after all, does not treat the lives of saints or heroes: it does not attempt to portray the absolute commitment to ultimate issues—the total commitment which transcends, tragically and heroically, the everyday world that we know. Shakespeare does not present Prince Hal (as he might conceivably do in a tragic treatment) as a callous man, the scion of the "vile politician Bolingbroke." Hal will make a good ruler, and Falstaff would undoubtedly make a very bad ruler. Nor, on the other hand, is Falstaff portrayed as a villain: Falstaff, too, has his case. Falstaff's wit—most of it at least—is not merely amusing, trifling. It constitutes a criticism of the world of serious affairs, a criticism which, on certain levels, is thoroughly valid. The rulers of the world had better not leave it totally out of account.

If the prince must choose between two courses of action—and, of course, he must choose—we as readers are not forced to choose: indeed, perhaps the core of Shakespeare's ironic insight comes to this: that man must choose and yet that the choice can never be a wholly satisfactory one. If the play is a comedy in this sense, then the "comic" scenes of the play turn out to be only an aspect of, though an important aspect of, the larger comedy. To repeat, the reader must decide for himself whether he can accept the play as a fully unified organism. But the reader who can so accept it may well feel that it represents Shakespeare's most sophisticated level of comedy, a comedy, indeed, more fine-grained and "serious" than the romantic comedies such as *As You Like It* and written with a surer touch than the "bitter" comedies such as *All's Well That Ends Well*.

WILLIAM B. HUNTER, JR.

Prince Hal, His Struggle Toward Moral Perfection

Aside from Hamlet, I doubt whether another character in English literature has been the object of greater discussion than the fat knight, that reverend vice Sir John Falstaff. Somewhat like the melancholy Dane, he has been all things to all men. Sentimentalists see him as basically a good fellow, rejected at the end of the *Henry IV* plays by the prudish new King Henry V and finally killed by this blow. Perhaps they are led astray by admiration for the tremendous humor of the man, a quality which by and large they do not possess. One must remember that the frequently repeated

From *South Atlantic Quarterly*, L (January 1951), 86–95. Reprinted by permission of the author and Duke University Press. Originally entitled "Falstaff," the essay has been retitled by the author for its appearance here.

testimony as to the cause of his death—"The King has killed his
heart"—is spoken by Mistress Quickly, a most inaccurate reporter,
as witness her lines in the same scene on Sir John's "burning
quotidian tertian"—a fever never experienced in this world even
in the fanciful catalogues of diseases which the Renaissance has
bequeathed us. A broken heart is doubtful in that old ruffian's
case; the final results of overindulgence are more plausible.

Recent critics are, by and large, more sensible in their discussions of this "tun of man." They have been at pains to point out
that he derives from a whole family tree of rascals: the court jester,
the braggart soldier, the character of Vice in the earlier morality
plays. John Dover Wilson, one of the most stimulating and daring
of modern judges, has put forward this view, which seems emi-
nently sensible. But the estimate of Falstaff is not one which can
be reckoned apart from those of the other characters. If he is really
an old scalawag with a heart of gold beating some feet beneath
his rough hide, the Prince becomes, in Professor Bradley's words,
a man ready "to use other people as a means to his own ends"—
a heartless prig. His transformation to Shakespeare's picture of
him later as the ideal king, Henry V, is as great as that visited
upon St. Paul and an improbable transformation upon the stage
even between plays. On the other hand, if Falstaff is really evil,
there is the opportunity for the moral rehabilitation of Prince Hal
which Shakespeare seems to have intended; a truly good man would
have, perforce, to shun Sir John. Shakespeare himself has clearly
defamed the fat rascal in Part II. To take but one instance: the
impressment scene, only briefly described in Part I, is given in
realistic detail in the sequel. The groundlings, subject themselves
at times to just such a recruiting sergeant, would not have looked
upon Falstaff thereafter with any real affection.

Professor Wilson has given an able exposition of such points as
these. But he has mostly left out of account the fact that in the
first play there is a third participant in this mighty drama: Henry
Percy, the Hotspur of the North. Many people have contrasted
Hotspur with Prince Hal to the latter's detriment; as many have
compared the Prince with Falstaff; but only a few critics have considered all three together and hence have tried to present the whole
of their drama instead of only part of it. A complete theory must
account for all three in the First Part; for Falstaff, Hal, and the
Chief Justice in the Second Part; and for a consistent development

of Hal's character into that of Henry V in the final play of the group.

A clue in Part I lies in certain clear contrasts between Hotspur and Falstaff which must have been deliberate. Both speak of honor, though they have, of course, two very different ideas on the subject. The speeches are about equally well known. First, Hotspur asserts in almost extravagant terms the nobility of personal honor —a subject which links him with medieval chivalry:

> By heaven, methinks it were an easy leap
> To pluck bright honour from the pale-fac'd moon,
> Or dive into the bottom of the deep,
> Where fadom line could never touch the ground,
> And pluck up drowned honour by the locks.

Falstaff takes the exactly opposite position. Before he enters the Battle of Shrewsbury he rejects honor as a personal ideal. Why should he seek death, he asks:

> Well, 'tis no matter; honour pricks me on. Yea, but how if honour prick me off when I come on? How then? Can honour set to a leg? No. Or an arm? No. Or take away the grief of a wound? No. Honour hath no skill in surgery then? No. What is honour? A word. What is that word honour? Air. A trim reckoning! Who hath it? He that died a Wednesday. Doth he feel it? No. Doth he hear it? No. 'Tis insensible then? Yea, to the dead. But will it not live with the living? No. Why? Detraction will not suffer it. Therefore I'll none of it. Honour is a mere scutcheon.

Later, standing over the body of Sir Walter Blunt, he reiterates the same point of view.

Now surely, since Falstaff's speeches are soliloquies, we may look upon them as genuine utterances from character, as are all of Shakespeare's mature soliloquies. These who sympathize with Honest Jack either fail to note the real meaning of the lines or interpret them as mere clever exhibitionism. But why should they not be taken at face value? If so taken, we must condemn their speaker unless we disagree with the Elizabethans upon the value of a personal code of honor. Falstaff is clearly deficient in this prime attribute.

More difficult to see is that Hotspur's honor is not the ideal

goal either. Hotspur, like Mercutio, is one of Shakespeare's most
attractive creations. Everyone regrets his early passing. In this admiration we tend to forget that his honor in the long run destroys
him; more important, that it leads him into situations where he
shows up badly. At his very first appearance he insists because of
his honor on keeping prisoners whom, the play implies, the King
can rightly demand. Later in the same scene he even angers his
father and uncle by a similar hotheaded insistence. As Worcester
says of him:

> He apprehends a world of figures here,
> But not the form of what he should attend.

In Act III he very nearly breaks up the conspiracy by insulting
Glendower and demanding his rights to the last tithe. His father,
Northumberland, calls him "a wasp-stung and impatient fool" to
"break into this woman's mood," and Worcester again corrects
him to his face:

> In faith, my lord, you are too wilful-blame,
> And since your coming hither have done enough
> To put him [Glendower] quite besides his patience.
> You must needs learn, lord, to amend this fault.
> Though sometimes it show greatness, courage, blood—
> And that's the dearest grace it renders you—
> Yet oftentimes it doth present harsh rage,
> Defect of manners, want of government,
> Pride, haughtiness, opinion, and disdain;
> The least of which haunting a nobleman
> Loseth men's hearts, and leaves behind a stain.

The noble Hotspur has an excess, which occasionally leads him
astray and which does not serve him in the long run. Falstaff possesses a deficiency in the same virtue.

The presence of both the excess and the deficiency of a virtue
naturally suggests Aristotle's comprehensive theory of ethics. In
this book, which he addressed according to tradition to his son
Nicomachus, Aristotle presents his famous theory that virtuous
action or good action exists as a mean between two extremes both
of which are vicious. Virtue, he says, to quote from the translation

of W.D. Ross, "must have the quality of aiming at the intermediate." More particularly, "it is a mean between two vices, that which depends on excess and that which depends on defect; and again it is a mean because the vices respectively fall short of or exceed what is right in both passions and actions." For one example, he holds that "it is possible to desire honour as one ought, and more than one ought, and less." As to the mean of honor, he writes in a later chapter that it must be recognized, though unnamed; "now men desire honour both more than they should and less; therefore it is possible also to do so as one should; at all events this is the state of character that is praised, being an unnamed mean in respect of honour. Relatively to ambition it seems to be unambitiousness, and relatively to unambitiousness it seems to be ambition." These words seem to fit admirably with the words and actions of Hotspur and Falstaff.

If this be true, the golden mean, the ideal pattern of action in the play, must be Prince Hal, who is later to become the ideal king of England and in doing so must reject both extremes. The evidence is not far to seek. His enemy, Vernon, testifies to his excellence just before the battle. Throughout the play the young Prince does not falter, nor does he brag of his exploits. He "conquers" Falstaff at Gadshill against odds, just as he does Hotspur when he kills him in the last act. Never does the audience question his personal integrity. The clincher is his criticism of the honor of both Falstaff and Hotspur in Mistress Quickly's tavern. There he and Poins reveal to the world Falstaff's "cowardice" in running away at Gadshill. Most critics agree that Falstaff is not a coward: "he will not fight longer than he sees reason," as Poins says. On the other hand, in comparison with the Prince in the scene at the Boar's Head, he is surely panicky at the thought of fighting the rebels: "Tell me, Hal, art not thou horrible afeard? Thou being heir apparent, could the world pick thee out three such enemies . . . ? Art thou not horribly afraid? Doth not thy blood thrill?" If not the critics, at least the Prince thinks him serious and returns him a scornful answer.

Earlier in the same scene Hal laughs at Hotspur's excessive concern for honor. To Poins he confesses ironically, "I am not yet of Percy's mind, the Hotspur of the North; he that kills me some six or seven dozen of Scots at a breakfast, washes his hands, and says to his wife, 'Fie upon this quiet life! I want work.'" Even

more telling is his comparison of his deeds with those of Hotspur
when he is vowing to his father that he will reform: "I will redeem
all this on Percy's head," he avers, and goes on:

> And that shall be the day, whene'er it lights,
> That this same child of honour and renown,
> This gallant Hotspur, this all-praised knight,
> And your unthought-of Harry chance to meet.
> For every honour sitting on his helm,
> Would they were multitudes!

The Prince, as mean, is fundamentally opposed to both extremes, which, in turn, are most contrary to each other. As Aristotle says, "the greatest contrariety is that of the extremes to each
other, rather than to the intermediate." It is thus not surprising
that when they meet at last on the field of battle, Falstaff should
commit the indefensible act of stabbing the dead Hotspur. Even
in death he seems to fear him. We see the Prince's rejection of
both extremes in the course of the two parts of *Henry IV*: of Hotspur when Hal kills him at the end of the First Part; or Falstaff
when he disowns him at the same moment of the Second Part.
Together, then, the two plays show the Prince choosing and prac-
ticing the ideal mean and preparing for his emergence as ideal king.

If this analogy with Aristotle's ethics is justified, it may be helpful to look further into his series of moral virtues. Honor is by no
means the only one. In each case we should expect the Prince to
approach the golden mean of proper action and either Hotspur
or Falstaff or both to represent the vicious extremes. Consider
for example the mean of liberality as opposed to prodigality and
meanness. It can hardly be denied that the Prince is liberal, Falstaff prodigal, and Hotspur mean at least once in the aforesaid
argument over the division of spoils with Glendower and the other
conspirators. A similar comparison might be made of the moderation of Hal's good temper with Hotspur's irascibility and Falstaff's
utter lack of the quality. Indeed, Hal loses his temper only at the
illegal destruction of his baggage train by the French in *Henry V*;
there, since he "is angry at the right things and with the right people," he is still virtuous in Aristotle's eyes. Another of the virtues
is temperance. It is doubtful whether any other character in English literature is as intemperate as is Falstaff; on the other hand,

the Prince is moderate. Even a sense of humor appears as a mean in the *Ethics*; the contrast with the buffoon and the boor, marked between Falstaff and Prince John in the Second Part, is emphasized where the former says of the younger claimant to the throne just after an exit, "I would you had but the wit. 'Twere better than your dukedom. Good faith, this same young sober-blooded boy doth not love me; nor a man cannot make him laugh. But that's no marvel; he drinks no wine."

According to Aristotle the magnanimous or proud man represents the sum of all the virtues. Ross translates *megalopsychia* as *pride*, but *magnanimity* avoids the unpleasant connotations of this word. The magnanimous man, says Aristotle, "must be good in the highest degree"; his characteristic is "greatness in every virtue." Here appears the real key to Prince Hal, since magnanimity "seems to be a sort of crown of the virtues; for it makes them greater, and it is not found without them." Hence it is quite difficult to be truly magnanimous. Besides the need for perfection in all the virtues, Aristotle adds that this type of man is not disdainful or insolent—nor is he fond of just any danger. He will, however, "face great dangers, and when he is in danger he is unsparing of his life, knowing that there are conditions on which life is not worth having. And he is the sort of man to confer benefits, but he is ashamed of receiving them." Just so does Hal conduct himself during and after the Battle of Shrewsbury; he does not falter from danger even when his father warns him away. And he is willing to free the noble Douglas and give Falstaff the credit for killing Hotspur.

The magnanimous man, furthermore, will readily give help to anyone, gets along with all classes of people, and is "unassuming towards those of the middle class." He does not try for ordinary rewards but is "sluggish" and "holds back" unless great issues are at stake. Such a paragon is not overwhelmed by admiration, nor mindful of wrongs, nor a gossip, nor one who asks favors. All in all, one need not ask a better description of Henry as Prince and King. True, his father thought that he was a wastrel. True, Hotspur scorned him—to his sorrow—but then the extreme is opposed to the mean. True, Falstaff thinks that he will control the kingdom when the Prince comes to power. Even Poins, who is actually closer to Hal's real thoughts than Falstaff, cannot fathom his true character. Yet these are partial or biased witnesses. From the much-

debated soliloquy which ends his first appearance the audience itself is never in any doubt that the Prince is in fact good, whatever
others may think of him. If we accept this interpretation, he presents such a moral character as can properly develop into an ideal
king. Nor must we at the same time denigrate the more popular
and human—because sinning—Hotspur and Falstaff.

If the First Part of the play represents the final rejection by
death of Hotspur, the Second Part witnesses the rejection of the
other extreme in Falstaff—a neatly symmetrical arrangement. But
if this is true, we have a long five acts without a worthy opponent
for Sir John to replace the dead Hotspur. Instead the one vicious
extreme in the play is now opposed to the Lord Chief Justice, representative of law and order. He is clearly not the opposite vicious
extreme, for the new King Henry V sides with him and carries
out such policies as the Justice would sponsor, e.g., the execution
of Nym and Bardolph for robbing a church during the French
campaign. The theory of the moral unity of the plays would thus
break down, since there is no opportunity for the development of
anything more than justice versus injustice. Apparently Falstaff will
have to carry on alone.

It must be admitted that the sequel is not as dramatically powerful as the First Part. Under the impact of success, Shakespeare
probably gave Falstaff a proportionately much greater part. But
there are two significant differences btween the two plays. First,
the Prince, who had been Falstaff's close companion in the earlier
play, appears with him in the later for but part of a single scene
besides the renunciation. Shakespeare seems to have made a deliberate effort to keep them apart, probably to avoid smirching the
character of the man about to be crowned. The result accounts for
the falling off in Falstaff's wit in the Second Part. In the previous
play that "bolting hutch of beastliness" had an equal for cleverness
in the Prince, who called on Sir John's best for wit combats; in the
Second Part he has only the immensely inferior Bardolf or Shallow
or the ladies. As a result, he is reduced to soliloquy—a more contrived and hence less successful form of amusement.

Even so, the "swollen parcel of dropsies" retains a moral function in this play. If we turn over a few chapters in the *Nicomachean
Ethics*, we come to the last of the moral virtues, justice, represented in the play by the Lord Chief Justice, whom the Prince
meets on stage only in the final act. Now justice, Aristotle says, is

different from the other virtues. In the first place, it divides into the lawful, or universal justice, and the fair and equal, or particular justice. As to the lawful, it is "complete virtue" in relation to our neighbor; it is "complete virtue in its fullest sense, because it is the actual exercise of complete virtue." So conceived, justice becomes "not a part of virtue, but virtue entire; nor is contrary injustice a part of vice but vice entire." Like Falstaff, "the worst man is he who exercises his wickedness both towards himself and towards his friends."

This, then, is the legal aspect of justice. In the particular sphere Aristotle devotes a good deal of space to determining just how each man should conduct himself with respect to other men. His argument is a litle long for summary, but the conclusion is that "Justice is a kind of mean, but not in the same way as the other virtues, but because it relates to an intermediate amount, while injustice relates to the extremes." The just man acts by choice to give "what is equal in accordance with proportion"; injustice, on the contrary, is "related to the unjust, which is excess and defect, contrary to proportion, of the useful or hurtful. For which reason injustice is excess and defect, viz. because it is productive of excess and defect," quite an exact description of Sir John's failings. Indeed, the "just is the proportional; the unjust is what violates the proportion"; Falstaff qualifies in both plays as an example of the latter failure. As Bardolf says of his size, "You must needs be out of all compass—out of all reasonable compass, Sir John." One may even, Aristotle adds, "voluntarily, owing to incontinence, be harmed by another who acts voluntarily, so that it would be possible to be voluntarily treated unjustly." The scenes with the Hostess in Part II seem an explicit recognition of this characteristic of injustice. Actually, it is important to observe that Falstaff's relations with her are not primarily self-indulgent but a means of escaping arrest and—so to speak—protecting his financial interests. As Aristotle adds, "if one man commits adultery for the sake of gain and makes money by it," he is unjust in comparison with the man who does it merely for pleasure. So it is that Falstaff fears the law—it is an important source too of his wit—and has no better conception of it than "old father antic."

Clearly the Lord Chief Justice represents just action in both Aristotelian senses. His early warnings to Falstaff stress his excesses, but they go unheeded. Unlike the audience, the Justice believes with Falstaff that the new King Henry is on the side of the unjust; Falstaff says on learning of the coronation, "the laws of England are at my commandment. Blessed are they that have been my friends, and woe to my Lord Chief Justice." So when Henry meets the symbol of law and order, the Justice pleads his case: he represents the person and authority of the crown:

> The image of his power lay then in me;
> And in th' administration of his law,
> While I was busy for the commonwealth,
> Your Highness pleased to forget my place,
> The majesty and power of law and justice,
> The image of the King whom I presented.

These lines almost exactly represent Aristotle's reason why law is above the sway of any individual: "we do not allow a *man* to rule, but *rational principle*, because a man behaves thus in his own interests and becomes a tyrant." So would Falstaff have done. The true magistrate is the "guardian of justice" and as such will have no exceptional material reward; instead, he is due "honour and privilege; but those for whom such things are not enough become tyrants." As the new king says:

> You are right, Justice, and you weigh this well.
> Therefore still bear the balance and the sword;
> And I do wish your honours may increase.

So it is that the moral struggle develops in Aristotelian terms through the two *Henry IV* plays to eventuate in the actuality of an ideal king whose perfections had been foreshadowed through these first two plays. Henry V is not essentially different from Prince Hal, though he has matured and seems less human, perhaps because of the absence of close human associates; as king it is noteworthy that he is not represented as being intimate with any other characters. He has succeeded in avoiding the vicious extremes and practices the golden mean of virtue.

This is not, of course, to say that these plays are to be interpreted as a moral allegory, though some elements of the morality plays survive in them. Anyone who tries to limit Falstaff by a label and to say that he can be mounted like a dead elephant is doomed to

182

J. DOVER WILSON

falsify the evidence. He is far too real to be circumscribed by any
pat formula. The suggestion that he fits into the moral pattern of
the plays should not be interpreted as meaning that we can exhaust
his significance by tacking the name of extreme to him. A girth like
his can contain a multitude of considerations. Rather, the ethical
mean here advanced should indicate the belt which set a limit to
proportion and gave direction to the moral element of all these
plays. At the same time, Hal's importance, so often overlooked,
comes to the fore. He is the key character, though this position
has not been often accorded him; we must agree with Dr. Johnson, that the Prince is the real hero of both the comic and tragic
parts. Neither as Prince nor King does he catch the imagination
and sympathy as do Hotspur and Falstaff. But real virtue is not
spectacular, and we children of Adam do not find it particularly
enticing. "Men," as Aristotle noted, "think that acting unjustly
is in their power, and therefore that being just is easy. But it is
not."

J. DOVER WILSON

Falstaff and the Plan of Henry IV, Part I

Henry IV, a play much neglected by both actors and
critics, offers to our view the broadest, the most varied, and in
some ways the richest champaign in Shakespeare's extensive em-
pire. Much of this, and not the least alluring stretches, must be
ignored in what follows, or barely glanced at; Glendower's do-
main [1] in Part I, for example. Many characters can hardly be
touched; I shall have little to say about Ancient Pistol or Mistress

From *The Fortunes of Falstaff* (New York, 1944), pp. 15–35. Reprinted by permission of Cambridge University Press. Title added by Ed.
 [1] I refer to III, i of Pt. I, which was headed "The Archbishop of
Bangor's House in Wales" by Theobald and later editors, though without
any warrant in Shakespeare. Glendower behaves like a host throughout
the scene, which is clearly a family party.

Quickly, Hotspur or Prince John. The more subtle aspects of the play, its poetry, its dramatic light and shade, what may be called its atmospheric effects; all matters of first importance to anyone concerned in tracing the development of Shakespeare's art in the crucial and largely unexplored period that divides *Richard II* from *Hamlet*: these also lie beyond my present scope. The task I have set before me is at once narrow and simple. I am attempting to discover what Professor Charlton has called "the deliberate plan of Shakespeare's play" and, if such a plan existed, how far he succeeded in carrying it into execution.

My title, *The Fortunes of Falstaff*, will suggest the method to be followed. I propose to look for the outlines of Shakespeare's scheme by tracing the career of the knight of Eastcheap. This does not mean that I think him of greater structural consequence than Prince Hal. On the contrary, Falstaff's career is dependent upon Hal's favour, and Hal's favour is determined by that young man's attitude towards his responsibilities as heir to the throne of England. Yet if the Prince's choice spans the play like a great arch, it is Falstaff and his affairs that cover most of the ground.

The title I have selected has, moreover, the convenience of comprising the fortunes, or misfortunes, of the fat rogue outside the pages of Shakespeare. There are, for instance, his pre-natal adventures. He tells us that he "was born about three of the clock in the afternoon, with a white head and something of a round belly"; but all the world now knows that he was walking the boards in an earlier, pre-Shakespearian, incarnation, as a comic travesty of Sir John Oldcastle, the famous Lollard leader, who was historically a friend and fellow-soldier of Prince Hal in the reign of Henry IV, but was burnt as a heretic by the same prince when he became King Henry V. He still retained the name Oldcastle, as is also well known, in the original version of Shakespeare's play; until the company discovered, or were forcibly reminded, that the wife of the proto-protestant martyr they were guying on the public stage was the revered ancestress of the Cobhams, powerful lords at Elizabeth's court. Worse still, one of these lords was not only of strongly protestant bent, but also, as Lord Chamberlain, actually Shakespeare's official controller. Hasty changes in the prompt-book became necessary. How far they extended beyond a mere alteration of names can never be determined, though it seems possible that references to some of Oldcastle's historical or legendary characteristics would require modification. It is even more likely (as Alfred Ainger was, I believe, the first to point out) [2] that traces of Lollardry may still be detected in Falstaff's frequent resort to scriptural phraseology and in his affectation of an uneasy conscience. Of this I shall have something to say later.

First of all, however, I wish to deal with Falstaff's ancestral fortunes of a different kind. As he shares these to a large extent with Prince Hal, a consideration of them should prove helpful in bringing out the main lines of the plot which it is our object to discover.

RIOT AND THE PRODIGAL PRINCE

Falstaff may be the most conspicuous, he is certainly the most fascinating, character in *Henry IV*, but all critics are agreed, I believe, that the technical centre of the play is not the fat knight but the lean prince. Hal links the low life with the high life, the scenes at Eastcheap with those at Westminster, the tavern with the battlefield; his doings provide most of the material for both Parts, and with him too lies the future, since he is to become Henry V, the ideal king, in the play that bears his name; finally, the mainspring of the dramatic action is the choice I have already spoken of, the choice he is called upon to make between Vanity and Government, taking the latter in its accepted Tudor meaning, which includes Chivalry or prowess in the field, the theme of Part I, and Justice, which is the theme of Part II. Shakespeare, moreover, breathes life into these abstractions by embodying them, or aspects of them, in prominent characters, who stand, as it were, about the Prince, like attendant spirits: Falstaff typifying Vanity in every sense of the word, Hotspur Chivalry, of the old anarchic kind, and the Lord Chief Justice the Rule of Law or the new ideal of service to the state. [3]

Thus considered, Shakespeare's *Henry IV* is a Tudor version of a time-honoured theme, already familiar for decades, if not centuries, upon the English stage. Before its final secularization in

[2] V. Alfred Ainger, *Lectures and Essays*, 1905, i, pp. 140–55.

[3] In what follows I develop a hint in Sir Arthur Quiller-Couch's *Shakespeare's Workmanship*, 1918, p. 148: "The whole of the business [in *Henry IV*] is built on the old Morality structure, imported through the Interlude. Why, it might almost be labelled, after the style of a Morality title, *Contentio inter Virtutem et Vitium de anima Principis.*"

the first half of the sixteenth century, our drama was concerned with one topic, and one only: human salvation. It was a topic that could be represented in either of two ways: (i) historically, by means of miracle plays, which in the Corpus Christi cycles unrolled before spectators' eyes the whole scheme of salvation from the Creation to the Last Judgement; or (ii) allegorically, by means of morality plays, which exhibited the process of salvation in the individual soul on its road between birth and death, beset with the snares of the World or the wiles of the Evil One. In both kinds the forces of iniquity were allowed full play upon the stage, including a good deal of horse-play, provided they were brought to nought, or safely locked up in Hell, at the end. Salvation remains the supreme interest, however many capers the Devil and his Vice may cut on Everyman's way thither, and always the powers of darkness are withstood, and finally overcome, by the agents of light. But as time went on the religious drama tended to grow longer and more elaborate, after the encyclopaedic fashion of the middle ages, and such development invited its inevitable reaction. With the advent of humanism and the early Tudor court, morality plays became tedious and gave place to lighter and much shorter moral interludes dealing, not with human life as a whole, but with youth and its besetting sins.

An early specimen, entitled *Youth* [4] and composed about 1520, may be taken as typical of the rest. The plot, if plot it can be called, is simplicity itself. The little play opens with a dialogue between Youth and Charity. The young man, heir to his father's land, gives insolent expression to his self-confidence, lustihood, and contempt for spiritual things. Whereupon Charity leaves him, and he is joined by Riot,[5] that is to say wantonness, who presently introduces him to Pride and Lechery. The dialogue then becomes boisterous, and continues in that vein for some time, much no doubt to the enjoyment of the audience. Yet, in the end, Charity reappears with Humility; Youth repents; and the interlude terminates in the most seemly fashion imaginable.

No one, I think, reading this lively playlet, no one certainly who

---

[4] *The enterlude of youth,* ed. by W. Bang and R. B. McKerrow, Louvain, 1905.

[5] riot= "wanton, loose, or wasteful living; debauchery, dissipation, extravagance" (*O.E.D.*). Cf. the Prodigal Son, who "wasted his substance with riotous living" (Luke xv. 13).

has seen it performed, as I have seen it at the Malvern Festival, can have missed the resemblance between Riot and Falstaff. The words he utters, as he bounces on to the stage at his first entry, give us the very note of Falstaff's gaiety:

> Huffa! huffa! who calleth after me?
> I am Riot full of jollity.
> My heart is as light as the wind,
> And all on riot is my mind,
> Wheresoever I go.

And the parallel is even more striking in other respects. Riot, like Falstaff, escapes from tight corners with a quick dexterity; like Falstaff, commits robbery on the highway; like Falstaff, jests immediately afterwards with his young friend on the subject of hanging; and like Falstaff, invites him to spend the stolen money at a tavern, where, he promises, "We will drink diuers wine" and "Thou shalt haue a wench to kysse Whansoeuer thou wilte"; allurements which prefigure the Boar's Head and Mistress Doll Tearsheet.

But Youth at the door of opportunity, with Age or Experience, Charity or Good Counsel, offering him the yoke of responsibility, while the World, the Flesh, and the Devil beckon him to follow them on the primrose way to the everlasting bonfire, is older than even the medieval religious play. It is a theme to which every generation gives fresh form, while retaining its eternal substance. Young men are the heroes of the Plautine and Terentian comedy which delighted the Roman world; and these young men, generally under the direction of a clever slave or parasite, disport themselves, and often hoodwink their old fathers, for most of the play, until they too settle down in the end. The same theme appears in a very different story, the parable of the Prodigal Son. And the similarity of the two struck humanist teachers of the early sixteenth century with such force that, finding Terence insufficiently edifying for their pupils to act, they developed a "Christian Terence" by turning the parable into Latin plays, of which many examples by different authors have come down to us.[6] In these plot and structure are much the same. The opening scene shows us Acolastus, the

<hr/>

[6] V. C. H. Herford, *The Literary Relations between England and Germany in the Sixteenth Century*, 1886, ch. III, pp. 84-95.

prodigal, demanding his portion, receiving good counsel from his father, and going off into a far country. Then follow three or four acts of entertainment almost purely Terentian in atmosphere, in which he wastes his substance in riotous living and falls at length to feeding with the pigs. Finally, in the last act he returns home, penniless and repentant, to receive his pardon. This ingenious blend of classical comedy and humanistic morality preserves, it will be noted, the traditional ratio between edification and amusement, and distributes them in the traditional manner. So long as the serious note is duly emphasized at the beginning and end of the play, almost any quantity of fun, often of the most unseemly nature, was allowed and expected during the intervening scenes.

All this, and much more of a like character, gave the pattern for Shakespeare's *Henry IV.* Hal associates Falstaff in turn with the Devil of the miracle play, the Vice of the morality, and the Riot of the interlude, when he calls him "that villainous abominable misleader of Youth, that old white-bearded Satan," [7] "that reverend Vice, that grey Iniquity, that father Ruffian, that Vanity in years," [8] and "the tutor and the feeder of my riots." [9] "Riot," again, is the word that comes most readily to King Henry's lips when speaking of his prodigal son's misconduct.[10] And, as heir to the Vice, Falstaff inherits by reversion the functions and attributes of the Lord of Misrule, the Fool, the Buffoon, and the Jester, antic figures the origins of which are lost in the dark backward and abysm of folk-custom.[11] We shall find that Falstaff possesses a strain, and more than a strain, of the classical *miles gloriosus* as well. In short,

[7] Pt. I, II, iv, 412; cf. l. 398: "Thou art violently carried away from grace, there is a devil haunts thee in the likeness of an old fat man."

[8] *Ibid.* II, iv, 404.

[9] Pt. II, V, v, 63 (66).

[10] Cf. Pt. I, I, i, 85: "Riot and dishonour stain the brow / Of my young Harry"; Pt. II, IV, iv, 62: "His headstrong riot hath no curb," IV, v, 135: "When that my care could not withhold thy riots, / What wilt thou do when riot is thy care?"

[11] In particular, the exact significance of the Vice is exasperatingly obscure. Cf. the discussion by Sir E. K. Chambers (*Medieval Stage*, ii, pp. 203–5), who concludes "that whatever the name may mean . . . the character of the vice is derived from that of the domestic fool or jester." I hazard the suggestion that it was originally the title or name of the Fool who attended upon the Lord of Misrule; *v.* Feuillerat, *Revels of the time of Edward VI*, p. 73: "One vyces dagger & a ladle with a bable pendante . . . deliuerid to the Lorde of Mysrules foole."

the Falstaff-Hal plot embodies a composite myth which had been centuries amaking, and was for the Elizabethans full of meaning that has largely disappeared since then: which is one reason why we have come so seriously to misunderstand the play.

Nor was Shakespeare the first to see Hal as the prodigal. The legend of Harry of Monmouth began to grow soon after his death in 1422; and practically all the chroniclers, even those writing in the fifteenth century, agree on his wildness in youth and on the sudden change that came upon him at his accession to the throne. The essence of Shakespeare's plot is, indeed, already to be found in the following passage about King Henry V taken from Fabyan's *Chronicle* of 1516:

> This man, before the death of his fader, applyed him unto all vyce and insolency, and drewe unto hym all ryottours and wylde disposed persones; but after he was admytted to the rule of the lande, anone and suddenly he became a newe man, and tourned al that rage into sobernesse and wyse sadnesse, and the vyce into constant vertue. And for he wolde contynewe the vertue, and not to be reduced thereunto by the familiarytie of his olde nyse company, he therefore, after rewards to them gyuen, charged theym upon payne of theyr lyues, that none of theym were so hardy to come within x. myle of such place as he were lodgyd, after a day by him assigned.[12]

There appears to be no historical basis for any of this, and Kingsford has plausibly suggested that its origin may be "contemporary scandal which attached to Henry through his youthful association with the unpopular Lollard leader" Sir John Oldcastle. "It is noteworthy," he points out, "that Henry's political opponents were Oldcastle's religious persecutors; and also that those writers who charge Henry with wildness as Prince find his peculiar merit as King in the maintaining of Holy Church and destroying of heretics. A supposed change in his attitude on questions of religion may possibly furnish a partial solution for his alleged 'change suddenly into a new man.'" [13] The theory is the more attractive that it would account not only for Hal's conversion but also for Oldcastle's degradation from a protestant martyr and distinguished soldier to what Ainger calls "a broken-down Lollard, a fat old sensualist, retaining

[12] Fabyan's *Chronicle*, 1516, p. 577.
[13] C. L. Kingsford, *The First English Life of King Henry the Fifth*, 1911, pp. xlii, xliii.

just sufficient recollection of the studies of his more serious days
to be able to point his jokes with them."

Yet when all is said, the main truth seems to be that the fifteenth and early sixteenth centuries, the age of allegory in poetry
and morality in drama, needed a Prodigal Prince, whose miraculous conversion might be held up as an example by those concerned
(as what contemporary political writer was not?) with the education of young noblemen and princes. And could any more alluring
fruits of repentance be offered such pupils than the prowess and
statesmanship of Henry V, the hero of Agincourt, the mirror of
English kingship for a hundred years? In his miracle play, *Richard
II*, Shakespeare had celebrated the traditional royal martyr; [14] in
his morality play, *Henry IV*, he does the like with the traditional
royal prodigal.

He made the myth his own, much as musicians adopt and ab-
sorb a folk-tune as the theme for a symphony. He glorified it, elabo-
rated it, translated it into what were for the Elizabethans modern
terms, and exalted it into a heaven of delirious fun and frolic; yet
never, for a moment, did he twist it from its original purpose,
which was serious, moral, didactic. Shakespeare plays no tricks
with his public. He did not, like Euripides, dramatize the stories of
his race and religion in order to subvert the traditional ideals those
stories were first framed to set forth. Prince Hal is the prodigal,
and his repentance is not only to be taken seriously, it is to be admired and commended. Moreover, the story of the prodigal, secu-
larized and modernized as it might be, ran the same course as ever
and contained the same three principal characters: the tempter, the
younker, and the father with property to bequeath and counsel to
give. It followed also the fashion set by miracle, morality and the
Christian Terence by devoting much attention to the doings of
the first-named. Shakespeare's audience enjoyed the fascination of
Prince Hal's "white-bearded Satan" for two whole plays, as perhaps no character on the world's stage had ever been enjoyed before. But they knew, from the beginning, that the reign of this
marvellous Lord of Misrule must have an end, that Falstaff must
be rejected by the Prodigal Prince, when the time for reformation
came. And they no more thought of questioning or disapproving of
that finale, than their ancestors would have thought of protesting

[14] V. pp. xvi–xix, lviii–lix of my Introd. to *Richard II*, 1939 ("The
New Shakespeare").

against the Vice being carried off to Hell at the end of the interlude.

The main theme, therefore, of Shakespeare's morality play is the growing-up of a madcap prince into the ideal king, who was Henry V; and the play was made primarily—already made by some dramatist before Shakespeare took it over—in order to exhibit his conversion and to reveal his character unfolding towards that end, as he finds himself faced more and more directly by his responsibilities. It is that which determines its very shape. Even the "fearful symmetry" of Falstaff's own person was welded upon the anvil of that purpose. It is probably because the historical Harry of Monmouth "exceeded the meane stature of men," as his earliest chronicler tells us; "his necke . . . longe, his body slender and leane, his boanes smale," [15]—because in Falstaff's words he actually was a starveling, an eel-skin, a tailor's yard, and all the rest of it— that the idea of Falstaff himself as "a huge hill of flesh" first came to Shakespeare.[16] It was certainly, at any rate in part, in order to explain and palliate the Prince's love of rioting and wantonness that he set out to make Falstaff as enchanting as he could.[17] And he succeeded so well that the young man now lies under the stigma, not of having yielded to the tempter, but of disentangling himself, in the end, from his toils. After all, Falstaff is "a devil . . . in the likeness of an old fat man," and the Devil has generally been supposed to exercise limitless attraction in his dealings with the sons

[15] Kingsford, op. cit. p. 16.

[16] Ainger tries to persuade himself that there was a tradition associating the Lollard, Oldcastle, with extreme fatness; but his editor, Beeching, is obliged to admit in a footnote that he is not aware of any references to this fatness before Shakespeare; v. Ainger, op. cit. pp. 126–30.

[17] Cf. H. N. Hudson, Shakespeare: his Life, Art and Characters (ed. 1888), ii, p. 83: "It must be no ordinary companionship that yields entertainment to such a spirit [as Prince Hal's] even in his loosest moments. Whatever bad or questionable elements may mingle with his mirth, it must have some fresh and rich ingredients, some sparkling and generous flavour, to make him relish it. Anything like vulgar rowdyism cannot fail of disgusting him. His ears were never organised to that sort of music. Here then we have a sort of dramatic necessity for the character of Falstaff. To answer the purpose it was imperative that he should be just such a marvellous congregation of charms and vices as he is." See also A. H. Tolman, Falstaff and other Shakespearian Topics, 1925, and W. W. Lawrence, Shakespeare's Problem Comedies, 1931, p. 64 (an interesting contrast between Hal and Falstaff, Bertram and Parolles).

of men. A very different kind of poet, who imagined a very different kind of Satan, has been equally and similarly misunderstood by modern critics, who no longer believing in the Prince of Darkness have ceased to understand him. For, as Professor R. W. Chambers reminded us in his last public utterance,[18] when Blake declared that Milton was "of the Devil's party without knowing it," he overlooked the fact, and his many successors have likewise overlooked the fact, that, if the fight in Heaven, the struggle in Eden, the defeat of Adam and Eve, and the victory of the Second Adam in *Paradise Regained*, are to appear in their true proportions, we must be made to realize how immeasurable, how indomitable, is the spirit of the Great Enemy. It may also be noted that Milton's Son of God has in modern times been charged with priggishness no less freely than Shakespeare's son of Bolingbroke.

Shakespeare, I say, translated his myth into a language and endued it with an atmosphere that his contemporaries would best appreciate. First, Hal is not only youth or the prodigal, he is the young prodigal *prince*, the youthful heir to the throne. The translation, then, already made by the chroniclers, if Kingsford be right, from sectarian terms into those more broadly religious or moral, now takes us out of the theological into the political sphere. This is seen most clearly in the discussion of the young king's remarkable conversion by the two bishops at the beginning of *Henry V*. King Henry, as Bradley notes, "is much more obviously religious than most of Shakespeare's heroes," [19] so that one would expect the bishops to interpret his change of life as a religious conversion. Yet they say nothing about religion except that he is "a true lover of the holy church" and can "reason in divinity"; the rest of their talk, some seventy lines, is concerned with learning and statecraft. In fact, the conversation of these worldly prelates demonstrates that the conversion is not the old repentance for sin and amendment of life, which is the burden, as we have seen, of Fabyan and other chroniclers, but a repentance of the renaissance type, which transforms an idle and wayward prince into an excellent soldier and governor. Even King Henry IV, at the bitterest moments of the scenes with his son, never taxes him with sin, and his only use of the word refers to sins that would multiply in the country, when

[18] *Poets and their Critics: Langland and Milton* (British Academy Warton Lecture), 1941, pp. 29–30.
[19] *Oxford Lectures*, p. 256.

> the fifth Harry from curbed licence plucks
> The muzzle of restraint.[20]

If Hal had sinned, it was not against God, but against Chivalry, against Justice, against his father, against the interests of the crown, which was the keystone of England's political and social stability. Instead of educating himself for the burden of kingship, he had been frittering away his time, and making himself cheap, with low companions

> that daff the world aside
> And bid it pass.

In a word, a word that Shakespeare applies no less than six times to his conduct, he is guilty of Vanity. And Vanity, though not in the theological category of the Seven Deadly Sins, was a cardinal iniquity in a young prince or nobleman of the sixteenth and seventeenth centuries; almost as heinous, in fact, as Idleness in an apprentice.

I am not suggesting that this represents Shakespeare's own view. Of Shakespeare's views upon the problems of conduct, whether in prince or commoner, we are in general ignorant, though he seems to hint in both *Henry IV* and *Henry V* that the Prince of Wales learnt some lessons at least from Falstaff and his crew, Francis and his fellow-drawers, which stood him in good stead when he came to rule the country and command troops in the field. But it is the view that his father and his own conscience take of his mistreadings; and, as the spectators would take it as well, we must regard it as the thesis to which Shakespeare addressed himself.

When, however, he took audiences by storm in 1597 and 1598 with his double *Henry IV* he gave them something much more than a couple of semi-mythical figures from the early fifteenth century, brought up to date politically. He presented persons and situations at once fresh and actual. Both Hal and Falstaff are denizens of Elizabethan London. Hal thinks, acts, comports himself as an heir to the Queen might have done, had she delighted her people by taking a consort and giving them a Prince of Wales; while Falstaff symbolizes, on the one hand, all the feasting and

[20] Pt. II, IV, v, 131.

good cheer for which Eastcheap stood, and reflects, on the other, the shifts, subterfuges, and shady tricks that decayed gentlemen and soldiers were put to if they wished to keep afloat and gratify their appetites in the London underworld of the late sixteenth century. It is the former aspects of the old scoundrel that probably gave most pleasure to those who first saw him on the stage; and, as they are also those that we moderns are most likely to miss, I make no apology for devoting most of the rest of this chapter to an exposition of them.

SWEET BEEF

Riot invites Youth, it will be remembered, to drink wine at a tavern, and tavern scenes are common in other interludes, especially those of the Prodigal Son variety. But Shakespeare's tavern is more than a drink-shop, while his Riot is not only a "huge bombard of sack" but also a "roasted Manningtree ox with the pudding in his belly."

The site of the Boar's Head tavern in Eastcheap is now as deep-sunk in the ooze of human forgetfulness as that of the palace of Haroun. But it was once a real hostelry, and must have meant much to Londoners of the reigns of Elizabeth and James. Records are scanty, but the very fact that Shakespeare makes it Falstaff's headquarters suggests that it was the best tavern in the city. And the further fact that he avoids mentioning it directly, though quibbling upon the name more than once,[21] suggests, on the one hand, that he kept the name off the stage in order to escape complications with the proprietors of the day, and on the other that he could trust his audience to jump to so obvious an identification without prompting. In any event, no other tavern in Eastcheap is at all likely to have been intended, and as Eastcheap is referred to six times in various scenes, there can be little real doubt that what Falstaff once calls "the king's tavern"[22] is the famous Boar's Head, the earliest known reference to which occurs in a will dat-

---

[21] V. Pt. I, II, iv, 100: "That damned brawn"; Pt. II, I, i, 19: "Harry Monmouth's brawn"; II, ii, 143 (159): "Doth the old boar feed in the old frank? / At the old place, my lord, in Eastcheap"; and II, iv, 224 (250): "Thou whoreson little tidy Bartholomew boar-pig."

[22] Pt. I, II, ii, 49. This designation perhaps implies a claim to royal patronage on the proprietor's part, possibly connected with the quasi-historical incident known as the Hurling in Eastcheap, an affray which arose among their retinue while Hal's brothers, the princes John and

ing from the reign of Richard II.[23] Whether there is anything or
not in Skeat's conjecture that the Glutton in *Piers Plowman* made
it the scene of his exploits like Falstaff,[24] it was a well-known
house of entertainment more than two hundred years before Shakespeare introduced it into his play, and had come therefore by his
day to be regarded as a historic hostelry, for which reason it was
probably already associated in popular imagination with the float-
ing legends of the wild young prince. What, however, seems to
have escaped the attention of modern writers is that the house, with
a name that symbolized good living and good fellowship above
that of any other London tavern, was almost certainly even better
known for good food than for good drink.

Eastcheap, there is plenty of evidence to show, was then, and
had long been, the London centre at once of butchers and cook-
shops. Lydgate, writing in the reign of Henry V, puts the following
words in the mouth of his *London Lyckpenny:*

> Then I hyed me into Estchepe;
>   One cryes 'rybbes of befe and many a pye';
> Pewter pots they clattered on a heap;
>   There was a harp, pype, and minstrelsy.

The street was famed, in short, not only for meat and drink, but
also for the "noise" of musicians, which belonged to "the old
Tauerne in Eastcheap" in *The Famous Victories,* and which
"Mistress Tearsheet would fain hear" in Part II of *Henry IV.*[25] As
for "rybbes of befe," though we never see or hear of Falstaff eating, or desiring to eat, anything except Goodwife Keech's dish of
prawns [26] and the capon, anchovies and halfpenny worth of bread
recorded with "an intolerable deal of sack" in the bill found upon
him while asleep,[27] Shakespeare none the less contrives to associate him perpetually with appetizing food by means of the imagery
that plays about his person. For the epithets and comparisons

Thomas, were taking supper at a tavern (unnamed) in Eastcheap, on
St John's Eve, 1410, as is related by Stow (*v.* Kingsford, *op. cit.* p. xxxix).

[23] V. "East Cheap" in Sugden's *Topographical Dictionary to the Works
of Shakespeare.*

[24] V. note on *Piers Plowman*, Passus v, l. 313, ed. Skeat (Clarendon
Press).

[25] Pt. II, II, iv.

[26] *Ibid.* II, i, 94 (102) ff.

[27] Pt. I, II, iv, 479–485.

which Hal and Poins apply to him, or he himself makes use of, though at times connected with his consumption of sack, are far more often intended to recall the chief stock-in-trade of the victuallers and butchers of Eastcheap, namely meat of all kinds, and meat both raw and roast.

Falstaff is once likened to a "huge bombard," [28] once to a "hogshead," [29] once to a "tun," [30] and twice to a "hulk," that is, to a cargo-boat; the nature of the cargo being specified by Doll, who protests to Mistress Quickly, "There's a whole merchant's venture of Bourdeaux stuff in him, you have not seen a hulk better stuffed in the hold." [31] But beyond these there is little or nothing about him in the vintner's line. When, on the other hand, Shakespeare promises the audience, through the mouth of his Epilogue in Part II, to continue the story, with Sir John in it, "if you be not too much cloyed with fat meat," the phrase sums up the prevailing image, constant in reference though ever-varying in form, which the physical characteristics of Falstaff presented to his mind's eye, and which he in turn was at pains to keep before the mind's eye of his public. Changes in London, and even more, changes in the language, have obliterated all this for the modern reader, so that what was intended, from the first, as little more than a kind of shimmering half-apprehended jest playing upon the surface of the dialogue, must now be recovered as a piece of archaeology, that is, as something long dead. The laughter has gone out of it; yet I shall be disappointed if the reader does not catch himself smiling now and again at what follows.

"Call in Ribs, call in Tallow" is Hal's cue for Falstaff's entry in the first great Boar's Head scene; and what summons to the choicest feast in comedy could be more apt? For there is the noblest of English dishes straightaway: Sir John as roast Sir Loin-of-Beef, gravy and all. "Tallow," a word often applied to him, generally in opprobrium, is not rightly understood, unless two facts be recalled: first, that it meant to the Elizabethans liquid fat, as well as dripping or suet or animal fat rendered down; second, that human sweat, partly owing perhaps to the similarity of the word to "suet," was likewise thought of as fat, melted by the heat of the

[28] *Ibid.* II, iv, 402.
[29] Pt. II, II, iv, 59 (69).
[30] Pt. I, II, iv, 399.
[31] Pt. II, II, iv, 59–61 (69–71).

body. The most vivid presentation of Falstaff served up hot, so to say, is the picture we get of him sweating with fright in Mistress Page's dirty linen basket, as it was emptied by her servants into the Thames; and though *The Merry Wives* does not strictly belong to the Falstaff canon, the passage may be quoted here, as giving the clue to passages in *Henry IV* itself. For however different in character the Windsor Falstaff may be from his namesake of Eastcheap, he possesses the same body, the body that on Gad's Hill "sweats to death, and *lards* the lean earth, as he walks along." [32]

"And then," he relates to the disguised Ford,

> to be stopped in, like a strong distillation, with stinking clothes that fretted in their own grease! Think of that, a man of my kidney! think of that—that am as subject to heat, as butter; a man of continual dissolution and thaw; it was a miracle to 'scape suffocation. And in the height of this bath, when I was more than half stewed in grease, like a Dutch dish, to be thrown into the Thames, and cooled, glowing-hot, in that surge, like a horse-shoe. Think of that—hissing hot: think of that, Master Brook! [33]

The "greasy tallow-catch," [34] again, to which the Prince compares him, much to the bewilderment of commentators, betokens, I believe, nothing more mysterious than a dripping-pan to catch the fat as the roasting joint turned upon the spit before the fire. Or take the following scrap of dialogue:

> L. CHIEF JUSTICE. What, you are as a candle, the better part burnt out.
> FALSTAFF. A wassail candle, my lord, all tallow—if I did say of wax, my growth would approve the truth.
> L. CHIEF JUSTICE. There is not a white hair on your face, but should have his effect of gravity.
> FALSTAFF. His effect of gravy, gravy, gravy.[35]

Falstaff's repeated "gravy" is a quibble, of course. But it is not just a feeble jest upon his table manners, as seems to be usually assumed: it follows upon the mention of "tallow" and refers to the drops of sweat that never cease to stand upon his face. In fact, to use a seventeenth-century expression, applicable to one bathed

[32] Pt. I, II, ii, 95–96.
[33] *Merry Wives of Windsor*, III, v, 103–12 (114–24).
[34] Pt. I, II, iv, 206.
[35] Pt. II, I, ii, 155–61 (182–4).

in perspiration, he may be said perpetually to "stew in his own gravy." [36]

Indeed, he glories in the fact. Was it not, according to the physiological notions of the time, the very warrant of his enormous vitality? Never is he more angered to the heart than when the Prince likens him one day to a dry withered old apple-john. His complexion is merely sanguine; heat and moisture mingle to form the element he moves in; except in moods of mock-repentance he leaves to baser earth the cold and dry of melancholy.[37]

Once we have the trick of it, all sorts of other allusions and playful terms of abuse are seen to belong to the same category, while the analogy between that vast carcase, as a whole or in its parts, and roasts of various kinds is capable of almost infinite elaboration. "Chops," for instance, as he is twice called,[38] carries the double significance of "fat cheeks" and "cutlets"; "guts," the Elizabethan word for "tripe," is an epithet that occurs no less than five times; [39] and "sweet beef" as a term of endearment [40] requires no explaining. Nor is he only served up as beef; pork, still more appropriate to the Boar's Head, though brought in less often, provides some magnificent examples. The term "brawn," which means a large pig fattened for the slaughter, is applied to him on two occasions; [41] on his return from Wales the Prince, enquiring of Bardolph, "Is your master here in London? . . . Where sups he? doth the old boar feed in the old frank?" [42] refers to the familiar inn-sign; Falstaff himself declares that he walks the streets followed by the diminutive page "like a sow that hath overwhelmed all her litter but one"; [43] last, and best of all, when Doll salutes him between her "flattering busses" as her "whoreson little tidy Bartholomew boar-pig," [44] she is alluding to the tender sweet-fleshed little sucking-pigs which formed the chief delicacy at Bartholomew Fair.

[36] V. *O.E.D.* "gravy."
[37] V. p. 224, *Edinburgh University Journal,* Summer 1942 (art. on "Shakespeare's Universe").
[38] Pt. I, I, ii, 118; Pt. II, II, iv, 211 (234).
[39] Pt. I, II, iv, 205, 235, 403; *ibid.* III, iii, 136, 138.
[40] Pt. I, III, iii, 158.
[41] Pt. I, II, iv, 100; Pt. II, I, i, 19.
[42] Pt. II, II, ii, 143 (169).
[43] *Ibid.* I, i, 11–12 (13–14).
[44] *Ibid.* II, iv, 224–5 (250).

The mention of Bartholomew Fair, the most popular annual festivity of Elizabethan and Jacobean London, may be linked with two other comparisons, which take us beyond the confines of Eastcheap and help to bestow on Falstaff that "touch of infinity" which Bradley discovers in him, associating him, as they do, with feasting on a vast and communal scale. The first, already quoted above, is the Prince's description of him as a "Manningtree ox with the pudding in his belly," [45] in other words, as an ox roasted whole and stuffed with sausages, after the fashion of the annual fairs at Manningtree, an Essex town famed for the exceeding fatness of its beasts. But the extremest inch of possibility is reached by Poins when he asks Bardolph "How doth the Martlemas, your master?" [46] Martlemas, or the feast of St Martin, on 11 November, was in those days of scarce fodder the season at which most of the beasts had to be killed off and salted for the winter, and therefore the season for great banquets of fresh meat. Thus it had been for centuries, long before the coming of Christianity,[47] and thus it remained down to the introduction of the cropping of turnips in the eighteenth century. In calling him a "Martlemas" Poins is at once likening Falstaff's enormous proportions to the prodigality of fresh-killed meat which the feast brought, and acclaiming his identity with Riot and Festivity in general.[48] But perhaps the best comment upon Falstaff as Martlemas comes from Spenser's procession of the seasons in the Book of Mutabilitie. His November might almost be Falstaff himself, though the dates prove that the two figures must be independent:

> Next was Nouember, he full grosse and fat,
> As fed with lard, and that right well might seeme;
> For, he had been a fatting hogs of late,
> That yet his browes with sweat did reek and steem,
> And yet the season was full sharp and breem.[49]

[45] Pt. I, II, iv, 403.

[46] Pt. II, II, ii, 100 (110).

[47] V. Sir E. K. Chambers, *Medieval Stage*, ch. XI, "The Beginning of Winter."

[48] I owe this point to the late Lord Ernle: writing in *Shakespeare's England* (i, p. 356), he notes: "To Shakespeare's mind the prodigious plenty of Martlemas suggested Falstaff in its proportions."

[49] *The Faerie Queene*, Bk. VII, canto vii, st. 40.

One might go to the other end of the scale and point out that the objects Falstaff chooses as a contrast to his person, objects excessively thin, wizened or meagre, are likewise often taken from the food-shops. There is, for instance, the shotten herring, the soused gurnet, the bunch of radish, the rabbit-sucker or poulter's hare, and wittiest of all perhaps, the carbonado—the rasher of bacon, we should say—which he will only allow Hotspur to make of him, if he is foolish enough to come in his way.[50] But enough to have shown that by plying his audience with suggestions of the choicest food that London and Eastcheap had to offer, whenever the person of Falstaff is mentioned, Shakespeare lays as it were the physical foundations of his Falstaff myth.

The prodigiously incarnate Riot, who fills the Boar's Head with his jollity, typifies much more, of course, than the pleasures of the table. He stands for a whole globe of happy continents, and his laughter is "broad as ten thousand beeves at pasture." [51] But he is Feasting first, and his creator never allows us to forget it. For in this way he not only perpetually associates him in our minds with appetizing images, but contrives that as we laugh at his wit our souls shall be satisfied as with marrow and fatness. No one has given finer expression to this satisfaction than Hazlitt, and I may fitly round off the topic with words of his:

> Falstaff's wit is an emanation of a fine constitution; an exuberance of good-humour and good-nature; an overflowing of his love of laughter and good-fellowship; a giving vent to his heart's ease, and over-contentment with himself and others. He would not be in character, if he were not so fat as he is; for there is the greatest keeping in the boundless luxury of his imagination and the pampered self-indulgence of his physical appetites. He manures and nourishes his mind with jests, as he does his body with sack and sugar. He carves out his jokes, as he would a capon or a haunch of venison, where there is *cut and come again*; and pours out upon them the oil of gladness. His tongue drops fatness, and in the chambers of his brain "it snows of meat and drink." He keeps perpetually holiday and open house, and we live with him in a round of invitations to a rump and dozen. . . . He never fails to enrich his discourse with allusions to eating and drinking, but we

[50] Pt. I, V, iii, 56.
[51] George Meredith, *The Spirit of Shakespeare.*

never see him at table. He carries his own larder about with him, and is himself "a tun of man." [52]

MONSIEUR REMORSE

Like all great Shakespearian characters Falstaff is a bundle of contradictions. He is not only Riot but also Repentance. He can turn an eye of melancholy upon us, assume the role of puritan sanctimony, and when it pleases him, even threaten amendment of life. It is, of course, *mock*-repentance, carried through as part of the untiring "play extempore" with which he keeps the Prince, and us, and himself, entertained from beginning to end of the drama. And yet it is not mere game; Shakespeare makes it more interesting by persuading us that there is a strain of sincerity in it; and it almost completely disappears in Part II, when the rogue finds himself swimming on the tide of success. There is a good deal of it in Part I, especially in the earliest Falstaff scenes.

> But, Hal, I prithee, trouble me no more with vanity. I would to God thou and I knew where a commodity of good names were to be bought.
> Thou hast done much harm upon me, Hal—God forgive thee for it: before I knew thee, Hal, I knew nothing, and now am I, if a man should speak truly, little better than one of the wicked: I must give over this life, and I will give it over: by the Lord, an I do not, I am a villain. I'll be damned for never a king's son in Christendom.[53]

One of his favourite poses is that of the innocent, beguiled by a wicked young heir apparent; he even makes it the burden of his apologia to the Lord Chief Justice at their first encounter. It serves too when things go wrong, when resolute men who have taken £1000 on Gad's Hill are left in the lurch by cowardly friends, or when there's lime in a cup of sack:

> There is nothing but roguery to be found in villainous man, yet a coward is worse than a cup of sack with lime in it. A villainous coward! Go thy ways, old Jack, die when thou wilt, if manhood, good manhood, be not forgot upon the face of the earth, then am I a shotten herring. . . . There lives not three good men un-hanged in England, and one of them is fat, and grows old. God

[52] *Characters of Shakespeare's Plays* (Hazlitt's *Works*, ed. A. R. Waller and A. Glover, 1902, i. 278).
[53] Pt. I, I, ii, 70–73, 80–85.

help the while! a bad world, I say. I would I were a weaver—I could sing psalms or anything.[54]

But beside this talk of escaping from a wicked world and the toils of a naughty young prince, there is also the pose of personal repentance. At his first entry Poins hails him as Monsieur Remorse, an indication that this is one of his recognized roles among Corinthians and lads of mettle. And we may see him playing it at the opening of Act 3, Scene 3, when there is no Hal present to require entertaining.

> Well, I'll repent, and that suddenly, while I am in some liking. I shall be out of heart shortly, and then I shall have no strength to repent. An I have not forgotten what the inside of a church is made of, I am a peppercorn, a brewer's horse. The inside of a church! Company, villainous company, hath been the spoil of me.

Such passages, together with the habit of citing Scripture, may have their origin, I have said, in the puritan, psalm-singing, temper of Falstaff's prototype—that comic Lollard, Sir John Oldcastle in the old *Henry IV*.[55] But, if so, the motif, adapted and developed in Shakespeare's hands, has come to serve a different end. In this play of the Prodigal Prince it is Hal who should rightly exhibit moods of repentance; and on the face of it, it seems quite illogical to transfer them to Falstaff, the tempter. Yet there are reasons why Hal could not be thus represented. In the first place, as already noted, repentance in the theological sense, repentance for sin, is not relevant to his case at all, which is rather one of a falling away from political virtues, from the duties laid upon him by his royal vocation. And in the second place, since Henry V is the ideal king of English history, Shakespeare must take great care, even in the days of his "wildness," to guard him from the breath of scandal. As has been well observed by a recent editor: "His riots are mere frolics. He does not get drunk and is never involved in any scandal with a woman." [56] And there is a third

[54] *Ibid.* II, iv, 111–119.

[55] *V. supra*, p. 16 and ch. iv note 20.

[56] *V.* p. xi of ɪ *Henry IV*, ed. by G. L. Kittredge (Ginn & Co.). I fancy Hal is just a little tipsy at the beginning of Pt. I, II, iv, but the point is, in general, sound enough, and the more striking that the chroniclers do not hide the fact that Prince Henry was given to sexual intemperance; *v.* Kingsford, *op. cit.* p. 17: "he exercised meanelie the

reason, this time one of dramatic technique not of morals, why the repentance of the Prince must be kept in the background as much as possible, viz. that as the only satisfactory means of rounding off the two parts, it belongs especially to the last act of the play.

Yet Monsieur Remorse is a good puppet in the property-box of the old morality, and may be given excellent motions in the fingers of a skilful showman, who is laying himself out, in this play especially, to make fun of the old types. Why not shape a comic part out of it, and hand it over to Falstaff, who as the heir of traditional medieval "antics" like the Devil, the Vice, the Fool, Riot and Lord of Misrule, may very well manage one more? Whether or not Shakespeare argued it out thus, he certainly added the ingredient of melancholy, and by so doing gave a piquancy to the sauce which immensely enhances the relish of the whole dish. If only modern actors who attempt to impersonate Falstaff would realize it!

Falstaff, then, came to stand for the repentance, as well as the riotous living, of the Prodigal Son. And striking references to the parable, four of them, seem to show that his creator was fully aware of what he was doing. "What, will you make a younker of me? shall I not take mine ease in mine inn but I shall have my pocket picked?" [57] Sir John indignantly demands of Mistress Quickly, on discovering, or pretending to discover, the loss of his grandfather's seal-ring. The word "younker" calls up a scene from some well-known representation of the parable, in picture or on the stage, a scene to which Shakespeare had already alluded in the following lines from *The Merchant of Venice*:

> How like a younker or a prodigal
> The scarféd bark puts from her native bay,
> Hugged and embracéd by the strumpet wind!
> How like a prodigal doth she return,
> With over-weathered ribs and ragged sails,
> Lean, rent, and beggared by the strumpet wind! [58]

feates of Venus and of Mars, and other pastimes of youth, for so longe as the Kinge his father liued."

[57] Pt. I, III, iii, 69–70. "The alternative title for the Prodigal Son was the 'younger,' as the alternative for the good brother was the 'elder'" (Richmond Noble, *Shakespeare's Biblical Knowledge*, p. 277).

[58] *The Merchant of Venice*, II, vi, 14–19; cf. 3 *Henry VI*, II, i, 24: "Trimmed like a younker, prancing to his love."

Equally vivid is Falstaff's description of the charge of foot he led into battle at Shrewsbury as so "dishonourable ragged" that "you would think that I had a hundred and fifty tattered prodigals, lately come from swine-keeping, from eating draff and husks." [59] And seeing that he calls them in the same speech "slaves as ragged as Lazarus in the painted cloth, where the Glutton's dogs licked his sores," we may suppose that, here too, he is speaking right painted cloth, from whence he had studied his Bible; [60] an inference which seems borne out by his third reference, this time from Part II. Having, you will remember, already honoured Mistress Quickly by becoming indebted to her for a hundred marks, that is for over £65, he graciously condescends to borrow £10 more from her. And when she protests that to raise the sum she must be fain to pawn both her plate and the tapestry of her dining-chambers, he replies: "Glasses, glasses, is the only drinking—and for thy walls, a pretty drollery or the story of the Prodigal or the German hunting in waterwork is worth a thousand of these bed-hangers and these fly-bitten tapestries." [61] This is not just the patter of the confidence-trickster; Falstaff, we must believe, had a real liking for the Prodigal Son story, or why should that tactful person, mine Host of the Garter Inn, have gone to the trouble of having it painted, "fresh and new," about the walls of the chamber that he let to the greasy philanderer who assumed the part of Sir John, in Windsor.[62] Not being a modern critic, the good man could not know that his guest was an impostor.

But jollification and mock-repentance do not exhaust Falstaff's roles. For most of *Henry IV* he plays the soldier, taking a hand in a couple of campaigns, the first culminating in the death of Hotspur at Shrewsbury, and the other in the encounter between Prince John and the Archbishop of York at Gaultree Forest, where the rebels are finally overthrown. In both of these he performs the useful dramatic function of supplying the light relief, and in so doing he exhibits himself as at once the supreme comic soldier of English literature and a variation of a time-worn theme, the *miles gloriosus* of Plautus. . . .

[59] Pt. I, IV, ii, 27–31.

[60] Cf. *As You Like It*, III, ii, 271 (290): "I answer you right painted cloth, from whence you have studied your questions."

[61] Pt. II, II, i, 143–7 (155–9).

[62] *The Merry Wives*, IV, v, 7.

ARTHUR C. SPRAGUE

Gadshill Revisited [1]

For about a hundred and eighty years after Sir John Falstaff for the first time ran roaring from Gadshill, the fact of his cowardice was taken for granted. Falstaff was immensely popular with readers and playgoers alike. In the seventeenth century, allusions to him are far more numerous, by actual count, than those to any other Shakespearian character,[2] and the terms in which he is referred to are quite unambiguous. "A thrasonical puff, and emblem of mock valour," Tom Fuller calls him;[3] and Dryden, not, I think, inaccurately, describes him as "old, fat, merry, cowardly, drunken, amorous, vain, and lying." Yet Falstaff's individuality, as Dryden perceived, lay elsewhere:

> That wherein he is singular is his wit, or those things he says . . .
> unexpected by the audience; his quick evasions, when you expect
> him surprised, which, as they are extremely diverting of them-
> selves, so receive a great addition from his person.[4]

And Dr. Samuel Johnson, agreeing with Dryden, pronounces Falstaff a coward and defines his wit as consisting "in easy escapes and sallies of levity." [5]

It was not until 1777 that heresy began. In that year appeared a long essay of a good deal of subtlety, and even charm, *On the Dramatic Character of Sir John Falstaff*, by Maurice Morgann.

From *Shakespeare Quarterly*, IV (April 1953), 125–137. Reprinted by permission of the author and the Shakespeare Association of America.
[1] A paper read at the Shakespeare Conference at Stratford-on-Avon in August 1951.
[2] G. E. Bentley, *Shakespeare and Jonson* (Chicago [1945]), chap. vii.
[3] *The History of the Worthies of England*, ed. P. Austin Nuttall (London, 1840), II, 455.
[4] "An Essay of Dramatic Poesy," in *Dramatic Essays*, "Everyman's Library," p. 43.
[5] *The Plays of William Shakespeare*, ed. Johnson (London, 1765), IV, 356.

Morgann, a middle-aged civil servant of "uncommon powers,"
acknowledges that his book was written on a dare, and he dreads
that it might be taken, as, indeed, it was by many, as a mere exercise in paradox. He recognizes "how universally the contrary opinion prevails"; and that "the appearances" in this case are all
against him. Falstaff is involved, almost immediately, "in circumstances of apparent dishonour"; he is called a coward; is seen "in
the very act of running away," and "betrayed into those *lies* and
braggadocioes, which are the usual concomitants of cowardice in
military men, and pretenders to valour." What was more, these
things are "thrust forward, pressed upon our notice as the subject
of our mirth." [6] The grounds for his own belief that Sir John was
no coward were of quite another sort, and he asks patience of the
reader while he sets forth what "lies so dispersed, is so latent, and
so purposely obscured" [7]—the "secret impressions upon us of courage." [8]

Though Morgann's ideas were to prevail, they were not unop-
posed in his own day. A carefully reasoned reply by Richard Stack
appeared in *The Transactions of the Royal Irish Academy*. Dr.
Johnson's opinion was twice asked and given. "Why, Sir," Boswell
quotes him as saying, "we shall have the man come forth again;
and as he has proved Falstaff to be no coward, he may prove Iago
to be a very good character." [9] Thomas Davies, too, the actor and
bookseller, spoke out, and the point he made was, I think, a telling one: "If the knight is proved to be a man of courage, half the
mirth he raises is quite lost and misplaced." [10] What is more curious, Falstaff on the stage remained unregenerate. As he had once
been, in this matter of cowardice, so he has remained right down
to the present—though such fine actors as Sir Ralph Richardson
and (at Stratford) Mr. Anthony Quayle and the late Roy Byford,
have dispensed with most of the traditional buffoonery which once
disfigured the role.

We have come, indeed, to a parting of ways, the actors keeping
straight on as they had been going, the critics, with few excep-

[6] *An Essay on the Dramatic Character of Sir John Falstaff* (London,
1820), pp. 2, 3.
[7] *Ibid.*, p. 4.
[8] *Ibid.*, p. 13.
[9] James Boswell, *Life of Samuel Johnson,* ed. G. B. Hill and L. F.
Powell (Oxford, 1934), IV, 192 note.
[10] *Dramatic Miscellanies* (London, 1784), I, 272.

tions, straying obscurely to the left. Nor was Morgann, with his notion of appearance and reality, his "secret impressions" of courage, a safe guide. Thus, William Lloyd would have Falstaff's delightfully spontaneous rejoinder to the Prince's "Where shall we take a purse tomorrow, Jack?" "Zounds, where thou wilt, lad! I'll make one," a bit of crafty duplicity, with the speaker fully conscious of the incongruity of what he says.[11] And Hazlitt fancies that Falstaff's bill, with its "out-of-the-way charge for capons and sack with only one half-penny-worth of bread," may have been planted for the Prince to find.[12] (One might question, with equal propriety, whether at the moment of the reading of the bill Sir John, for all his snoring, was really asleep!)

The starting point for such divagations remains the denial of what in the theater seems obvious, the fact of cowardice. Yet Bradley and even Kittredge are among those who have denied it. Bradley, indeed, is not without misgivings. The manner of Falstaff's flight at Gadshill troubles him, if only in a footnote: "It is to be regretted . . . that in carrying his guts away so nimbly he 'roared for mercy'; for I fear we have no ground for rejecting Henry's statement to that effect." [13] He grants, too, that "Falstaff sometimes behaves in what we should generally call a cowardly way." But conduct is not a certain indication of character. "If the word [coward] means a person who feels painful fear in the presence of danger, and yields to that fear in spite of his better feelings and convictions, then assuredly Falstaff was no coward." [14] As for Kittredge, strangely, as it always seemed to me, he had no doubts whatsoever. Even the roaring at Gadshill he denied, or explained away. For once, dramatic evidence went by the board with him, and his Falstaff was *sans peur*, if not quite *sans reproche*.

Among the minority-critics who have held out for cowardice (and John Bailey was one), the foremost is, of course, Professor Stoll. Time after time he has returned to the question, bringing to it his broad knowledge of popular drama and its enduring conventions.[15] Thus, he shows that Falstaff's behavior on the battle-

[11] *Essays on Shakespeare* (1858), in *1 Henry IV*, Furness Variorum Edition, p. 135.
[12] *Characters of Shakespeare's Plays*, Bohn ed. (1892), p. 135.
[13] *Oxford Lectures on Poetry* (London, 1909), p. 268 note.
[14] *Ibid.*, p. 266.
[15] *Shakespeare Studies* (New York, 1927); "Recent Shakespeare Criticism," *Shakespeare Jahrbuch*, LXXIV (1938); *Shakespeare and Other*

field—his cracking jokes, for instance, or capturing a prisoner of his own, the redoubtable Colevile of the Dale—cannot be taken as evidence of courage, since the mere type-cowards and comic butts of earlier and cruder plays do the like. Sir John's ancestors are a shabby lot, but their existence may as well be acknowledged. In fact, a late-comer to this controversy, who has convinced himself that Falstaff was no braver than he should be, is likely to discover that many of his best arguments have already been used, somewhere, by Mr. Stoll. That they have been so largely disregarded is a little puzzling.

Finally, Professor J. Dover Wilson, though he repeatedly invokes the authority of Johnson in combatting the Romantic critics, is ambiguous on this matter of timidity; or, rather, as it seems to me, he would have it both ways. Falstaff, during the overpowering of the travelers at Gadshill, is described as "dancing with rage, on the fringe of the scuffle," and his subsequent flight becomes as ignominious as the older actors were accustomed to make it. Indeed, if the Gadshill Scene stood alone, Mr. Wilson is satisfied that the audience would accept Sir John as "an absolute coward"—which he will not admit.[16] The representation of cowardice by the right sort of comedian will (he thinks) have produced an effect upon us very different from what might be expected—affection, even, rather than a "jeering contempt." [17] The impression of cowardice is dissolved in the mirth of the Tavern Scene. Falstaff, sensing the plot against him, deliberately exaggerates, winking to the audience at the moment he begins to do so. The groundlings might miss the point; there would be others to whom the question of cowardice was left open to debate. And Falstaff's "magnificent display of stoutness of heart" when the Sheriff comes to arrest him, is "the final answer to the Prince's slanderous story of the events on Gad's Hill, and to our own receding impressions." [18]

Yet as we pass to still later episodes, it is curious to find Mr. Wilson taking issue repeatedly with the contentions of the Mor-

Masters (Cambridge [Massachusetts], 1940); From Shakespeare to Joyce (New York, 1944); "Symbolism in Shakespeare," Modern Language Review, XLII (1947).

[16] The Fortunes of Falstaff (Cambridge and New York, 1944), pp. 44, 45.

[17] Ibid., p. 47.

[18] Ibid., p. 58.

gann school. Falstaff's presence in the thick of battle is no longer accepted as evidence of valor. His "military reputation is not only complete bogus, but one of the best jokes in the whole drama." [19] Had Colevile of the Dale resisted, "we may surmise that another sham death would have followed the exchange of a few blows." [20] Even the turning out of poor swaggering Pistol is left to Bardolph, "while Falstaff, sword in hand, follows up at a discreet distance behind." [21]

On this whole question of cowardice, then, the earlier critics, and the actors, are on one side; the later critics, with few exceptions, on the other. Either, that is to say, Falstaff is an egregious coward; or he is—here there is some want of agreement—a veteran soldier, usually, and a realist in war; trusted, and not wholly undeserving of trust; wily, and of great presence of mind; no Hotspur, of course, but just as certainly, not a coward. The chief arguments of Morgann and his followers, the arguments against cowardice, are familiar—Morgann, himself, thought up most of them—and I shall present them only summarily, though I hope with fairness.

There is, first of all, Morgann's bold challenge to the impartial reader: "We all like *Old Jack*" though we so constantly abuse him! But could we like him, vicious as he is, were he actually a coward? Cowardice seems incompatible with our impression of the character as a whole. Our feeling toward Falstaff is altogether different from our feeling toward, say, the cowardly Parolles in *All's Well that Ends Well*.

From impressions and their analysis we pass to inference. Falstaff's military reputation is pointed to with confidence as evidence of desert. Thus, in the dark days before Shrewsbury, the Prince himself entrusts him with the command of a company of foot. Falstaff is present at the King's Council of War; and in the premature account of the outcome of the battle is prominently mentioned among the casualties—"And Harry Monmouth's brawn, the hulk Sir John, Is prisoner." Later we hear of "a dozen Captains" searching anxiously for him while he sups with Mistress Tearsheet. Then, too, a rebel of some note, a knight, Colevile of the Dale, surrenders at once upon hearing who his antagonist is: "I think you are Sir John Falstaff, and in that thought yield me."

[19] *Ibid.*, p. 89.
[20] *Ibid.*, p. 87.
[21] *Ibid.*, p. 107.

Much is made, also, of a relatively inconspicuous episode at the close of the great Tavern Scene in 1 *Henry IV*. Bardolph rushes in, with a good deal of nasal clamor, to interrupt the play which Falstaff and Prince Hal are acting: "O, my lord, my lord! the sheriff with a most monstrous watch is at the door"—looking of course, for certain thieves. Falstaff, it is urged, might well be expected to show alarm at this, or even terror. On the contrary, he merely takes hiding behind the arras, where he is presently discovered, not quaking with fear but asleep, and "snorting like a horse."

Later in the same play we have Sir John on the field of battle—and in time, too! He tells us in soliloquy that he has led his poor soldiers where they were slaughtered. He finds himself in the very thick of the fight. Hotspur contends with Prince Hal in single combat. The terrible Douglas suddenly attacks Falstaff. Whereupon Falstaff, no match of course for such an adversary, but never losing his coolness and presence of mind, has recourse to a brilliant stratagem by which he escapes: lives, as is hopefully said of him, to fight another day. As no coward could have slept, earlier, so no coward could now have outwitted death by seeming to die!

The complicated happenings at Gadshill, Morgann takes up last of all, and he admits the possibility that Falstaff in this single instance yielded to a momentary and quite understandable terror (even Bradley, as we saw, was troubled by Sir John's *roaring* as he ran). For an uncompromising defence of the fat hero at this point, one goes to Kittredge. Falstaff, he urges, is under no sort of obligation to fight it out. On the contrary, as a thief caught in the act, it behooves him to take to his heels. "How the fat rogue roar'd!" says Poins, at the end of the Gadshill Scene. But this refers to Falstaff's "vociferous swaggering"—his "Down with them . . . whoreson caterpillars" and so on—as he set upon the travellers—or encouraged poor Bardolph and the others to set upon them! And when the roaring is again mentioned and its precise character specified ("and, Falstaff, you carried your guts away as nimbly . . . and roar'd for mercy, and still run and roar'd, as ever I heard bullcalf"), it is the "only departure from accuracy in Prince Hal's story."

These, then, are the principal arguments which have been used by those who deny that Falstaff was a coward, despite those circumstances of "apparent dishonour" and appearances "singularly strong and striking" which Morgann recognized as likely to sway the judgment of a simple reader. They are arguments which vary a good deal in force; but each of them can, I think, be fairly met.

There is Morgann's argument, first of all, that we could not like "plump Jack" as we do if to his other failings, and quite tipping the balance, were added cowardice. But this is to leave out of account Sir John's years, and it might be added his corpulence. He is obviously disqualified as a combatant—"blasted with antiquity." [22] To expect valor of him is, indeed, to expect too much! And in the Play Scene when, speaking in the person of Prince Hal, he has occasion to praise himself, he makes a point of this: "But for sweet Jack Falstaff, kind Jack Falstaff, true Jack Falstaff, valiant Jack Falstaff, and therefore more valiant being, as he is, old Jack Falstaff. . . ." Nor need the argument remain hypothetical. For it is quite obvious that Dr. Johnson liked Falstaff, though recognizing the rogue's numerous vices and insisting upon his cowardice.

As for his military reputation, I am tempted merely to repeat Professor Dover Wilson's comprehensive description of it as "complete bogus" and "one of the best jokes in the whole drama." Colevile of the Dale has only to learn who his antagonist is, and yields without striking a blow. (His alacrity in yielding does not, indeed, escape comment: "It was more, his courtesy than your deserving," says Prince John to Falstaff, unpleasantly enough.) But if Pistol, the complete coward, is able to take a prisoner on the field of battle, why not his old master, the better man of the two? And Colevile, though his words are not abject like those of Pistol's Frenchman, seems scarcely formidable. Falstaff speaks of him with suspicious emphasis as "a most furious knight and valorous enemy" and of his own "pure and immaculate valour" in taking such a prisoner. Perhaps, the first tribute is as unsubstantial as the second?

But the Prince entrusted Falstaff with the command of a company shortly before Shrewsbury? And this same company, it might be answered, will afford occasion for one of Sir John's happiest monologues; is fully justified, in terms of dramatic economy, by the use made of it! The Prince, too, seems to take the matter lightly. "I'll procure this fat rogue a charge of foot," he says, adding, not I think without relish, "and I know his death will be a march of twelve score." He wants to see Falstaff larding the lean earth

[22] 2 *Henry IV*, I, ii, 207.

once more! Meanwhile, there will be the pleasure of telling him
the news:

> I have procured thee, Jack, a charge of foot.
> *Falstaff.* I would it had been of horse.

Later, by the way, Hal entrusts despatches of obvious importance
to—of all messengers—Bardolph!

He slept behind the arras—slept soundly and snored. Now this
fact has been taken as incontestable proof of high fortitude on the
snorer's part. But is it? I would not so far belittle Sir John's sagacity
as to believe that what even a minor member of the gang (Gadshill)
recognized would not have been perceived by Falstaff—that on
this particular expedition they stole "as in a castle, cocksure." [23]
The Prince of Wales, deeply involved as he is, himself, must needs
"(if matters should be look'd into) for [his] own credit sake make
all whole." Falstaff might well sleep soundly, and, sleeping, con-
tribute to the forwarding of the plot by allowing his pockets to be
picked. What is natural in itself has reason as well in the economy
of the play as a whole; most of dramatic technique (as I have come
to believe) consisting in a playwright's ability to kill more than one
bird with a single stone.

Falstaff's behavior at Shrewsbury and Gadshill remains to be
considered. At Shrewsbury, then, he led his ragamuffins where
they were peppered; is found, himself, where the fighting is fiercest,
and escapes death by means of a quite legitimate stratagem. The
passing allusion to the destruction of the ragamuffins is impressive
when taken out of context. Nor would I impute a sinister motive
to old Jack and believe that the securing of their death pay was his
object here.[24] Were this so, one would expect some intimation of
it in the text. They fell, in any case, almost to a man—and it is
convenient for the playwright certainly, and perhaps for Sir John,
to have them out of the way. Meanwhile, the soliloquy in which
we hear of their fate is worth examining. "Though I could scape
shot-free at London," Falstaff begins, "I fear the shot here." Then,
starting at the sight of one who has paid his score—"There's honour
for you!" "I am as hot as molten lead," he mutters, "and as heavy
too. God keep lead out of me! I need no more weight than mine

[23] *1 Henry IV*, II, i, 77.
[24] Cf. J. W. Fortescue, in *Shakespeare's England*, I, 123.

own bowels." For an Elizabethan audience—for, I think, any popular audience—the character of the speech will already have been determined. It is addressed to them, designed for their amusement—a comic monologue spoken by one who does, indeed, "fear the shot" and who will have recourse to whatever shifts he can devise to save that precious carcass of his.

Such shifts and stratagems, far from being incompatible with cowardice on the stage, were its familiar concomitants. Not to go further for an illustration, one turns to *The Famous Victories of Henry the Fifth*. In the old play of that name, well known, it would seem, to Shakespeare, the "Clown" Dericke is an egregious coward; yet he has his wits about him, and most of all when his need is greatest. He boasts of having tickled his nose with a straw, gained in this way the title of "the bloodie souldier," and so escaped combat duty.[25] Taken prisoner, ignominiously enough, during the raid upon the English camp at Agincourt, he manages by an elaborate and very implausible trick to secure his captor's sword, *"hurles him downe"* and is about to kill him when the Frenchman escapes in turn. "What, is he gone?" says Dericke, "Masse, I am glad of it. For, if he had staid, I was afraid he wold have sturd again, and then I should have beene spilt." [26]

"Enter *Douglas*. He fighteth with *Falstaff*, who falls down as if he were dead." I recall a very good performance of *1 Henry IV* at an American repertory theater before a small audience. In the row behind me were two very young girls who clearly had not read the play but, as clearly, were greatly enjoying it. And the happy comment of one of them, wholly spontaneous as it was, delighted me: "He's playing possum!" It came, as I noted, a moment or two after Sir John's descent. To her, as to a good many in that first audience of long ago, he must have seemed to have died indeed. And when, upon the talk of embowelling, Falstaff rose, there came amusement and relief. Though the expedient he practised was, as an eighteenth-century critic stated, "very natural to a coward," [27] and one which an unfortunate fat man of the same name repeats in *The Merry Wives of Windsor*, it is not, I should say, conclusive evidence of cowardice any more than it is of valor. Relief and

[25] *Chief Pre-Shakespearean Dramas*, ed. J. Q. Adams (Boston, etc. [1924]), p. 688.
[26] *Ibid.*, pp. 686, 687.
[27] Richard Stack, in *1 Henry IV*, Furness Variorum Edition, p. 417.

amusement come first, and beyond such feelings I doubt if the ordinary spectator goes. Long ere this, he will have made up his mind on the matter of cowardice and will interpret this episode accordingly. And if we, away from the theater, disputing as we do over niceties, are in need of further enlightenment, it comes in the speech immediately following. "The better part of valour is discretion," Falstaff rationalizes. Then, as he looks about him, come thoughts of another sort. "Zounds, I am afraid of this gunpowder Percy, though he be dead. How if he should counterfeit too, and rise?" And, accordingly, to "make him sure," he will thrust his sword into the dead body. If, he adds as an afterthought, he takes upon himself the glory of having slain Hotspur, he may succeed in brazening it out. "Why may not he rise as well as I?" he repeats. There is a double incentive for what he does—fame, yes, but caution as well. Tom Davies who, knowing as he did a great deal about the practical theater, remained undazzled by the brilliance of Maurice Morgann, gave this passage the emphasis it deserves: "If any proof of [Falstaff's] timidity be yet wanting, we have, in this scene, such as bids defiance to all question; for Falstaff, not satisfied with seeing the dead body of Percy before him, to make all sure, wounds the corpse in the thigh." [28]

The circumstances of the Gadshill robbery Morgann, for obvious reasons, examined last of all. In the play, it is of some consequence, however, that the episode comes very early. Shakespeare's practice in matters of exposition is remarkably consistent. Facts and impressions, once imparted, are rarely contradicted, and then in quite unmistakable terms. Even Iago, who for a few moments may appear to have something of a case against his master, a still unknown Moor, is soon shown in his true colors as a designing villain. What is more, the cowardice of Falstaff is not lightly referred to, or joked about; it receives in the Gadshill episode what amounts, in dramatic terms, to demonstration.

As Poins outlines the plan, he and the Prince are to set upon Falstaff, Bardolph, Peto, and Gadshill, and rob them of their newly acquired booty. The Prince, not unnaturally, wonders whether "they will be too hard for us"—four men against two. But Poins reassures him:

Well, for two of them, I know them to be as true-bred cowards as ever turn'd back; and for the third, if he fight longer than he

[28] *Dramatic Miscellanies, I,* 273.

sees reason, I'll forswear arms. The virtue of this jest will be the incomprehensible lies that this same fat rogue will tell us when we meet at supper: how thirty, at least, he fought with; what wards, what blows, what extremities he endured; and in the reproof of this lies the jest.

Thus, two things are promised: that Falstaff, to translate understatement by understatement, is not likely to do much fighting; and that, in keeping with his timidity and making it truly diverting, his tales of prowess afterwards will be infinite ("incomprehensible"). Hal is satisfied—and, indeed, Poins knows his man!

At Gadshill, Falstaff has first to endure the distress of being deprived of his horse—that unfortunate animal!—but being Falstaff is soon able to play upon the familiar theme of his own bulk quite as happily as his tormenters. He hears that the travellers are numerous. "Zounds," he cries, "will they not rob us?" And the Prince: "What, a coward, Sir John Paunch?" "Indeed," he answers, "I am not John of Gaunt, your grandfather; but yet no coward, Hal." "Well, we leave that to the proof." And the proof is soon forthcoming. The travelers, easing their legs by walking down the hill, are pounced upon and relieved of their money, Falstaff setting up a prodigious clamor while this is going on. Once more, to keep these complicated happenings clear, the prince comments:

> The thieves have bound the true men. Now could thou and I rob the thieves and go merrily to London, it would be argument for a week, laughter for a month, and a good jest for ever.

But Falstaff, returning with the booty, is full of satisfaction:

> Come, my masters, let us share, and then to horse before day. An the Prince and Poins be not two arrant cowards, there's no equity stirring. There's no more valour in that Poins than in a wild duck.

It is the note he will sound insistently at the beginning of the Tavern Scene. They are the cowards, not he! He may even believe it, himself. Then,

> as they are sharing, the Prince and Poins set upon them. They all run away, and Falstaff, after a blow or two [he is, of course, less nimble than the rest], runs away too, leaving the booty behind them.

> PRINCE. Got with much ease. Now merrily to horse.
>   The thieves are scattered, and possess'd with fear

> So strongly that they dare not meet each other.
> Each takes his fellow for an officer.
> Away, good Ned. Falstaff sweats to death
> And lards the lean earth as he walks along.
> Were't not for laughing, I should pity him.
> POINS.   How the fat rogue roar'd!

So in A *Midsummer Night's Dream*, Bully Bottom's companions
had fled in panic at sight of the ass's head.

George Bartley, a distinguished Falstaff of the early years of the
last century and for a long time stage-manager at Covent Garden
Theatre, is described as "a courteous, discreet gentleman." He had,
nevertheless, a very low opinion of the intelligence of audiences.

> "Sir," he would say . . . , "you must first tell them you are go-
> ing to do so and so; you must then tell them you are doing it, and
> then that you have done it; and then, by G-d" (with a slap on his
> thigh), "*perhaps* they will understand you!" [29]

Shakespeare in the present instance might almost be anticipating
the precautions recommended. We are told what will happen; told,
as well, what has happened. And if the actual encounter can
scarcely be interpreted while it is taking place, it is, in Shakespeare's
theater, no encounter of phantom-shapes, of dimly outlined sil-
houettes, but one clearly visible by honest daylight. Misunderstanding could not well have existed. "But yet no coward, Hal. . . .
Well, we leave that to the proof."

More still was promised: "the virtue of this jest . . . the incomprehensible lies." And Falstaff fairly outdoes expectation. In the
study, one may forget or overlook, the visual impressiveness of
his entrance. He and his followers carry battered weapons, their
clothes are stained with blood ("Tell me now in earnest," the
Prince asks later, "how came Falstaff's sword so hack'd?" and
Peto explains, "Why, he hack'd it with his dagger, and said he
would swear truth out of England but he would make you believe
it was done in fight, and persuaded us to do the like"). It is he,
Sir John, who makes complaint, "A plague of all cowards, I say."
Deserted, as he found himself, by those who should have fought
beside him, he had yet borne himself magnificently and escaped
only "by miracle." Poins had prophesied he would claim to have
fought with "thirty, at least," and he reaches fifty—"two or three

[29] J. R. Planché, *Recollections and Reflections* (London, 1872), II, 208.

and fifty upon poor old Jack." Then, before the fun of the mounting figures is yet exhausted, he is led to mention casualties: "two rogues in buckram . . . pepper'd." The same two, as we recognize, who are so eagerly listening to him now, who can wait, nonetheless, and give their great fish more line, for he is surely caught!

For the actor to wink at his audience, somewhere here, as Mr. Dover Wilson would have him do, seems to me purely arbitrary. (The meaning of innumerable passages in Shakespeare could be perverted by means of extra-textual winkings, and it is to be hoped that the present vogue for imagining them does not spread to tragedy!) Arbitrary, and also confusing, dividing the audience at a moment when they should be at one and sharing their pleasure as good audiences ever do. Above all, for Sir John to appear conscious of his danger thus early, is to anticipate our pleasure in his escape. Whereas, if we are to judge from the text alone, this comes as a magnificent surprise. He seems doomed.

> PRINCE. Mark now how a plain tale shall put you down. Then did we two set on you four and, with a word, outfac'd you from your prize, and have it; yea, and can show it you here in the house. And, Falstaff, you carried your guts away as nimbly, with as quick dexterity, and roar'd for mercy, and still run and roar'd, as ever I heard bullcalf. . . . What trick, what device, what starting hole canst thou now find out to hide thee from this open and apparent shame?
>
> POINS. Come, let's hear, Jack. What trick has thou now?

And then, and only then (and the actor will not fail to bring out the sudden and dramatic change of speed which marks the moment), Falstaff replies:

> By the Lord, I knew ye as well as he that made ye. Why, hear you, my masters. Was it for me to kill the heir apparent? Should I turn upon the true prince? Why, thou knowest I am as valiant as Hercules; but beware instinct. The lion will not touch the true prince.

Falstaff, as Davies recognized, "is never in a state of humiliation; he generally rises superior to attack, and gets the laugh on his side in spite of truth and conviction." [30] Nevertheless, it is the Prince who recurs to this episode with enjoyment, still gloating over it in *The Second Part of Henry the Fourth*. And Falstaff, having out-

[30] *Dramatic Miscellanies*, I, 237, 238.

done himself with his glorious lion and a prince whose legitimacy is *now*, he says, established (as if there might have been some slight reason to doubt it before!) significantly changes the subject:

> Gallants, lads, boys, hearts of gold, all the titles of good fellowship come to you! What, shall we be merry? Shall we have a play extempore?
>
> PRINCE. Content—and the argument shall be thy running away.
>
> FALSTAFF. Ah, no more of that, Hal, an thou lovest me!

As Professor Waldock asked in *The Review of English Studies* some years ago, "What point would there be in such a reply . . . if Falstaff had had the laugh on them all along?" [31] He has extricated himself—"in spite of truth and conviction"—and we in the audience are glad of it. Yet Poins and Prince Hal were right; and for them Gadshill will be, as prophesied, "argument for a week, laughter for a month, and a good jest for ever."

It will be seen, if we look back, that the arguments of those who have denied that Falstaff was a coward are of many different sorts. For the most part, they are suggestive of the study rather than the playhouse. Some, indeed, are abstract, or even syllogistic, like Morgann's *We do not like cowards; we like Falstaff; therefore, Falstaff is not a coward.* Some, again, are based on inferences, sound enough, perhaps, in real life, but untrustworthy in the case of popular drama, as that a coward is unlikely to be found in the thick of the fighting. Often, it is as if the critics were determined to impose their own sense of naturalness on what, in the theater, is the more effective for being extreme—Falstaff's "incomprehensible" lying, for example. Yet Bradley himself perceived that "Shakespeare's comic world" was one of make-believe, "not merely as his tragic world is, but in a further sense—a world in which gross improbabilities are accepted with a smile. . . ." [32]

It remains possible, of course, that with this great character Shakespeare was not contented to work on a single level; so that at one instant we may be back with the Clowns of primitive drama (with Dericke, say, in *The Famous Victories*) and at another are not far from the amiable philosopher of the romantic critics. Thus, the soliloquy on honor seems to me something more than a very

---

[31] A. J. A. Waldock, "The Men in Buckram," *Review of English Studies*, XXIII (1947), 19.

[32] *Oxford Lectures on Poetry*, p. 270.

witty apology for the speaker's cowardice—though is it not that, as well? We read of an American actor whose fame is associated with this role:

> the shudder with which Hackett spoke the words about Honor, "Who hath it? he that-*died*-o'Wednesday," with its obvious revulsion from even the thought of death, was wonderfully expressive of *Falstaff's* animal relish of life, and also it was supremely comic.[33]

For the cowardice of Falstaff as a comic assumption gives added point to speech after speech, and to deprive the actors of it is to deprive them of a constant source of merriment. "Where," as John Bailey asked, "would be the humour of 'a plague of all cowards' if the speaker were a brave man? Where would be the fun of the 'plain tale' that put his preposterous boastings down if, as we are told, he never meant to be believed?"[34] I would not defend the farcical enormities which have been committed in Falstaff's name by unworthy comedians. Descriptions of the older stage business, whether at Gadshill or Shrewsbury, are sometimes far from edifying. But suppose, merely for the sake of argument, that Sir John *was* a coward—a fat, old, witty, boastful coward.

Early in the *Second Part of King Henry the Fourth*, he seeks to avoid a meeting with the Lord Chief Justice, attempts to hide, then feigns deafness. "Go pluck him by the elbow," the Justice tells his Servant, who does so. (Kittredge, I remember, used to describe this Servant as the Justice's "personal attendant," a "young lawyer," who "thought a lot of himself.") "Sir John!" And Falstaff, as if shocked: "What? A young knave, and begging? Is there not wars? . . . Doth not the King lack subjects?" and so on, all very humiliating to the young man. "You mistake me, sir," he says, but Falstaff continues—and goes too far.

> Why, sir, did I say you were an honest man? Setting my knighthood and my soldiership aside, I had lied in my throat if I had said so.
> SERVANT. I pray you, sir, then set your knighthood and your soldiership aside, and give me leave to tell you you lie in your throat if you say I am any other than an honest man.

[33] William Winter, *Shakespeare on the Stage: Third Series* (New York, 1916), p. 359.
[34] *Shakespeare* (London, New York, and Toronto, 1929), p. 128.

FALSTAFF. I give thee leave to tell me so? I lay aside that which
grows to me? If thou get'st any leave of me, hang me; if thou
tak'st leave, thou wert better be hang'd. You hunt counter.
Hence! avaunt!

Is it not the fact of timidity, here thinly disguised in bluster, which
makes the episode diverting? [35]

When the attempt to arrest Falstaff is resisted, a little later, his
own part in the ensuing scuffle is not easy to determine. As Professor Shaaber, the Variorum editor, notes, much is left to the
actors here; yet he adds, wisely, I think, "There is perhaps a hint
in the fact that almost every word Falstaff says is by way of putting
Bardolph up to active measures of defense." On the other hand, I
should allow Sir John a major share in the routing of Ancient Pistol,
in the Tavern Scene. Though Bardolph is at hand, once more, to
give assistance, his master seems to have put on a magnificent show
of belligerency, at the least; is reported to have hurt Pistol in the
shoulder and has to be quieted at last by Doll, who points out that
"the rascal's gone." Afterwards, we have speeches of purring self-
gratulation ("A rascal bragging slave! The rogue fled from me like
quicksilver"), as, to use Mr. Stoll's words, he "prolongs the precious
moment, unique and unparalleled in his experience, by continually
recurring to it." [36] And perhaps we remember (as we should) Sir
John's own description of his opponent earlier in the scene as "a
tame cheater. . . . You may stroke him as gently as a puppy greyhound. He'll not swagger with a Barbary hen if her feathers turn
back in any show of resistance."

Finally, I would suggest that even single lines and phrases may
take on an unexpected impressiveness for us if we return to the
earlier conception of the character: to a Falstaff of dexterous
evasions and miraculous escapes, lawless in his exaggerations, redoubtable only in repute, and the funnier for being fat and old
and a coward. So, in the theater, I have heard Ned Poins lay a
sudden emphasis upon two words, just before the Gadshill robbery: "Sirrah Jack, thy horse stands behind the hedge. When thou
need'st him, there thou shalt find him. Farewell and *stand fast*";
and their portentousness was of exactly the sort that Sir Toby

[35] Stoll brackets Falstaff's sidling off at this moment with his behaviour
towards Poins in *1 Henry IV*, II. iv, 131, an episode which seems to me
less clear in its implications (*Shakespeare Studies*, p. 421).

[36] *Ibid.*, p. 425.

Belch, sometimes, imparts to a phrase in Sir Andrew's letter: "Fare thee well, and *God have mercy upon one of our souls!*" I conceive, too, of a glint in Falstaff's eye, a certain morbid insistence in his voice, as, at another time, he dwells on the strength of the rebels.

> But tell me, Hal, art not thou horrible afeard? Thou being heir apparent, could the world pick thee out three such enemies again as that fiend Douglas, that spirit Percy, and that devil Glendower? Art thou not horribly afraid? Doth not thy blood thrill at it?

A veteran talking to a young soldier, you may say of the passage— and perhaps it is merely that. Just before Shrewsbury they are talking in a somewhat similar vein.

> FALSTAFF. Hal, if thou see me down in the battle and bestride me, so! 'Tis a point of friendship.

It is delivered with a flourish—almost as if in imagination he saw the Prince of Wales standing over and defending a gallant old soldier wounded (at any rate, *fallen*) in battle. Hal's quibbling reply gives him cold comfort: "Nothing but a Colossus can do thee that friendship. Say thy prayers, and farewell." And Falstaff: "I would 'twere bedtime, Hal, and all well."

The last instance I shall give is from a soliloquy, in which the Elizabethan actor, standing in the midst of his hearers, would have directly and familiarly addressed them. Falstaff speaks of Prince John, who does not appreciate him and cannot be made to laugh. No wonder, he says, for "this same young sober-blooded boy" does not drink as he should:

> There's never none of these demure boys come to any proof; for thin drink doth so over-cool their blood, and making many fish-meals, that they fall into a kind of male greensickness; and then, when they marry, they get wenches. They are generally fools and cowards—which some of us should be too, but for inflammation.

For an instant, the joke has become one between Falstaff and ourselves. He pauses after "cowards"; then, "which some of us" (Sir John himself, no less!) would certainly be too, except (triumphantly) for the effects of drinking sack! And who could accuse him of negligence in that regard? *You thought I was confessing, did you?*

I would not seem to attach an undue importance to these passages. They can be reconciled, each of them, with the Morgann Falstaff. "Would 'twere bedtime, Hal, and all well" is a sentiment which can be responded to by plenty of soldiers on a level quite different from that of comic cowardice. And the loss to the actor—though there is loss—will not be irreparable. On the other hand, it may be that the consensus among early readers and critics deserves more emphasis than I have given it. The burden of proof, as even Morgann recognized, rests upon those who deny cowardice. Samuel Johnson, as I said earlier, referred twice to Morgann's *Essay*. On the second occasion, when it is Malone who records the Doctor's words, they are splendidly comprehensive: "all he shd. say, was, that if Falstaff was not a coward, Shakespeare knew nothing of his art." [37]

[37] Boswell, *Life of Johnson*, iv, 515.

E. M. W. TILLYARD

On the Structure of Henry IV

In an article on *Structural Unity in the two Parts of "Henry IV"* R. A. Law maintains that Part Two is a new structure, an unpremeditated addition. I think so decidedly the other way that I shall treat the two parts as a single play (as Dover Wilson does in the *Fortunes of Falstaff*). Indeed Shakespeare almost goes out of his way to advertise the continuity by keeping the action patently incomplete at the end of the first part. In IV, iv the Archbishop of York is shown preparing for the rebellious action which is the main political theme of Part Two but which is almost irrelevant to Part One. In V, ii there is a probable reference forward to the second part. Here Worcester refuses to inform Hotspur of the king's generous consent to confine the battle to a duel between Hotspur and the Prince and of his generous offer of a

From *Shakespeare's History Plays*, by E. M. W. Tillyard, pp. 264–266. Copyright 1946 by The Macmillan Company and used with their permission. Title added by the Ed.

pardon to all the rebels. Worcester distrusts Henry and probably
without reason. Shakespeare was thinking ironically of John of
Lancaster's offer of pardon made to the other rebels in the second
part, which, though insincere, was trusted. And the first part ends
with Henry's sending Prince John and Westmoreland to deal with
Northumberland and the Archbishop; an action which is taken
up immediately in the second part. Finally, one of the most striking
anticipations, pointing to Shakespeare's having planned ahead with
much thought, is the talk between Falstaff and the Prince on
justice in the scene that first brings them in. The Prince has
slipped into the talk of robberies by moonlight an unpleasant reference to the gallows. Falstaff, not relishing it, seeks to turn the
conversation with

> And is not my hostess of the tavern a most sweet wench?

But the Prince turns the conversation back to the unpleasant
theme. Falstaff again turns the conversation; but the thought of
the gallows is too strong for him and he can't help asking,

> Shall there be gallows standing when thou art king? and resolu-
> tion thus fobbed as it is with the rusty curb of old father antic
> the law?

The Prince does not say no to this. But the questions are not answered till the end of the second part—indeed they cannot arise
again in the first part because the Prince is not yet king—but there
Resolution, or Falstaff and his gang, are indeed fobbed with the
rusty curb of the Lord Chief Justice or old father antic the law.

The reason why Law wishes to separate the two parts is that he
thinks their motives are different. According to him Part One
shows the struggle of the Prince and Hotspur culminating in the
Battle of Shrewsbury, while Part Two, in strong contrast, shows
the Prince in the background not fighting but fought over, as in
the Moralities, by the royal household and the Lord Chief Justice
on the one hand and by Falstaff, the epitome of the Seven Deadly
Sins, on the other. Law was right in seeing the Morality pattern
in Part Two, but wrong in not seeing it in Part One likewise. The
struggle between the Prince and Hotspur is subordinate to a larger
plan.

The structure of the two parts is indeed very similar. In the first
part the Prince (who, one knows, will soon be king) is tested in

the military or chivalric virtues. He has to choose, Morality-fashion, between Sloth or Vanity, to which he is drawn by his bad companions, and Chivalry, to which he is drawn by his father and his brothers. And he chooses Chivalry. The action is complicated by Hotspur and Falstaff, who stand for the excess and the defect of the military spirit, for honour exaggerated and dishonour. Thus the Prince, as well as being Magnificence in a Morality Play, is Aristotle's middle quality between two extremes. Such a combination would have been entirely natural to the Elizabethans, especially since it occurred in the second book of the *Fairy Queen*. Guyon is at once the Morality figure fought over by the Palmer and Mammon and the man who is shown the Aristotelian allegory of Excess Balance and Defect in Perissa Medina and Elissa. Near the end of the play the Prince ironically surrenders to Falstaff the credit of having killed Hotspur, thus leaving the world of arms and preparing for the motive of the second part. Here again he is tested, but in the civil virtues. He has to choose, Morality-fashion, between disorder or misrule, to which he is drawn by his bad companions, and Order or Justice (the supreme kingly virtue) to which he is drawn by his father and by his father's deputy the Lord Chief Justice. And he chooses Justice. As in the first part the Aristotelian motive occurs, but it is only touched on. After Falstaff has exchanged words with John of Lancaster about his captive Sir John Colevile, he remains on the stage to soliloquise. He calls John a "sober-blooded boy" and blames him for not drinking sack. John is thus cold-blooded and addicted to thin potations; Falstaff himself is warm-blooded and addicted to strong drink. The Prince is the mean, cold-blooded by inheritance but warmed "with excellent endeavour of drinking good and good store of fertile sherris." Temperamentally he strikes the balance between the parsimony of John and the extravagance of Falstaff. He does the same too in his practice of justice. The justice of John of Lancaster in his cold-blooded treatment of the rebels verges on rigour; Falstaff has no general standard of justice at all; Henry V uses his justice moderately in the way he treats his old companions—at least by Elizabethan standards.

M. A. SHAABER

The Unity of Henry IV

The fact that, in the last three or four years, two persuasive and influential critics have offered us interpretations of Shakespeare's *Henry IV* plays which assume that these plays form a unified whole invites us once more to consider this assumption. There is nothing new about it (it is at least as old as Dr. Johnson), but it has rarely been assumed so confidently or worked into so elaborate an interpretation. Since, however, as often as it has been made it has been questioned—among others, by Dr. J. Q. Adams, whose scholarly distinction and rare friendliness we commemorate—it seems desirable to ascertain whether or not Professor Wilson and Dr. Tillyard have been able to put it on a new or a firmer footing.

Professor Dover Wilson proclaimed the unity of the two plays in *The Fortunes of Falstaff* (1943), but without making much attempt to prove it. He says:

> (1) . . . Shakespeare must have kept his intentions for Part II steadily in mind all the time he was writing Part I, and (2) . . . Part II . . . is a continuation of the same play, which is no less incomplete without it than Part II is itself unintelligible without Part I. In any case, the unity and continuity of the two parts is a cardinal assumption of the following study. As we shall find, it is impossible otherwise to make sense of Falstaff's character, to say nothing of Prince Hal's [p. 4].

But in his edition of 1 *Henry IV* (1946) he offers some justification of his opinion:

> 1 *Henry IV* . . . is . . . patently only part of a whole, inasmuch as at its close all the strands of the plot are left with loose ends. [1] The rebels, Northumberland and Archbishop Scroop,

From *Joseph Quincy Adams Memorial Studies* (Washington, D.C., 1948), pp. 217–227. Reprinted by permission of the Folger Shakespeare Library and the author.

are still at large after the battle of Shrewsbury; and [2] the Archbishop is introduced and given a scene to himself in 4. 4 in order to prepare the audience for the expedition of Prince John in Part 2. [3] The relations of the Prince with his father, eased by the interview in 3. 2 and his brilliant conduct in battle, still await that final clarification which, as Elizabethan auditors acquainted with the merest outline of the life of Henry of Monmouth would know, belonged to the death-bed scene in the Jerusalem chamber. [4] Most striking of all perhaps is that stone of stumbling to modern interpreters, the soliloquy at the end of the second scene of Part 1, which looks forward not only to the coronation of Henry V but also to the rejection of Falstaff, neither of which occurs until the very end of Part 2. If Part 1 be an integral drama, and Part 2 a mere afterthought, the soliloquy is inexplicable . . . In short, the political and dynastic business of this history play, which is twofold, the defeat of the rebels and the repentance of the Prince including his reconciliation with his father, is only half through at the end of Part 1. . . . [5] Yet another indication of planning is the symbolic arrangement, which excludes the Lord Chief Justice from Part 1, though there are indications that he appeared early in the pre-Shakespearian version, restricts that part to the theme of the truant prince's return to Chivalry, and leaves the atonement with Justice, or the Rule of Law, as a leading motive for its sequel [p. x ff.].

Dr. E. M. W. Tillyard, in *Shakespeare's History Plays* (1944), argues for the unity of the two plays as follows:

[6] [Shakespeare keeps] the action patently incomplete at the end of the first part. [7] In IV, iv the Archbishop of York is shown preparing for the rebellious action which is the main political theme of Part Two but which is almost irrelevant to Part One. [8] In V, ii there is a probable reference forward to the second part. Here Worcester refuses to inform Hotspur of the king's generous consent to confine the battle to a duel between Hotspur and the Prince and of his generous offer of a pardon to all the rebels. Worcester distrusts Henry and probably without reason. Shakespeare was thinking ironically of John of Lancaster's offer of pardon made to the other rebels in the second part, which, though insincere, was trusted. . . . [9] Finally, one of the most striking anticipations, pointing to Shakespeare's having planned ahead with much thought, is the talk between Falstaff and the Prince on justice in the scene that first brings them in. . . .

"Shall there be gallows standing when thou art king? and reso-

lution thus fobbed as it is with the rusty curb of old father antic the law?"
The Prince does not say no to this. But the questions are not answered till the end of the second part . . . there Resolution, or Falstaff and his gang, are indeed fobbed with the rusty curb of the Lord Chief Justice or old father antic the law [p. 264 ff.].

It is apparent that 1 and 6, 2 and 7 are the same arguments and that 4 and 9 come to almost the same thing. Except for 8, which I think need not be taken seriously, I shall discuss them seriatim.

[1, 6] The incompleteness assumed by both interpreters is not apparent to me. Of course, the reign of Henry IV is incomplete; as long as Shakespeare chose to make the Battle of Shrewsbury the climax of his play it could not be otherwise. The rebels, to be sure, are not completely quelled, but then they never are. The announcement that they have been thoroughly scotched a moment before Henry IV dies is an invention of Shakespeare's intended, I think, to add a poignant irony to the king's death. But the inheritors of their quarrel rise up against Henry V at the beginning of his reign, and indeed it is the argument of Dr. Tillyard's book that the rebel cause draws its motive from the wrong done Richard II, a wrong which plagues Henry IV and his successors all their lives and is not expiated till the end of the Wars of the Roses. So far as the play is incomplete, it is incomplete because history is an endless chain, and Shakespeare is dramatizing history. And if the theme of 1 Henry IV is what Dr. Tillyard says it is, I do not understand how the play can be called incomplete.

In the first part [he says] the Prince . . . is tested in the military or chivalric virtues. He has to choose, Morality-fashion, between Sloth or Vanity, to which he is drawn by his bad companions, and Chivalry, to which he is drawn by his father and his brothers. And he chooses Chivalry.[1]

[1] Op. cit., p. 265. I accept this statement of Dr. Tillyard's so as to keep the discussion on the unity of the two plays, but I have uncomfortable misgivings about it. It could equally well be argued that the prince is never really tempted by Sloth and Vanity. He tolerates them; he plays the madcap in their company; but he is never deceived by them. "I know you all," he says, and why may we not take him at his word? Hal does not *choose* Chivalry; he *is* Chivalry from the beginning to the end of the play. There is no visible struggle. The conflict is not between his better and his worser nature, but between his real nature and the common opinion of him. These are not precisely the terms I would choose to

Indeed he does, unequivocally and completely. Fully reconciled
with his father, he seems to have set the issue between them completely at rest. I cannot think what need have or could have been
added to show that Hal was indeed the true prince.

[2, 7] 1 *Henry IV*, IV, iv is very commonly pointed out as a
reason for taking the two plays as a unit. It has even been said that
this appearance of the archbishop "has no meaning unless his
conspiracy was to follow." [2] On the contrary, the scene has an obvious meaning in the dramatic scheme of 1 *Henry IV* and is not
"almost irrelevant" to it. Its business is to foreshadow the outcome
of the Battle of Shrewsbury. There the rebels are to meet with a
decisive check, and Shakespeare, after his usual fashion, anticipates
what is to come. This scene signifies that the rebel cause is in a
bad way indeed if one of its ringleaders has grave misgivings about
it. The same thing might have been, and is, signified otherwise, but
this is by no means the only place where Shakespeare, even near
the end of a play, has brought forward a new character to serve
some purpose of the moment and dismissed him as soon as his
work was done. If 1 *Henry IV* had never had a sequel, Shakespeare,
judged by his practice elsewhere, might well have put this scene
into his play.

[3, 4, 9] The idea that the relations of the prince and the king,
"eased by the interview in 3. 2 and his brilliant conduct in battle,"
still await "final clarification" is adroitly stated. Much virtue in
eased. Is there really the slightest hint in 1 *Henry IV* that the king
and the prince are not completely and triumphantly reconciled?
Does "Thou hast redeem'd thy lost opinion" (V, iv, 47) really
mean "I feel a bit easier about you than I did before, but the final
showdown is still to come"? I cannot think that the impression
left by 1 *Henry IV* is anything but that of a complete vindication
of the prince in his father's eyes. To be sure, in 2 *Henry IV* we find
him as much misunderstood as ever, but to interpret the first part
by the second is what Professor Wilson himself objects to as "the
fallacy of omniscience, that is, of treating a play like a historical

---

describe the play, but they seem to me to correspond with Shakespeare's
text at least as well as Dr. Tillyard's interpretation. It is amazing how
small a place is allowed Hotspur in this interpretation. Dr. Tillyard is
right in saying that Hotspur is not the hero of the play, but how can one
ignore the fact that his combat with the prince is the climax?

[2] *Shakespeare, Works* (Eversley ed., 1899), vi, 253 ff.

document and collecting evidence in support of a particular reading of character or situation from any point of the text without regard to its relation to the rest." [3] If one does not fall into this fallacy, there is no reason whatever for supposing that the end of 1 *Henry IV* is anything but an end. The prince has broken through the clouds "that did seem to strangle him," has falsified men's hopes; the premises from which the play took its start have been carried to a conclusion.

In another sense, however, Professor Wilson and Dr. Tillyard have a point here. There is no doubt that, from the first, Shakespeare knew that the scene at the death-bed of Henry IV and the rejection of Falstaff were parts of the legend of Prince Hal with high dramatic possibilities. But this is really no argument that 2 *Henry IV* was conceived and planned with its predecessor. No one thinks that, as he wrote 1 *Henry IV*, Shakespeare did not have a sequel in mind—a sequel approximately like the play we know as *Henry V*. I have no notion how clearly Shakespeare had devised a scheme for this sequel while at work on 1 *Henry IV*, but, whether clear or highly nebulous, his plan could easily have included the idea of beginning with the rejection of Falstaff or even with the death of Henry IV. The coronation would be a natural starting-place for a history of the reign of Henry V, especially when it is immediately preceded by one highly dramatic episode and followed by another. Therefore, since Shakespeare certainly had a play on Henry V in mind when he wrote 1 *Henry IV*, the anticipations in the latter of the death of Henry IV and the rejection of Falstaff cannot be used to prove that he also had 2 *Henry IV* in mind, for these episodes might appropriately have begun the projected *Henry V*. If 2 *Henry IV* is an unpremeditated sequel, Shakespeare of course transferred them to the new play he was constrained to fabricate.

[5] I cannot say much against Professor Wilson's idea that the appearance of the Chief Justice in 2 *Henry IV* is a proof of a unified plan for both plays, for I do not know how an idea of this kind can be proved or disproved. Professor Wilson thinks that the late appearance of the Chief Justice must be the result of planning; I think it could equally well be the result of a search for new material to make a play not contemplated until Falstaff became a tremendous hit. Thought is free, and neither of us can adduce real

[3] *The Fortunes of Falstaff*, p. 3 ff.

evidence to support his point of view. I doubt that Professor Wilson would rest his case on this argument alone and I would not think that I had disposed of his case if I could squelch it utterly.

Besides imputing weakness to the arguments in favor of a unified plan, I submit that there are other reasons for viewing the idea skeptically. The first is the similarity of the structure of the two plays. Structurally 2 *Henry IV* is almost a carbon copy of the first play. According to the scene-division of modern editions, there is exactly the same number of scenes in both plays; according to that of the folio, there are three more in the first part. By either count the number of scenes is exactly the same in the first, second, and last acts. What is more impressive, the sequence of scenes developing the historical plot and that of the comic scenes is almost exactly the same. The following table shows the order of the historical and the comic scenes in both plays.

	Part 1	Part 2		Part 1	Part 2
I, i	H	H	IV, i	H	H
I, ii	C	C	IV, ii	C	H
I, iii	H	H	IV, iii	H	C
II, i	C	C	IV, iv	H	H
II, ii	C	(H), C	IV, v		H
II, iii	H	H	V, i	H, C	C
II, iv	C	C	V, ii	H	H
III, i	H	H	V, iii	H, C	C
III, ii	H	C	V, iv	H, C	C
III, iii	C		V, v	H	H, C

In the first two acts the correspondences are remarkably close. I, iii represents a conference of the rebels in both plays; II, iii is a domestic scene among the Percies; II, iv is a tavern scene. The last is, I think, especially significant. In the third act the plan is, in a very general way, the same (historical matter followed by a Falstaff scene), but in 2 *Henry IV* the comic material outweighs the historical. In the fourth act the correspondence is perhaps closer than the table shows, for in 2 *Henry IV* there are really only two scenes (corresponding to i–iii and iv–v). In both plays the act is devoted to the historical plot except for one irruption on the part of Falstaff. There are real divergences in the fifth act. In 1 *Henry IV* the historical and the comic material are interwoven; in 2 *Henry IV* they are separated until the last scene. The question is, then, would Shakespeare be more likely to plan the plays in this fashion if he were working out, in a single fit of creation, a play of ten acts or if, after 1 *Henry IV* proved a resounding success, he aimed at repeating it? To me the latter view is the more probable.

Another reason for hesitating to see the two plays as one is, I think, the fact that in the second the clock is turned back most flagrantly. At the end of 1 *Henry IV* the king and the prince are *en rapport* and united against the Welsh; in 2 *Henry IV* we find them estranged all over again so that they must be reconciled a second time. No new cause of misunderstanding is shown; the situation simply reverts to what it was in the beginning. Shakespeare sets the clock back adroitly, but set it back he does. I know that Professor Wilson will have it otherwise: the king and the prince are only tentatively reconciled at the end of 1 *Henry IV*; their relations are only "eased." I can only repeat what I have said above, that I defy a candid reader to detect any flaws in the understanding between them as it is presented at the end of 1 *Henry IV*. What becomes of the triumphant close of the play if the king and the prince are still somewhat at odds? How could this imperfect sympathy possibly be acted? Thus the question arises, if Shakespeare planned both plays as a whole, would he have planned to bring the king and the prince together, separate them covertly, and then bring them together once more? Would he have invented the reconciliation at the Battle of Shrewsbury, about which *The Famous Victories* and Holinshed are silent, knowing that there was a second reconciliation to come later? Or is it more likely that he would have done what he did because the immoderate popularity of 1 *Henry IV* forced him to write an unpremeditated sequel for which he needed the death-bed scene as climax? It is hard for me to believe that an experienced playwright who from the first contemplated making the death-bed scene the climax of his picture of the relations of father and son would have anticipated their reconciliation in his version of the Battle of Shrewsbury and the events leading up to it.

Finally, the question of the unity of *Henry IV* raises larger questions about cyclical plays. Professor Wilson sees the implications of his argument clearly and faces them boldly. "Part II," he says, "was written to be played immediately, or at not more than

twenty-four hours' interval, after Part I." [4] And indeed his interpretation is highly esoteric unless the plays were so performed.
What is the likelihood that they were?

So far as I know, there are no recorded performances of the two
plays on the same day or on successive days before the twentieth
century.[5] In the absence of contemporary records of performances
of Shakespeare, we have nothing to judge by but Henslowe's *
records. They are not decisive. Henslowe records a number of performances of the two parts of *Tamburlaine* on successive days,[6] a
few more of a two-part *Hercules* [7] and a two-part *Tamar Cam*,[8] and
one of a two-part *Seaser*.[9] But at the same time he also records independent performances of both parts of the same plays. We can
infer very little from these facts even if we assume that the Chamberlain's men would always do just what Henslowe's companies
did. 1 and 2 *Henry IV* may have been acted both successively and
separately in Shakespeare's day.

Perhaps the practice of other playwrights will help us to estimate
the likelihood of Shakespeare's having planned *Henry IV* as a unit.
In the sixteenth and seventeenth centuries, I cannot find a real
example of an integrated cycle of plays, of two or more plays which
must be considered as one if their import is to be grasped.[10] I find
a number of examples of linked plays and of plays on contiguous
subjects, but none of a cycle like Professor Wilson's version of
Henry IV. The nearest thing would seem to be, strangely enough,
Heywood's *Iron Age*, in which the story of the siege of Troy (plus
other matter) is divided between the two parts as if the audience
were expected to follow it from the beginning, but to speak of the
unity of so naïve a cycle is a little absurd. *The Conquest of Granada*

[4] *The Fortunes of Falstaff*, p. 91.
[5] Both parts may have been performed at court during the holiday
season of 1612–1613; at least two plays for which the King's men were
rewarded—*The Hotspur* and *Sir John Falstaffe*—have been so identified
(see Chambers, *The Elizabethan Stage*, iv, 180). But there is nothing to
show that they were acted on successive nights.
* Philip Henslowe (d. 1616), a theatrical manager. Ed.
[6] *Henslowe's Diary*, ed. Greg. i, 21–42.
[7] *Ibid.*, i, 24–7.
[8] *Ibid.*, i, 42.
[9] *Ibid.*, i, 24.
[10] I have not considered a few Cavalier two-part plays because I think
they must be quite outside any tradition which may throw light on
Shakespeare's practice.

almost answers the specifications. The two parts are closely integrated; there is no final resolution of anything at the end of the
first and some familiarity with the first is demanded to understand
the second. But the fact remains that both parts were often played
independently,[11] apparently without baffling audiences or sending
them home unsatisfied.*

It would seem then that, if *Henry IV* is a fully integrated unit,
it is virtually unique. What Shakespeare did no other playwright
of his time attempted. Obviously Shakespeare is by no means de-
barred from venturing upon untrodden ground and the singularity
of such a scheme hardly disproves it. But one may still ask what
Shakespeare would have gained by it, what advantage a highly integrated scheme gave him in attracting audiences to the theater.
From a purely practical point of view, surely none at all; successive
performances, separated by an interval of not more than twenty-
four hours, require a degree of cooperation of the audience difficult
to obtain. For obviously such a cycle of plays can achieve its full
effect only so far as the same audience attends both performances.
According to Professor Wilson, any spectator who sees *1 Henry IV*
alone goes away unsatisfied and any one who sees *2 Henry IV* alone
cannot understand it. Presumably such an outcome must be fore-
stalled. But Professor Wilson cannot suppose that, in the sixteenth
century, every member of the audience who saw *1 Henry IV* on
Monday was able, even if willing, to come back on Tuesday to see
the second part. Or that on Tuesday auditors who could not show
that they had seen the first part on Monday were turned away from
the door. The practical difficulties of achieving what Professor Wilson requires are very great.

So great, indeed, that I cannot imagine an experienced playwright, in his right wits, doing anything of the kind. I doubt that
such a playwright would ever think of writing a play which, by
itself, had not sufficient dramatic interest to stand on its own legs,
which would be unintelligible without some other play which the
audience may not see or have seen, which would not fully reward
any audience that happened to gather to see it. This is not to say
that there are no links between the two parts of *Henry IV* or that

[11] Dryden, *Works* (Nonesuch ed., 1932), iii, 13.
* Note 12, omitted here, lists a number of two-part plays of the sixteenth and seventeenth centuries each part of which, Professor Shaaber
contends, can stand as an adequate dramatic unit. Ed.

the experience of seeing 2 *Henry IV* is not the richer for having seen the first part. It is only to say that I cannot square what I think a knowledgeable playwright would do in writing two linked plays with Professor Wilson's description of *Henry IV*, and that therefore I am suspicious of his description. The unity which he attributes to the two plays seems to me to be a theatrical impossibility.[13]

We must conclude, I think, that the unity of the *Henry IV* plays is an assumption which Professor Wilson and Dr. Tillyard have not proved and which implies some things difficult to believe. Accordingly, interpretations of the plays based on their assumptions cannot win a hearty assent.

One word more. I hope I do Professor Wilson and Dr. Tillyard no injustice by inferring that when they defend the unity of *Henry IV* they think they are vindicating Shakespeare's art, they think that a unified *Henry IV* is artistically superior to two plays linked by catch-as-catch-can methods. To that assumption I would demur. The logic of a play is no necessary cause of its greatness and at most but a minor cause. According to Professor Wilson, it is impossible to make sense of Falstaff's character or of the prince's unless we look at the two plays as a unified whole. Let us suppose that he is right. What do we gain? Something which increases or intensifies our enjoyment of Falstaff's antics or the prince's exploits as we watch a performance of the play? I think not. Making sense of the play, rationalizing its diversity is an *ex post facto* operation; it cannot even begin before all the materials which it fits into rational patterns have been unfolded. It seems to me therefore largely a work of supererogation, with some interest of its own but no great importance to the understanding or the enjoyment of drama. Assuming it to be all-important is the capital fallacy of Professor Wilson's and Dr. Tillyard's discussions of the play. What worries

[13] The structure which Professor Wilson attributes to the two plays is, I suspect, equally impossible. According to him (*1 Henry IV*, p. xi ff.), the normal dramatic curve of a five-act Shakespearian play here encompasses ten acts. Now the structure of an effective play presses the spectator forward at an accelerating pace till his interest is carried to the climax and is satisfied by the dénouement. There are minor relaxations of the tension along the way, but there can be no real interruption of this continuous and progressive interest without disastrous results. How is it possible to send him home overnight midway in this continuous and progressive development without seriously impairing its effect? What experienced playwright would ever dream of doing such a thing?

234 M. A. SHAABER

them seems to me largely beside the point. "Part II is itself unintelligible without Part I," says Professor Wilson. Who asks for intelligibility—the kind of intelligibility that Part I can confer on
Part II—in a play? "The soliloquy is inexplicable." Who asks to
have it explained? "Falstaff's false claim to the *spolia opima* of
Harry Hotspur . . . [is] the key to his character in Part 2." [14]
Who pays his penny at the door to have keys to character put in
his hand? "Once its unity is accepted . . . , it will stand revealed
as one of the greatest of dramatic masterpieces." [15] Unity—Professor Wilson's kind of unity—is the test of a masterpiece? It cannot
be. For two hundred years captious critics have been trying to make
sense of Falstaff's hyperbolical account of the action on Gadshill,
trying to make it acceptable to our minds. They have not succeeded. But the scene remains ineffable comedy just the same; in
other words, whether the mind can accept it has very little to do
with the matter. Sense is only sense; it is not drama. Critics who
put so heavy an emphasis on it are barking up the wrong tree. What
happens in Shakespeare's plays (like what happens in human life)
sometimes defies explanation, especially easy explanation, but if
this fact is of any importance to the profound and lasting impressions that the plays make it is because our interest is quickened and
our impressions heightened, as in life itself, by what is not trans-
parently clear. Explain away the puzzles, the incongruities, the
diversities and you take away some of the amazement, the awe, the
sense of the complexity and the inscrutability of life which they
excite. We do not need to impose an airtight logical scheme on
Shakespeare's plays to justify them artistically; we come much
closer to the radiant core of their interest by other avenues of
approach.

[14] *1 Henry IV*, p. x f.
[15] *Ibid.*, p. xiii.

MADELEINE DORAN

Imagery in Richard II and in Henry IV †

It is a commonplace that the development of Shakespeare's style is away from verbal ingenuity and exuberance for their own sake and towards concentrated expression under control for dramatic ends. What I shall have to say here is nothing very new in itself, but it may be said in such a way as to give new significance to an old subject. I shall be concerned only with imagery, and with that only in two plays which come at crucial stages in Shakespeare's poetic and dramatic growth: *Richard II* about 1595, at the end of his "experimental" years, and *1 Henry IV* a year or two later, when he has unmistakably attained his majority. Most of the work on Shakespeare's imagery has had to do with its content and its distribution. But the quality of an image—its fabric and structure and relation to its immediate context—is also interesting and may, as is recognized, be important in revealing something of the poetic process. Much may yet be done in the way of examining Shakespeare's images from this intensive point of view.

On reading the First Part of *Henry IV* immediately after *Richard II* one is struck, along with evidences of greater maturity in other matters, by the difference in the handling of the images. I shall begin with a general statement which will obviously need qualification and if pushed too far will distort the picture, but

From *Modern Language Review*, XXXVII (April 1942), 113–122. Reprinted by permission of the Modern Humanities Research Association and the author. Footnotes have been renumbered.

† It will be evident in this paper how much I owe to the rather pervasive influence in our time of I. A. Richards and William Empson. But I wish to acknowledge a more specific debt to E. M. W. Tillyard's profoundly stimulating book, *Poetry Direct and Oblique*, London, 1934. Some of the terms I use (*directness, statement, obliquity*) will be recognized as coming from him. Since it is the point of view of the book as a whole that has been important to me, I can give references to particular pages only in a few instances.

which, for convenience, has nevertheless to be made at the outset. It may be said that the images in *Richard II* tend to be direct or explicit, complete, correspondent, point by point, to the idea symbolized, and separate one from another; whereas the images in 1 *Henry IV* tend to be richer in implicit suggestion and in ambiguity, not fully developed, fluid in outline and fused with one another.

These qualities will be evident in the following illustrations:

> RICHARD. I have been studying how I may compare
> This prison where I live unto the world:
> And for because the world is populous
> And here is not a creature but myself,
> I cannot do it; yet I'll hammer it out.
> My brain I'll prove the female to my soul,
> My soul the father; and these two beget
> A generation of still-breeding thoughts,
> And these same thoughts people this little world,
> In humours like the people of this world,
> For no thought is contented. The better sort,
> As thoughts of things divine, are intermix'd
> With scruples and do set the word itself
> Against the word:
> As thus, 'Come, little ones,' and then again,
> 'It is as hard to come as for a camel
> To thread the postern of a small needle's eye.'
> Thoughts tending to ambition, they do plot
> Unlikely wonders; how these vain weak nails
> May tear a passage through the flinty ribs
> Of this hard world, my ragged prison walls,
> And, for they cannot, die in their own pride.
> Thoughts tending to content flatter themselves
> That they are not the first of fortune's slaves,
> Nor shall not be the last; like silly beggars
> Who sitting in the stocks refuge their shame,
> That many have and others must sit there;
> And in this thought they find a kind of ease,
> Bearing their own misfortunes on the back
> Of such as have before endured the like.

Thus play I in one person many people,
And none contented.   (*Richard II*, v, v, 1–32)

Except for the compact and allusive "do set the word itself Against
the word," etc. (ll. 11–13), which at once strikes one because it
is so unlike the style of the rest of the play, the passage is explicit
throughout. Notice the completeness of the image on the peopling
of the world with thoughts, and with the equation of terms—brain
to mother, soul to father, thoughts to children with all varieties of
temperament who will in turn grow up to breed more of their kind,
equally discontented. And then the discontented thoughts are
enumerated one by one, each equated with an image more or less
fully worked out. In the remainder of the speech, not quoted,
it will be recalled how extensively treated is Richard's conceit of
himself as a clock. With such a subject, requiring a listing of
ideas, the separation of the images is perhaps not as indicative as
in some other places. All of Richard's long speeches tend to show
this succession of separate images [1] and it may be objected that
from the speeches of a character so specially conceived as is Richard we have no right to draw too general conclusions about Shakespeare's style. To this point I shall return later. But it may be
noted here that the qualities I have been remarking on in the
passage quoted occur generally in the speeches of other characters
throughout the play, though Richard's long speeches afford the best
examples to illustrate the presence of all of them in any one place. [2]
Now consider this passage from *1 Henry IV*:

The skipping King, he ambled up and down
With shallow jesters and rash bavin wits,
Soon kindled and soon burnt; carded his state;

[1] See III, ii, 144–56; III, iii, 143–71; the speeches in the deposition scene,
IV, 1.

[2] For other noteworthy examples of fully worked out images see the
latter half of Bolingbroke's speech in III, iii (ll. 54–67), where he first
compares the meeting of himself and Richard to the meeting of fire and
water, and then compares Richard's appearance to that of the sun; also
the Queen's and Bushy's talk about her premonition of sorrow (II, ii),
where Bushy compares her emotionally distorted visions to the view of
a "perspective," and where the comparison of her premonitions to a child
she is about to be delivered of runs throughout the whole episode.

> Mingled his royalty with cap'ring fools;
> Had his great name profaned with their scorns
> And gave his countenance, against his name,
> To laugh at gibing boys and stand the push
> Of every beardless vain comparative;
> Grew a companion to the common streets,
> Enfeoff'd himself to popularity;
> That, being daily swallowed by men's eyes,
> They surfeited with honey and began
> To loathe the taste of sweetness, whereof a little
> More than a little is by much too much.
> So, when he had occasion to be seen,
> He was but as the cuckoo is in June,
> Heard, not regarded—seen, but with such eyes
> As, sick and blunted with community,
> Afford no extraordinary gaze,
> Such as is bent on sunlike majesty
> When it shines seldom in admiring eyes;
> But rather drows'd and hung their eyelids down,
> Slept in his face, and rend'red such aspect
> As cloudy men use to their adversaries,
> Being with his presence glutted, gorg'd, and full.
>
> (III, ii, 60–84)

Notice the rapid succession of images, the quick suggestion rather than elaboration in such compact and elliptical lines as "To laugh at gibing boys . . ." (ll. 66–67) and "Enfeoff'd himself to popularity" (l. 69), the fusion of one image with another: the skipping and capering with the quick burning of faggots ("rash bavin") and with the adulteration suggested by carding; the enfeoffment with the idea of surfeit (itself boldly linked with eyes), it in turn with the common sight of the cuckoo in June and with the drowsiness of men in constant sunshine, and this latter image shifting ground with "cloudy men." In contrast to the way in which the firm outlines of the images in Richard's speech hold the mind within certain limits set by the close equation of idea and image, the rapidity, complexity, and fluidity of the images in Henry's speech help (as well as their substance) to increase their obliquity. Fewer doors are closed.

It is obvious that the interweaving of images such as one finds in

the following speech of the Duchess of Gloucester is not the same
thing as the fusion in the speech from *Henry IV* just quoted:

> Edward's seven sons, whereof thyself art one,
> Were as seven vials of his sacred blood,
> Or seven fair branches springing from one root:
> Some of those seven are dried by nature's course,
> Some of those branches by the Destinies cut;
> But Thomas, my dear lord, my life, my Gloucester,
> One vial full of Edward's sacred blood,
> One flourishing branch of his most royal root,
> Is crack'd, and all the precious liquor spilt,
> Is hack'd down, and his summer leaves all faded,
> By envy's hand and murder's bloody axe.
>
> (*Richard II*, I, ii, 11–21)

The vials and the branches retain their distinctness, and their relation to the idea is rather tediously explored. Again, take a genuinely
complex figure from *Richard II*:

> for within the hollow crown
> That rounds the mortal temples of a king
> Keeps Death his court, and there the antic sits,
> Scoffing his state and grinning at his pomp,
> Allowing him a breath, a little scene,
> To monarchize, be fear'd and kill with looks,
> Infusing him with self and vain conceit,
> As if this flesh which walls about our life
> Were brass impregnable, and humour'd thus
> Comes at last and with a little pin
> Bores through his castle wall, and farewell king!
>
> (III, ii, 160–70)

"Death" hesitates ambiguously in "Keeps Death his court" between Death as a ruler holding court and Death as a jester holding
the real power in the king's court, then shifts certainly to "Death
the antic" (still *within* the hollow crown), and then shifts again to
a borer from without. Set this passage against one from *Henry IV*:

> Those opposed eyes
> Which, like the meteors of a troubled heaven,

> All of one nature, of one substance bred,
> Did lately meet in the intestine shock
> And furious close of civil butchery,
> Shall now in mutual well-beseeming ranks
> March all one way and be no more oppos'd
> Against acquaintance, kindred, and allies.   (i, i, 9–16)

Here the fusion of images results in a syntactical boldness seldom found in *Richard II*. Moreover, for all the complexity of structure in the passage on Death, the images are fully explicatory; whereas in the passage from *Henry IV* the meanings of "opposed eyes" and "meteors of a troubled heaven" are almost wholly implicit.

The differences observed in the passages already quoted are exhibited in certain other ways, namely, in respect to similes, allegorically handled metaphor, and words retaining both a literal and a figurative meaning.

My first impression was that similes were more common in *Richard II* than in *Henry IV*. In a simile, stated as an equation, there is, at least formally, no fusion of idea and image. A closer examination of the two plays does not, in point of fact, bear out my first impression of greater frequency of similes in *Richard II*. But numerical difference is not so important as the character of the similes themselves, and it is true that in *Henry IV* there are fewer fully extended similes of the type here illustrated from *Richard II*:

> See, see, King Richard doth himself appear,
> As doth the blushing discontented sun
> From out the fiery portal of the east,
> When he perceives the envious clouds are bent
> To dim his glory and to stain the track
> Of his bright passage to the occident.   (iii, iii, 62–7) [3]

Two examples of a similar kind in *Henry IV* occur in set speeches, and two occur in a passage where a scene is being vividly described.[4]

[3] Similar extended similes in *Richard II* occur at ii, ii, 16–24; iii, ii, 6–11; iv, i, 181–89; v, i, 29–34; v, ii, 23–28.

[4] (1) Prince Hal's soliloquy (i, ii) and Glendower's courtly promise to Mortimer of a song from his daughter (iii, i, 213–19); (2) Vernon's comparison of Prince Hal mounting his horse to Mercury or an angel mounting Pegasus, and Hotspur's comparison of the coming of the king's forces to sacrifices to the maid of war, etc. (iv, i, 104–10, 113–17).

But most of the similes in *Henry IV* are brief and colloquial: they are the "unsavoury similes" applied by Hal and Falstaff to one another; the homely comparisons in the talk of Falstaff and his companions (skin like an old lady's loose gown, withered like an old apple John, roaring like a bullcalf, ragged as Lazarus, vigilant as a cat to steal cream, dank as a dog, stung like a tench); the quick, vivid figures in Hotspur's overflowing speech (fresh as a bridegroom, perfumed like a milliner, tedious as a tired horse or a railing wife, worse than a smoky house). It is characteristic of the style of the play that Hotspur's objection to Kate's swearing (III, i, 245–253), which begins with a simile, "Heart, you swear like a comfitmaker's wife" (itself by no means a simple statement), leads into an image that embodies a whole nest of subsidiary images, complex and confused:

> And givest such sarcenet surety for thy oaths
> As if thou ne'er walk'st further than Finsbury.
> Swear me, Kate, like a lady as thou art,
> A good mouth-filling oath; and leave 'in sooth'
> And such protest of pepper gingerbread
> To velvet guards and Sunday citizens.

It is surely not insignificant that one finds allegorical use of metaphor only in *Richard II*, not in *Henry IV*. Allegory is sustained metaphor.[5] One expects it to have a definite core of statement, of clear correspondence between figure and idea, with however much peripheral suggestion it may be enriched. The little allegory of the garden scene (III, iv), in its exact correspondence of figure and idea, point by point, is explicit and little else. The only places where it achieves obliquity are in the implicit allusion in "our sea-walled garden" (l. 43) to John of Gaunt's speech, and in the allusion to Eden and the fall of man in the Queen's address to the Gardener as Adam (ll. 72–80). In the latter allusion a profounder meaning is suggested than is stated.

In *Henry IV* there are a number of single words which, together with a figurative meaning, retain their literal meaning and greatly enrich the context by this ambiguity. A good example is *balk'd* in Henry's statement that

[5] See Tillyard's Chapter IV, "Some Terms Discussed," especially pp. 57–8, 60–2.

> Ten thousand bold Scots, two-and-twenty knights
> Balk'd in their own blood did Sir Walter see
> On Holmedon's plains.   (i, i, 68–70)

Professor Kittredge (in his notes to the play) defines a *balk* as "a ridge between two furrows." Hence, the statement means literally that the bodies are "piled up in ridges and soaked in blood"; but it also means that the Scots have been thwarted and defeated. The more immediately apprehended figurative meaning is deepened and modified by the force of the literal meaning. Other words in the play which get a similar re-enforcement from two layers of meaning are *malevolent* (i, i, 97), *countenance* (i, ii, 25), *baffle* (i, ii, 88), *frontier* (i, iii, 19), *nettled* (i, iii, 239), *bombast* (ii, iv, 291), *teeming* (iii, i, 28), *bootless* (iii, i, 67), *common-hackney'd* (iii, ii, 40), 'stain'd nobility' (v, iv, 12). This use of words is not the same thing as the play on John of Gaunt's name in *Richard II* (ii, i, 73–84 and 115), although it springs, of course, from the same alertness to the suggestive power of words. In the passage in *Richard II*, the meanings are all made explicit; in *Henry IV*, they are left implicit, without statement, and often without special emphasis. Moreover, the use in question is not the same thing as an implied pun, for in the former the meanings are overlaid and mutually enriching, in the latter generally disparate and incongruous. In a really good pun, of course, the obvious incongruity may cover a deeper congruity, as in Falstaff's remark to Prince Hal, who finds a bottle of sack in Falstaff's pistol case, "There's that will sack a city." But in the use under discussion in the words from *Henry IV*, there is no incongruity.

Words used with this special re-enforcement of meaning are rarer in *Richard II*. An example is *down* in Richard's great climactic speech when he surrenders to Bolingbroke:

> Down, down I come; like glistering Phaethon,
> Wanting the manage of unruly jades.
> In the base court? Base court, where kings grow base,
> To come at traitors' calls and do them grace.
> In the base court? Come down? Down, court! down, king!
> For night-owls shriek where mounting larks should sing.
> (iii, iii, 178–83)

But even here, the secondary meaning of *down* is made explicit, and *base* is played upon as Gaunt's name is played upon.[6]

Bearing in mind Coleridge's distinction between *fancy* as "the aggregative and associative power" and *imagination* as "the shaping and modifying power" or "the fusing power," * one is tempted to call the images from *Richard II* so far given fanciful, and those from *Henry IV* imaginative. One need not commit oneself to Coleridge's theory of faculty psychology to find the terms useful as descriptive of differences of effect, by whatever mental operation produced. But the matter is too complex to allow of such a simple distinction. A speech such as the Queen's at the sight of Richard coming on his way to the Tower (v, i, 7–15) is an aggregate of separate images, yet at least two of them, "My fair rose" and "the model where old Troy did stand" are imaginative in their evocation of meanings not stated. Moreover, Richard *is* the rose; the two terms have coalesced and mutually modify one another, *Richard* contributing all that we have seen throughout the play of his fresh colouring, youth, and charm, the *rose* bringing in a whole aura of associations from experience and literature—colour, freshness, fragrance, beauty, youth, sensuous pleasure, love, evanescence, the *carpe diem* ** theme. A passage of similar structure is Gaunt's speech on England (II, i, especially ll. 40–59), where, though the rapidly succeeding images (throne, scepter'd isle, seat of Mars, Eden, fortress, little world, precious stone, nurse, teeming womb) are not fused, they are individually more or less rich in suggestion and the whole speech is intense with feeling. However, I do not wish to raise an issue over terms or make the discussion as complex as their just application would entail. I have approached the matter from a somewhat different point of view and have found a different set of terms to be helpful: distinct and fused, explicit and implicit, extended and quickly suggested, and so on. Briefly, the differences in the handling of the images so far exhibited are the differences between enunciation and suggestion.[7]

---

* See *verge* and *waste*, examples of effective ambiguity, in II, i, 100–15.

* See Chapters XII–XIII of Coleridge's *Biographia Literaria*. Ed.

** See Horace, *Odes*, I. xi. 8: "*carpe diem, quam minimum credula postero*": enjoy today, trust little to tomorrow. Ed.

[7] Tillyard (op. cit., p. 124) uses these two terms in discussing Shirley's "The glories of our blood and state."

The examples have been carefully selected, of course, to make the point, and, although they are typical, there are many exceptions. Not all the images in *Richard II* are extended, separate, and enunciatory, and not all in *Henry IV* are brief, fused, and more implicit than explicit. It seems to me significant, however, that there are more exceptions in *Richard II* than in *Henry IV*. This is what one would expect if the difference is a sign, not just of the differences between subject-matter and characters, but of the maturing powers of the writer. The later manner is likely to appear long before it becomes predominant, and *Richard II* is at most only two years earlier than *Henry IV*; but once the later manner has been fully achieved, the earlier manner will almost certainly disappear except when it is consciously adopted for some specific purpose: Gertrude's pretty and formalized description of the death of Ophelia comes to mind. (As a parallel case of stylistic development compare Yeats.) There are, for instance, almost no conceits that can be strictly so called in *Henry IV*; the most striking exception is Hotspur's description of the fight between Mortimer and Glendower on the banks of the frightened Severn (I, iii, 95–107), and the effect of rhetorical exaggeration is intended. The king's response is, "Thou dost belie him, Percy, thou dost belie him!"

It is interesting that the exceptions to the type in *Richard II* occur almost always in passages describing what the effect of war will be on English soil:

> For that our kingdom's earth should not be soil'd
> With that dear blood which it hath fostered;
> And for our eyes do hate the dire aspect
> Of civil wounds plough'd up with neighbours' sword;
> And for we think the eagle-winged pride
> Of sky-aspiring and ambitious thoughts,
> With rival-hating envy, set on you
> To wake our peace, which in our country's cradle
> Draws the sweet infant breath of gentle sleep;
> Which so roused up with boisterous untuned drums,
> With harsh-resounding trumpets' dreadful bray,
> And grating shock of wrathful iron arms,
> Might from our quiet confines fright fair peace
> And make us wade even in our kindred's blood;
> Therefore, we banish you our territories. (I, iii, 125–39)

Here the fusion of images is combined with the same sort of syntactical boldness we have observed in the passage from *Henry IV* on opposed eyes.[8] The oblique allusion contained in the imagery of the opening lines of *Henry IV* to these fine passages in *Richard II* re-enforces with powerful effect the sense of continuity established by the explicit allusion to events in the earlier play:

> No more the thirsty entrance of this soil
> Shall daub her lips with her own children's blood.
> No more shall trenching war channel her fields,
> Nor bruise her flow'rets with the armed hoofs
> Of hostile paces.   (ɪ, i, 5–9)

The idea of war on English soil was evidently one which called forth from Shakespeare an intense imaginative response.

I said I should return to the objection that the imagery in *Richard II* is what it is because of the kind of character Richard is and therefore should not be pressed for another significance. It is true enough that its appropriateness is so great that anything better to exhibit his character can hardly be imagined. But I should like to raise the question whether or not Shakespeare would have been tempted by just such a figure at any time very much later in his career. The question is not idle. Although I have not carefully examined the imagery of all the early plays with respect to the qualities here considered, I suspect that it will be found to be generally of the same kind as in *Richard II*; certainly it is in *Romeo and Juliet*. *King John,* though perhaps exceptional in the abundance of imaginative images, is strongly marked, nevertheless, by the elaborate type so frequent in *Richard II*.[9] But in the case of *Richard II,* these characteristics of the imagery are especially striking because they are so beautifully adapted to exhibit the central character. The perfection of the play, within its limits, is the perfection of union between character and a style that Shakespeare had mastered at that stage of his career. He had it at his fingers' ends and he found a character for whom it was dramatically right.

[8] See p. 116. Other vividly imaginative passages in *Richard II* on this subject (only one, however, with the degree of fusion exhibited in the passage quoted) occur at ɪɪɪ, iii, 42–8, 93–100, 161–63; ɪv, i, 137–44.

[9] See Constance's speeches, especially the one on Death, in ɪɪɪ, iv; and Arthur's speech on the irons Hubert is heating, ɪv, i, 60–70.

But 1 *Henry IV* is a stage beyond *Richard II* in the welding of poetic imagination to dramatic need. This is best illustrated in the case of Hotspur. Dr. Tillyard says that there is no profound obliquity in Richard's character and that a good deal of the play is the poetry of statement.[10] Richard's character is exhibited directly. He is a poet and he speaks poetically. But Hotspur is a hater of poetry who speaks some of the most vivid and the most beautiful poetry in the play. In all of Richard's poetical speeches, he has nothing like Hotspur's speech on honour, so loaded with unexpressed meaning. Yet Hotspur's animadversions on poets and poetry remain convincing. It will not do to say that we do not take him at his word. That is a very superficial view of his character and of Shakespeare's art. We do take him at his word if we pay attention to the play. He is an entire man of action, as he says he is, without artistic habits or interests. He is intensely imaginative, certainly, but imagination is not enough to make a poet. Whereas Richard's speeches are the poems that Shakespeare puts into his mouth as his own compositions, Hotspur's speeches are Shakespeare's poetry to express the mind of a character who could not himself compose a poem at all. This is a very high degree of obliquity in the use of artistic means. It is accomplishment of an altogether different order from the minor perfection of *Richard II*.

It might prove fruitful to examine the imagery of the rest of the plays from the point of view I have suggested in this paper. Miss Spurgeon and Professor G. Wilson Knight have already shown, in different ways, how the "modifying and shaping power" of the imagination has in the great tragedies produced a kind of running imagery contributory to the tone of each play. One would expect this same power to produce, along with greater boldness in syntax and greater condensation in statement, greater concentration, greater fluidity of outline, and greater suggestiveness in the imagery. The highest achievement of the "fusing power" of the imagination one feels to be, however, not complexity, but something beyond— utter simplicity of form to express multiplicity of meaning. One thinks of *Antony and Cleopatra*, part of whose great obliquity surely arises from its imagery. *Rich* is not an adequate word to describe it. At its greatest, it is evocative of things that can have no statement:

[10] Op. cit., p. 244.

there is nothing left remarkable
Beneath the visiting moon.

MILTON CRANE

The Worlds of Prose and Verse
in Henry IV, Part 1

Nowhere in Shakespeare are the boundaries of two worlds
so clearly delimited by the use of prose and verse as in the *Henry
IV* plays (1597, 1598). The scenes relating to the historical matter are in verse, the scenes of Falstaff and his followers in prose.
There are trifling exceptions: the conventional usages, as in Hotspur's letter (II, iii); Hotspur's short comic dialogue with his lady
(III, i), with its startling shifts between prose and verse; and the
mock verse of Pistol. One can hardly say of plays which fall so
neatly into two actions and two spheres of influence that the form
of either action is basic and the form of the other is the exception.
Between the two worlds lies a huge and fundamental opposition,
but each is autonomous within itself; Pistol's verse in the Boar's
Head tavern is burlesque, not a sadly distorted recollection that
the "serious business" of the play is going on elsewhere in verse.

Falstaff is Shakespeare's most brilliant speaker of comic prose,
as Hamlet is his most gifted speaker of a prose which defies categories. But why does Falstaff speak prose? This may seem an idle
question: Falstaff is a clown, although a nobleman, and must therefore speak prose; he must, furthermore, represent "the whole world"
that Hal has to banish before he can become England's Harry, and
Falstaff must therefore be opposed in every conceivable way to the
world of high action and noble verse in which Hal is destined to
move. But beyond all this, Falstaff speaks prose because it is in-
conceivable that he should speak anything else. He is the incarna-

tion of realism, who, in George Orwell's words, "sees very clearly the advantages of staying alive with a whole skin . . . He it is who punctures your fine attitudes and urges you to look after Number One, to be unfaithful to your wife, to bilk your debts, and so on and so forth." [49] He is the soldier who carries, not unlike Bernard Shaw's Bluntschli, a bottle of sack in his holster, and who remains on the battlefield to question the meaning of honor after the rest have gone forth to seek it. Verse in his mouth is but a mockery of verse, and as such he speaks it. Prose in Shakespeare's earlier chronicle-histories has been the rough speech of Jack Cade and his ragamuffins. Falstaff's prose is the very honey of Hybla. The devil may speak through him, but such is his utterance that the angels are easily worsted.

Burlesque lies near the heart of Shakespearean comedy, from *The Comedy of Errors* to *As You Like It*. In the two *Henry IV* plays, the Falstaff-plot offers the broadest conceivable burlesque on the serious action. Falstaff derides the chivalric ideal, the forms of noble behavior, the law itself; he robs the travelers, suffers himself to be robbed in turn without fighting, and at last lies grossly and complacently about the whole affair and is totally unabashed at being found out. He is an unrepentant sinner, and, notwithstanding, is handsomely rewarded for his evil life until the moment of his banishment. He is a particularly noisome stench in the nostrils of the godly. His burlesque of their world is conducted on every plane: he robs them, flouts their ideals, and corrupts their prince. And, because he is in such constant opposition to their world, it is only fitting that he should never really speak its language. The powerful contrast is expressed on the level of speech as on every other, and thus Falstaff speaks prose because of what he represents as well as what he is.

Most of the characters can be assigned easily enough to one group or the other—Hal's position remaining always ambiguous—but Hotspur's case is somewhat odd. He accepts the code completely; he is honor's fool, and is killed for it. But he is a very downright man, whose hard and realistic common sense makes him impatient with both poetry and milk-and-water oaths; language must speak clearly, directly, and forcefully, or he will have none of it. It is therefore inevitable that he should speak the very best of lan-

[49] George Orwell, "The Art of Donald McGill," in *Dickens, Dali and Others* (New York, 1946), p. 136.

guage, and that especially in verse. His verse is so hard, colloquial, and simple that he really has no need for prose. George Rylands says that Hotspur's speech marks an important stage in the development of Shakespeare's verse style, a stage at which Shakespeare incorporated into his verse many of the qualities of his prose.[50] And yet one feels that Shakespeare must have known what he was about when he made Hotspur speak much more verse than prose. Hotspur belongs, after all, to the world of the knights, and he must speak their idiom even if only to mock them in it. Occasionally he uses prose, and very well, as in the prose letter in II, iii—a furious stream of prose: letter, comment, and vituperation, all well jumbled together. But as soon as Lady Percy enters, we have verse dialogue. The prose of this first long monologue should perhaps be put down to a combination of conventional epistolary prose and the dramatic necessity for continuing the letter scene in prose, even after the reading of the letter is finished.

In III, i, where Hotspur taunts and enrages the fiery Glendower, he begins in broken verse:

> Lord Mortimer, and cousin Glendower,
> Will you sit down?
> And uncle Worcester. A plague upon it!
> I have forgot the map. (III, i, 3–6)

Glendower's reply has been rearranged as most irregular verse by Pope from the prose of the Quartos. Hotspur's next speech is in prose, whereas Glendower at once breaks into the pompous, inflated verse so characteristic of him. Hotspur then varies between prose and verse; the length of the individual speech appears to be the only determinant. Thus he says at first:

> Why, so it would have done at the same season, if your mother's cat had but kitten'd, though yourself had never been born. (18–20)

But, a moment later, he goes on:

> And I say the earth was not of my mind,
> If you suppose as fearing you it shook.

. . . .

[50] H. W. Rylands, *Words and Poetry* (London, 1928), pp. 147, 148.

O, then the earth shook to see the heavens on fire,
And not in fear of your nativity.
Diseased nature oftentimes breaks forth
In strange eruptions; oft the teeming earth
Is with a kind of colic pinch'd and vex'd
By the imprisoning of unruly wind
Within her womb, which, for enlargement striving,
Shakes the old beldame earth and topples down
Steeples and mossgrown towers. At your birth
Our grandam earth, having this distemp'rature,
In passion shook. (22–23, 25–34)

After Glendower's reply, Hotspur returns to prose for a two-line retort, and, a little later, speaks verse again. Hotspur's prose in this scene appears to be restricted to short gibes, whereas he speaks verse when he becomes aroused.

He uses prose again, briefly, toward the end of the scene, when he jokes with his wife and reproaches her for her genteel swearing. It is difficult to assign any specific reason for this prose, largely because of the general uncertainty of media in this passage (225–258). Hotspur speaks prose, then verse, then prose again; after the Welsh lady's song, Hotspur's protest against his lady's "in good sooth" begins in prose and drops suddenly into verse. His last speech is again in prose. The Quartos and Folio disagree on the setting of the mixed speech. The Quartos have

> Not yours, in good sooth? Heart! you swear like a comfit-maker's wife. 'Not you, in good sooth!' and 'as true as I live!' and 'as God shall mend me!' and 'as sure as day!'

> And givest such sarcenet surety for thy oaths
> As if thou ne'er walk'st further than Finsbury,
> Swear me, Kate, like a lady as thou art,
> A good mouth-filling oath; and leave 'in sooth'
> And such protest of pepper gingerbread
> To velvet guards and Sunday citizens.
> Come, sing. (245–254)

which is the form generally accepted by modern editors. The Folios, however, make verse of lines 245–247, ending the lines at *sooth? wife, live,* and *day.* The Quartos are doubtless correct in their reading; but one's confusion finds honorable precedents.

The Prince, in general, takes his cue from his company, speaking prose in the tavern and verse in the court with equal facility. His one violation of this division is, consequently, all the more striking. He enters in V, iii, to find Falstaff moralizing over the corpse of Sir Walter Blunt. Hal is now no longer the boon companion, but the valiant knight, and reproves Falstaff in straightforward verse. Falstaff replies with a jest in prose, and the rest of the scene—a matter of a half-dozen speeches—is wound up in prose. But Falstaff himself has brought his prose into a verse scene, one of noble words and deeds, and he has used Sir Walter's "grinning honour" as a telling proof of his conclusions in his own catechism of honor. The scene thus contains a double contrast between prose and verse, and the old use of prose and verse characters within a single scene is here given a new and effective turn.

In V, i, Falstaff is for the first time brought into the world of the court, and at once sets about his favorite task of deriding it. Worcester pleads his innocence, and to the King's ironic question about the rebellion, "You have not sought it! How comes it then?" (V, i, 27), Falstaff interjects a reply: "Rebellion lay in his way, and he found it." Only Hal's injunction to remain quiet keeps Falstaff from making further comments on the action of the scene. He must needs hold his peace until the nobles have left, but immediately thereafter rediscovers his vein. Hal is short with him, for he is keenly aware of the seriousness of the situation. And so Falstaff must wait for even Hal to leave before he can make his most devastating comment on the ideals of a world he so ambiguously serves.

Shakespeare was too keen a dramatist not to have understood that the most powerful impression a scene creates in the mind of an audience is the final one. The first scene of Act V begins with King Henry, Worcester and the rest; but it ends with Falstaff. The *dramatic* point of the scene is well made and the main action is appreciably advanced. But at the side, and attempting always to intrude, is Falstaff, and when the rest have left, he has the stage entirely to himself. The net effect is produced not by the heroics of the nobles, but by the cynical realism of Falstaff. This is not to say that Falstaff dominates the play as he dominates this scene; as Professor Van Doren has well expressed it: "History is enlarged here to make room for taverns and trollops and potations of sack, and the heroic drama is modified by gigantic mockery, by the roared voice of truth; but the result is more rather than less reality, just as a cathedral, instead of being demolished by merriment among its aisles, stands more august." [51]

Hal must, as he says, "imitate the sun," and Falstaff's charm must be made so great as to convince the spectator that Hal's enjoyment of low life is not caused by a natural preference for the stew or the alehouse. But so charming (to use the word strictly) is Falstaff that Hal's necessary renunciation of him cannot be anything but priggish. The more obvious viciousness of Falstaff's actions in 2 *Henry IV* is an indication that Shakespeare was obliged to degrade deliberately the tempter who had succeeded only too well. The damage, as far as the reader or spectator is concerned, is past repair.

[51] Mark Van Doren, *Shakespeare* (New York, 1939), p. 116.

II

SAMUEL JOHNSON

The Unimitable Falstaff

. . . *Falstaff* unimitated, unimitable *Falstaff*, how shall I describe thee? Thou compound of sense and vice; of sense which may be admired but not esteemed, of vice which may be despised, but hardly detested. *Falstaff* is a character loaded with faults, and with those faults which naturally produce contempt. He is a thief, and a glutton, a coward, and a boaster, always ready to cheat the weak, and prey upon the poor; to terrify the timorous and insult the defenceless. At once obsequious and malignant, he satirises in their absence those whom he lives by flattering. He is familiar with the prince only as an agent of vice, but of this familiarity he is so proud as not only to be supercilious and haughty with common men, but to think his interest of importance to the duke of *Lancaster*. Yet the man thus corrupt, thus despicable, makes himself necessary to the prince that despises him, by the most pleasing of all qualities, perpetual gaiety, by an unfailing power of exciting laughter, which is the more freely indulged, as his wit is not of the splendid or ambitious kind, but consists in easy escapes and sallies of levity, which make sport but raise no envy. It must be observed that he is stained with no enormous or sanguinary crimes, so that his licentiousness is not so offensive but that it may be borne for his mirth.

The moral to be drawn from this representation is, that no man is more dangerous than he that with a will to corrupt, hath the power to please; and that neither wit nor honesty ought to think themselves safe with such a companion when they see *Henry* seduced by *Falstaff*.

From *The Plays of William Shakespeare* (London, 1765), IV, 356.
Title added by Ed.

MAURICE MORGANN

The Courage of Falstaff

I do not clearly discern that Sir *John Falstaff* deserves to
bear the character so generally given him of an absolute Coward;
or, in other words, that I do not conceive *Shakespeare* ever meant
to make Cowardice an essential part of his constitution. . . . Cowardice *is not* the *Impression* which the *whole* character of *Falstaff*
is calculated to make on the minds of an unprejudiced audience;
tho' there be, I confess, a great deal of something in the *composi-
tion* likely enough to puzzle, and consequently to mislead the
Understanding. . . . It is strange . . . that it should now be a
question, whether *Falstaff* is or is not a man of Courage; and
whether we do in fact contemn him for the want, or respect him
for the possession of that quality: And yet I believe the reader will
find that he has by no means decided this question, even for himself.—If then it should turn out that this difficulty has arisen out
of the Art of *Shakespeare*, who has contrived to make secret Impressions upon us of Courage, and to preserve those Impressions
in favour of a character which was to be held up for sport and
laughter on account of actions of apparent Cowardice and dishonour, we shall have less occasion to wonder, as *Shakespeare* is a
Name which contains All of Dramatic artifice and genius. . . .
Perhaps, after all, the *real* character of *Falstaff* may be different
from his *apparent* one; and possibly this difference between reality
and appearance, whilst it accounts at once for our liking and our
censure, may be the true point of humour in the character, and
the source of all our laughter and delight. We may chance to find,
if we will but examine a little into the nature of those circumstances which have accidentally involved him, that he was intended to be drawn as a character of much Natural courage and

From *An Essay on the Dramatic Character of Sir John Falstaff* (1777)
reprinted from *Eighteenth Century Essays on Shakespeare*, ed. D. Nichol
Smith (Glasgow, 1903), pp. 218–231. Title added by Ed.

resolution; and be obliged thereupon to repeal those decisions which may have been made upon the credit of some general tho' unapplicable propositions. . . . With respect to every infirmity, except that of Cowardice, we must take him as at the period in which he is represented to us. If we see him dissipated, fat,—it is enough;—we have nothing to do with his youth, when he might perhaps have been modest, chaste, *"and not an Eagle's talon in the waist."* But *Constitutional Courage* extends to a man's whole life, makes a part of his nature, and is not to be taken up or deserted like a mere Moral quality. It is true, there is a Courage founded upon *principle*, or rather a principle independent of Courage, which will sometimes operate in spite of nature; a principle which prefers death to shame, but which always refers itself, in conformity to its own nature, to the prevailing modes of honour, and the fashions of the age.—But Natural courage is another thing: It is independent of opinion; It adapts itself to occasions, preserves itself under every shape, and can avail itself of flight as well as of action. . . . That Courage which is founded in nature and constitution, *Falstaff*, as I presume to say, possessed;—but I am ready to allow that the principle already mentioned, so far as it refers to reputation only, began with every other Moral quality to lose its hold on him in his old age; that is, at the time of life in which he is represented to us; a period, as it should seem, approaching to *seventy*.—The truth is that he had drollery enough to support himself in credit without the point of honour, and had address enough to make even the preservation of his life a point of drollery. The reader knows I allude . . . to his fictitious death in the battle of Shrewsbury. This incident is generally construed to the disadvantage of *Falstaff*: It is a transaction which bears the external marks of Cowardice. . . . Whatever there may be of dishonour in *Falstaff*'s conduct, he neither does or says any thing on this occasion which indicates terror or disorder of mind: On the contrary, this very act is a proof of his having all his wits about him, and is a stratagem, such as it is, not improper for a buffoon, whose fate would be singularly hard, if he should not be allowed to avail himself of his Character when it might serve him in most stead. We must remember, in extenuation, that the executive, the destroying hand of *Douglas* was over him: *"It was time to counterfeit, or that hot termagant Scot had paid him scot and lot too."* He had but one choice; he was obliged to pass thro' the ceremony of dying either in jest or in earnest; and we shall not be surprized at the event, when we remember his propensities to the former.— Life (and especially the life of *Falstaff*) might be a jest; but he could see no joke whatever in dying: To be chopfallen was, with him, to lose both life and character together: He saw the point of honour, as well as every thing else, in ridiculous lights, and began to renounce its tyranny. . . . The Courage of *Falstaff* is my Theme: And no passage will I spare from which any thing can be inferred as relative to this point. . . . And so with that attention to truth and candour which ought to accompany even our lightest amusements I proceed to offer such proof as the case will admit, that *Courage* is a part of *Falstaff's Character*, that it belonged to his constitution, and was manifest in the conduct and practice of his whole life.

A. C. BRADLEY

The Rejection of Falstaff

     The bliss of freedom gained in humour is the essence of Falstaff. His humour is not directed only or chiefly against obvious absurdities; he is the enemy of everything that would interfere with his ease, and therefore of anything serious, and especially of everything respectable and moral. For these things impose limits and obligations, and make us the subjects of old father antic the law, and the categorical imperative, and our station and its duties, and conscience, and reputation, and other people's opinion, and all sorts of nuisances. I say he is therefore their enemy; but I do him wrong; to say that he is their enemy implies that he regards them as serious and recognises their power, when in truth he refuses to recognise them at all. They are to him absurd; and to reduce a thing *ad absurdum* is to reduce it to nothing and to walk

From *Oxford Lectures on Poetry* by A. C. Bradley, pp. 262–268. Copyright 1909 by The Macmillan Company. By permission of Macmillan & Co. Ltd and St. Martin's Press, Inc.

about free and rejoicing. This is what Falstaff does with all the would-be serious things of life, sometimes only by his words, sometimes by his actions too. He will make truth appear absurd by solemn statements, which he utters with perfect gravity and which he expects nobody to believe; and honour, by demonstrating that it cannot set a leg, and that neither the living nor the dead can possess it; and law, by evading all the attacks of its highest representative and almost forcing him to laugh at his own defeat; and patriotism, by filling his pockets with the bribes offered by competent soldiers who want to escape service, while he takes in their stead the halt and maimed and the gaol-birds; and duty, by showing how he labours in his vocation—of thieving; and courage, alike by mocking at his own capture of Colvile * and gravely claiming to have killed Hotspur; and war, by offering the Prince his bottle of sack when he is asked for a sword; and religion, by amusing himself with remorse at odd times when he has nothing else to do; and the fear of death, by maintaining perfectly untouched, in the face of imminent peril and even while he *feels* the fear of death, the very same power of dissolving it in persiflage that he shows when he sits at ease in his inn. These are the wonderful achievements which he performs, not with the sourness of a cynic, but with the gaiety of a boy. And, therefore, we praise him, we laud him, for he offends none but the virtuous, and denies that life is real or life is earnest, and delivers us from the oppression of such nightmares, and lifts us into the atmosphere of perfect freedom.

. . . Falstaff is neither a liar nor a coward in the usual sense, like the typical cowardly boaster of comedy. He tells his lies either for their own humour, or on purpose to get himself into a difficulty. He rarely expects to be believed, perhaps never. He abandons a statement or contradicts it the moment it is made. There is scarcely more intent in his lying than in the humorous exaggerations which he pours out in soliloquy just as much as when others are by. Poins and the Prince understand this in part. You see them waiting eagerly to convict him, not that they may really put him to shame, but in order to enjoy the greater lie that will swallow up the less. But their sense of humour lags behind his. Even the Prince seems to accept as half-serious that remorse of his which passes so suddenly into glee at the idea of taking a purse, and his request to his friend to bestride him if he should see him down in the battle. . . .

* 2 *Henry IV*, IV, iii. Ed.

Again, the attack of the Prince and Poins on Falstaff and the other thieves on Gadshill is contrived, we know, with a view to the incomprehensible lies it will induce him to tell. But when, more than rising to the occasion, he turns two men in buckram into four, and then seven, and then nine, and then eleven, almost in a breath, I believe they partly misunderstand his intention, and too many of his critics misunderstand it altogether. Shakespeare was not writing a mere farce. It is preposterous to suppose that a man of Falstaff's intelligence would utter these gross, palpable, open lies with the serious intention to deceive, or forget that, if it was too dark for him to see his own hand, he could hardly see that the three misbegotten knaves were wearing Kendal green. No doubt, if he *had* been believed, he would have been hugely tickled at it, but he no more expected to be believed than when he claimed to have killed Hotspur. Yet he is supposed to be serious even then. Such interpretations would destroy the poet's whole conception. . . .

That Falstaff sometimes behaves in what we should generally call a cowardly way is certain; but that does not show that he was a coward; and if the word means a person who feels painful fear in the presence of danger, and yields to that fear in spite of his better feelings and convictions, then assuredly Falstaff was no coward. . . .

"Well," it will be answered, "but he ran away on Gadshill; and when Douglas attacked him he fell down and shammed dead." Yes, I am thankful to say, he did. For of course he did not want to be dead. He wanted to live and be merry. And as he had reduced the idea of honour *ad absurdum*, had scarcely any self-respect, and only a respect for reputation as a means of life, naturally he avoided death when he could do so without a ruinous loss of reputation, and (observe) with the satisfaction of playing a colossal practical joke. For *that* after all was his first object. If his one thought had been to avoid death he would not have faced Douglas at all, but would have run away as fast as his legs could carry him; and unless Douglas had been one of those exceptional Scotchmen who have no sense of humour, he would never have thought of pursuing so ridiculous an object as Falstaff running. So that . . . Poins is right when he thus distinguishes Falstaff from his companions in robbery: "For two of them, I know them to be as true-bred cowards as ever turned back; and for the third, if he fight longer than he sees reason, I'll forswear arms." And the event justifies this distinction. For it is exactly thus that, according to the original stage-direction, Falstaff behaves when Henry and Poins attack him and the others. The rest run away at once; Falstaff, here as afterwards with Douglas, fights for a blow or two, but, finding himself deserted and outmatched, runs away also. Of course. He saw no reason to stay. *Any* man who had risen superior to all serious motives would have run away. But it does not follow that he would run from mere fear, or be, in the ordinary sense, a coward.[1]

[1] It is to be regretted, however, that in carrying his guts away so nimbly he "roared for mercy"; for I fear we have no ground for rejecting Henry's statement to that effect, and I do not see my way to adopt the suggestion . . . that Falstaff spoke the truth when he swore that he knew Henry and Poins as well as he that made them.

E. E. STOLL

Falstaff

Falstaff's cowardice appears still more clearly when the Gadshill incident is viewed in detail. There is the testimony of the Prince, Poins, and Falstaff himself. Four times the Prince flatly calls him coward to his face. The only time he attempts to deny it—on Gadshill—the Prince replies, "Well, we leave that to the proof"; and it comes speedily. Clearer nothing could be: the question is raised, and Falstaff's roaring and running away the next moment are the all-sufficient answer. . . .

Poins's estimate of Falstaff's character just before this has been subjected to the most undramatic and hair-splitting comment imaginable:—"Well, for two of them, I know them to be as true-bred cowards as ever turned back; and for the third, if he fight longer than he sees reason, I'll forswear arms" (I, ii, 158). "As

From *Shakespeare Studies: Historical and Comparative in Method* (New York, 1927), pp. 415–424. Some footnotes have been omitted and those included renumbered.

for the third," echoes Morgann, solemnly; "as if the name of this veteran would have excited too strongly the ideas of courage and resistance." "What stronger evidence can we require," he cries, "than that Poins, the ill-disposed . . . than that this very Poins should not venture to put down Falstaff in the list of cowards?" Humour or the understanding of humour, particularly of that ancient Anglo-Saxon heritage the humour of understatement, which is the Englishman's possession to this hour, seems, as from most of us when saddled and ridden by a theory, to have been frequently withheld from this gifted man,—by a strange irony, the accepted chief expositor, now for a hundred and fifty years, of the foremost humorous character in literature.

Certainly the latter half of Poins's sentence contains no praise, however faint—the whole tone and context of the passage shows this; moreover, it is followed by the remark, still more explicit, about "the incomprehensible lies that this same fat rogue will tell us,—how thirty at least he fought with, and what wards, what blows, what extremities he endured," etc.—"a prediction," Morgann, faithfully but mournfully adds "unfortunately fulfilled, even beyond the letter of it,—a completion more incident, perhaps, to the predictions of a malice than of affection." What could Shakespeare have done with an audience of Morganns? Here or anywhere Poins, or Shakespeare himself in a comedy, is not the man to distinguish between conduct and character, principles and constitution, a skulker and a courageously consistent Epicurean; and the speech in question is a simple truth gilded with a pleasantry. Falstaff himself admits that he was "a coward on instinct," not on principle; and at Shrewsbury says to himself, "I fear the shot here,"—"I am afraid of this Percy," and makes his words good by stabbing the corpse. Against such an interpretation Morgann and his followers murmur, bidding us remember his age and his peculiar philosophy, the corrupting example of his associates, the odds against him, and the suddenness of the assault; but on the Elizabethan comic stage, or any popular stage, where of course there are no relentings towards cowardice . . . nobody confesses to fear but a coward, a child, or a woman. All Shakespeare's cowards, like his villains, bear their names written in their foreheads, and his true men . . . neither know nor understand what fear or dismay is. But the main objection to such considerations, as indeed to the general scheme and tenor of the prevailing Shake-

speare criticism, is, as Stack * well says, "its excessive refinement."
"Dramatic characters [particularly in comedy, I would add] are not
drawn for speculative ingenious men in their closets but for mankind at large." Such extenuations, the motives of malice, attributed
to "that Poins" and Lancaster, and the "secret impressions" of
valour,—all are inferences, "fine-spun deductions," to use Stack's
phrase; and the like things in comedy do not count because they
have not "a strong and immediate influence. . . ."

Nowhere is it more evident how little Morgann regarded dramatic method and stage-craft than at this early moment in the
episode:

> PETO. How many be there of them?
> GADSHILL. Some eight or ten.
> FAL. 'Zounds, will they not rob us?
> PRINCE. What, a coward, Sir John Paunch?
> FAL. Indeed, I am not John of Gaunt, etc.—(II, ii)

This is found to be hardly more of a confession on his part than
the Prince's remark to Poins on his own as they plan their trick
in the second scene of Act I: "Yea, but I doubt they will be too
hard for us." The latter remark is casual or else made in mockery,
but in either case it is meant only to call forth Poins's comment
(quoted above) on their companions' timorous natures; whereas
this speech of Falstaff's is uttered after the limelight has been
turned full upon him—the audience has been apprized of his cowardice, the business is afoot, and the booty at hand. Thus everything has been nicely calculated to give his abrupt exclamation full
comic value and "bring down the house," as would be seen by
anybody who on principle had not already blurred dramatic perspective and jumbled "values." And Falstaff's retort is, as Stack
rightly observes, a witty evasion; an effort to turn the laugh called
forth by his timorousness;—not, as Morgann would have it, a hint
at his discreetly courageous character, thrown out for the behoof
of the audience.

That Falstaff is not dissembling is still more evident from the
management of the ensuing incident, in the same scene, and of
the scene at the tavern. In the brief and fleeting moment of glory
immediately after the robbery of the travellers he calls Poins and

* Richard Stack, author of *Examination of Morgann's Essay on the*
Character of Falstaff (1788). Ed.

the Prince cowards, and swaggers. Now the coward charging the brave with cowardice, like the coward boasting of his courage, is a perennial situation, on the stage or off it. . . . Even in our time an audience knows as well what it means when such a charge comes from the lips of one already discredited as when a drunken man declares that he is not drunk and that others are. To clinch the business, immediately upon his words follows the ironical dramatic reversal and traditional comic situation of the robbery of the robber . . . and the fat rogue roaring and running off. What dunce in the audience would now fail to follow the drift? Morgann may think it not roaring if he pleases, for particulars in a play cannot be verified as in a history; but it is difficult to conceive how Poins could now say to the Prince on Gadshill, "How the fat rogue roared" unless he had just been doing it; or the Prince afterwards in Eastcheap could cast it up to Falstaff in the presence of all who heard him, without fear of denial—"roar'd for mercy, and still run and roar'd," and not like a lion, either, but "as ever I heard bull-calf." But to Morgann of course the play is not the whole story!

And when Falstaff with his craven crew, first bursts in, sweating to death, upon Prince Hal and Poins at the Boar's Head, he still cries out on cowards, again and again, as he drinks. Then, once he has caught his breath, come the "incomprehensible lies" of the men in buckram and Kendal green, the acting out of the combat—"wards," "blows," and "extremities"—and the swindling exhibition of battered buckler, bloodied garments, and hacked sword. And just like the coward denying his cowardice and the drunken man denying his drunkenness, he now cries, "I tell thee what, Hal, if I tell thee a lie, spit in my face, call me horse!" "Wilt thou believe me, Hal?" he says on a like occasion, again much misdoubting in his bluster; "three or four bonds apiece and a seal ring of my grandfather's." We have seen him fighting, we know his "old ward" and how he "bore his point," and at these we laugh as at the "eightpenny matter" (for so the Prince will have it) of the bonds and ring. Even if we should suspect him of saying it all for fun, on the spur of the moment, we now learn from blushing Bardolph of "his monstrous devices"—that like the cowardly Dericke of the *Famous Victories of Henry V* [1] he had persuaded them all to tickle

---

[1] 1585–88. As is well known, Shakespeare was acquainted with the play, and drew from it the traits of Falstaff's cowardice, thievishness, and loose living, the touches of repentance and sanctimoniousness, and his friendship with Prince Hal.

their noses with spear-grass, and to hack their swords with their daggers. As the precious coward Parolles, who thinks also of cutting his garments and breaking his Spanish sword, plans to do, he had given himself some hurts, though "slight" ones, and now swears he had "got them in exploit." [2] Here are all the conventional and traditional tricks of cowardice, and on the exposure of cowardice the comic effect of the scene depends as much on the reproof of the lies. . . . in the cowardice lies the whole point of twitting him with his boasting lies and excuses;—if in fun Falstaff had run away or lied what fun would there be in confuting him?—but twice in the scene the Prince calls him coward into the bargain, and casts it up to him that he had "hacked his sword and then said it was in fight." [3] "What a slave art thou!" Hal says truly.

Nor by his shifts and evasions, "I knew ye" and "on instinct," does he come off safe and sound. Throughout the rest of the scene, and even in Part II, he and his companions in cowardice are twitted with them. [4] It is the Prince that does the twitting, and the Prince should know. "No more of that, Hal," cries the fat knight, "an thou lovest me"; and that is not the tone of triumph. In the midst of this same scene his cowardice breaks out spontaneously anew. "Zounds," snarls Poins, "an ye call me coward, I'll stab thee." And the knight of Eastcheap sidles off, comically enough giving the words just on his lips the lie: "I call thee coward! I'll see thee damned ere I call thee coward; but I would give a thousand pound I could run as fast as thou canst. . . . Call you that backing of your friends? A plague upon such backing! give me them that will face me!" Just so he falters, and his bluster rings loud but hollow, when in Part II the servant of the Chief-Justice begs leave to tell him that he lies in his throat. "I give thee leave to tell me so! If thou gettest any leave of me, hang me!" Calls he this the facing of his foes? He shouts as he retreats, he barks as he runs, he jokes and quibbles to cover up his cowardice and confusion.

Through the rest of the play his cowardice is, as Morgann drolly confesses, still "thrust forward and pressed upon our notice." A coward Shakespeare will have him if Morgann won't. Even now,

---

[2] See *All's Well*, IV, i, for all these details; cf. Pistol, *Henry V*, V, i, 93–94;   And patches will I get unto these cudgell'd scars,
      And swear I got them in the Gallia wars.
[3] II, iv, 237; "Coward"; also lines 219, 441.
[4] II, iv, 254–331.

even after Gadshill, the dramatist, if so he had intended to do,
might have let Falstaff retrieve himself, by actions at least, and
not merely by wit or ingenuity, and induce the world to believe,
what without deeds the world to believe would be little inclined
—that his retreat was genuinely strategic, that he ran away only
to fight another day, that his cowardice had been a pretence or a
venial and momentary aberration. Instead, it is what Morgann will
not have it be—if not "constitutional," at least habitual. When
he hears the news of the uprising, he ingenuously asks the Prince
whether he is not horribly afeard, and in reply is told that the
Prince lacks some of his instinct. When told by the Prince that he
had been procured a charge of foot, he cries, "Well, God be thanked
for these rebels, they offend none but the virtuous. I laud them, I
praise them." Like a Stoic, in his own character he finds his con-
solation. And when he is ordered off to the North he wishes this
tavern were his drum; and on the eve of the fray whimpers, "I would
'twere bed-time, Hal, and all well," and then says his catechism of
dishonour. Standing by as Prince Hal and Hotspur come together,
he proves to be as good at encouraging others to fight as the white-
livered Moron and Panurge.[5] Then he falls flat and feigns death
as clowns and cowards did in the hour of danger, not in England
only but in contemporary Germany, Spain, and Italy; and above
all sets the seal on his cowardice by the dastardly blow and by
hatching the scheme to take the honour of killing Hotspur to himself. "I'll swear I killed him," he says, "nothing confutes me but
eyes and nobody sees me"; and could anything more effectually
contradict the opinion that he "stood on the ground of natural
courage only and common sense, and renounced that grinning idol
of military zealots, honour," than his undertaking, like the pitiful
poltroons, Pistol, Parolles, and Bessus,[*] to filch "bright honour,"
which the man fallen at his feet had boldly plucked? Men of principle, scorning glory, do not snatch at other men's. Such wreaking
of one's self on a dead body, moreover, is, like his "playing possum," one of the established *lazzi* [**] of the coward on the stage. . . .

---

[5] *Princesse d'Élide*, I, iii, intermède, where, perched in a tree, Moron
urges on the archers to kill the bear; and Rabelais, II, chap. 29, where
Panurge cheers on his master.

[*] Bessus, a cowardly captain in Beaumont and Fletcher's play *A King
and No King*. Ed.

[**] *Lazzi*, the farcical tricks of stage comedians. Ed.

in Shakespeare's time clowns played pranks on corpses both in England and Germany. Here in the battle, then, is a little heap of *lazzi*, or bits of "business," all stamped as those of a coward, not only intrinsically, but by immemorial custom; and it is difficult to see how Shakespeare could have effaced that impression had he tried.

J. W. DRAPER

Falstaff as an Elizabethan Soldier

Since the sources of *Henry IV* give only the slightest suggestion of Falstaff's character, the present writer proposes to seek his prototype in contemporary society; and, to this end, he presents two hypotheses: that actual Elizabethan conditions furnish ample analogies for the actions, and so for the character, of Falstaff; and that the audience, knowing such actions and such types of character in daily life, would see them, not as dramatic conventions, but as a holding of the mirror up to nature, and so judge them, not with nice ethical reasonings, as Bradley supposes, but in a rough-and-ready fashion, very much as they judged such people and such actions in the world around them.

Shakespeare clearly intended Sir John Falstaff to appear as an army officer; he is shown on a peace footing, with his soldier-comrades and his lady-loves, his food and lodging, his brawling and drinking, his chronic insolvency and his means of evading its consequences; he appears likewise at war, in preparation and recruiting, in military peculation, in actual battle, and in the dubious rewards of victory. Practically all the common elements of a soldier's life are involved; and, in a sense, they comprise practically all that Falstaff does in the three plays in which he appears. Logically then, one should study his character as an army officer, rather

From "Sir John Falstaff," *Review of English Studies,* VII (October 1932), 414–424. Reprinted by permission of the author and The Clarendon Press. Footnotes have been omitted. Title added by Ed.

than in any other group of Elizabethan society; and the following paragraphs propose to show how closely his behaviour squares with the actual doings of officers as depicted in the military books and other literature descriptive of the times.

Army life was on a very low plane, partly because the organisation and the method of recruiting were changing from the feudal to the modern professionalised system, and partly because Renaissance society, without the organised capital of modern industrialism, could hardly finance this new system which political necessity imposed. Soldiers, in consequence, were very little and very irregularly paid; and, as no provision was made for them in peace time or in old age, they often had to live by their wits and turn professional bully or downright highwayman; as Harman says ". . . the hardiest soldiers . . . if they escape all hazards, and return home again, if they be without relief of their friends they will surely desperately rob and steal." * This situation created a vicious circle; officers got their positions by favouritism—very much as Hal procured for Falstaff a "charge of foot"—and sometimes even by actual sale, and mis-used their commissions to enrich themselves. Therefore, men of probity avoided military service; and, therefore, the profession, "dispised of every man," sank lower and lower in the general esteem; Doll Tearsheet was voicing a general sentiment when she declared that captains such as Bardolph made "the word captain odious." Under such conditions, the few chivalrous exceptions, such as Sidney, were all the more conspicuous; and this decadence of army life explains why the worldly-wise Bacon advised Essex to seek civil rather than military preferment.

During war-time, the two main types of peculation practised by captains had to do with recruiting and with the padding of muster-rolls; and Falstaff seems to have been guilty of both.

. . . officers stole from their soldiers; and, even at that, their extravagant and disordered lives sometimes obliged them to pawn their own arms and come into battle, as Falstaff did, without full equipment. They stole the soldiers' pay, and even the money for their food; but the most lucrative form of peculation was the padding of muster-rolls, accomplished by enrolling one soldier in two different "bands" so that the Captain might draw pay for two, or by neglecting to report the dead and missing and so pocket-

* Thomas Harman, author of *A Caveat or Warening for Commen Cursetors* (1573). Ed.

ing their wages. This drawing of "dead pay," as it was called, made it profitable for a commander to lose in battle as many of his men as possible; and Digges declares that some would actually lead soldiers into "some desperate unfeasible Service . . . to have their throats cut, and then, having choice horses to save himself by flight, and his confederate Favorites, with the pay of the dead they may banquet and riot their fill." * Thus Falstaff, in spite of his cowardice, led his men to a place of danger so that "not three" of his "hundred and fifty" were left alive; for, indeed, as he says, he feared the "shot" (tavern-reckonings) of London even more than he did the "shot" of battle; and, knowing this abuse, surely an Elizabethan audience would infer that he had led his men to slaughter so that he might steal their "dead pay." Such were the means by which Bradley's "humorist of genius" attained his "godlike freedom."

If the officer on active service had his financial problems and his dubious ways of meeting them, the officer in peace time was no better off. The rigid system of nobility, clergy and guilds grouped the upper classes into sharply defined, closed corporations; and the widespread vagabondage of the day shows how little was the opportunity of the casual intruder. Society was too tightly organised to assimilate the numbers of soldiers or even of officers who returned from the wars; and the government assumed no responsibility. These outcast soldiers repaired to London, and lived a riotous life, very like that of Falstaff and his crew, sometimes begging from their friends, sometimes robbing as petty thieves, like the well-named Nym, or as highwaymen like Falstaff, and sometimes turning a doubtful penny by acting as "companion" to some wild young nobleman or as bully for some harlot such as Doll. . . .

Surely Shakespeare wrote the Falstaff comedies neither to make his hero the expression of some fine philosophy nor to concoct a clever compound of dramatic convention, although some of his characteristics may come from the tradition of the *miles gloriosus*. He seems rather to have aimed at contemporary realism with a lambent play of laughter. Not only Falstaff but his confederates are soldier-types of the period: Nym, whose very name suggests his "taking" ways; Bardolph, who carried his lantern in his nose; and Pistol, whose fantastic elegancies of speech bespoke a bowing acquaintance with the court; and Falstaff himself, who seems to

* Thomas Digges, *Foure Paradoxes, or Politique Discourses* (1604), pp. 19–20, 48. Ed.

represent the old military aristocracy run to seed, the foil of Henry V, in whom the Elizabethan saw epitomised the Golden Age of valour. Perhaps in Falstaff and his crew Shakespeare wished to satirise, by contrast with this Golden Age, the decadence of his own times, much lamented by Riche and other military writers of the day; but his touch is too light for satire, and his attitude too genial; and so the present writer would rather think that he aimed merely to depict men and things as they are, "to show virtue her own feature, scorn her own image, and the very age and body of the time his form and pressure."

FRANZ ALEXANDER

A Note on Falstaff

He [Falstaff] represents the deep infantile layers of the personality, the simple innocent wish to live and enjoy life. He has no taste for abstract values like honor or duty and no ambition. Man is only partially social. One part of his personality remains individualistic and resents the restrictions of social life and just these restrictions, especially if they go further than one can tolerate them, mobilize all the destructive instincts of man's nature such as discontent, ill spirit and a negative attitude toward the environment. This is the explanation of the popular belief that people who like to eat and drink well—that is to say, who treat the animal in themselves with consideration—are more amiable and less malicious. The opposite is true of the ascetic self-restricting characters often found among political fanatics and exponents of social doctrines for which they sacrifice their lives. Like Robespierre, the fanatic schoolmaster, under the guise of fighting for humanitarian ideals they can take revenge for all their self-imposed restrictions in destroying their opponents en masse. It is seldom difficult to recognize under the thin surface of their rationalizations,

From *Psychoanalytic Quarterly*, II (October 1933), 592–606. Reprinted by permission of the author and the publisher.

their real motives: hatred and revenge. Hotspur unquestionably belongs to this category of fanatic haters. The king offers him full consideration of all his complaints but what he seeks essentially is a fight. The conditions which he proposes to the king are unacceptable, and even his friends call him drunk with fury. He scarcely can await the battle: "Let the hours be short 'til fields and blows and groans applaud our sport."

Hotspur is the exponent of destruction, but destruction which serves not entirely selfish but also collective, that is, caste, interests. Falstaff is the personification of the wholly self-centered pleasure-seeking principle. Although he represents the opposite of destruction, the principle of life, libido, it is the most primitive manifestation of libido, the primary self-centered, narcissistic libido of the child which he stands for.

Prince Henry in the process of maturing must overcome both of these principles. When he kills Hotspur on the battlefield, he overcomes symbolically his own destructive tendency. In killing Hotspur, the arch-enemy of his father, he overcomes his own aggressions against his parent. But he must overcome also the Falstaff in himself if he is to become a fully balanced adult. In the history of the metamorphosis of Prince Henry, Shakespeare dramatically describes the characteristic course of the development of the male. There are two difficult emotional problems which must be solved by everyone in the course of his development; the first is the fixation to the early pregenital forms of instinctual life which expresses itself in oral receptiveness and narcissistic self-adoration. This old fellow, Sir John Falstaff, is a masterful dramatization of such an early emotional attitude. The second difficulty to be overcome is the hatred and jealousy directed against the father. Hotspur, the rebel, who strives against the life of the king is the personification of these patricidal tendencies. In the play, these inner processes find an externalized dramatic expression. After Prince Henry has overcome these two inner—in the drama, external—enemies he becomes an ideal king.

J. I. M. STEWART

The Birth and Death of Falstaff

If Shakespeare does indeed succeed in making the rejection [of Falstaff] palatable to persons adequately aware of traditional matters lying behind the play, it is yet in the theatre that he does so, for that the thing continues to *read* uncomfortably after all Dover Wilson has to say I believe there will be few to deny. What does this mean? It means that although Shakespeare doubtless relied on certain contemporary attitudes to Riot and the like, he relied even more on something perennially generated in the consciousness or disposition of an audience in a theatre—whether they belong to Elizabethan times or to our own. And it is here that I would knit the debate on Falstaff to the theme of the present book. For what I have tried to urge is simply this: that in the interpretation of Shakespeare a study of the psychology of poetic drama (which leads us to understand his *medium*) is at least as important as a study of the contemporary climate of opinion (which gives simply *conditions* under which he worked).

The second point concerns the emphatic and wonderful account in *Henry V* of the death of Falstaff. It is all very well for Dover Wilson to point to the promise of more Falstaff made in the Epilogue to 2 *Henry IV* and infer that the subsequent death was a matter of mere theatrical convenience. But surely the Epilogue to *Henry IV* is dramatically altogether less authoritative than the account of Falstaff's passing in the later play; and what Shakespeare there wrote appears to me (because it is so wonderful) much less like an expedient dictated by changes in personnel in his company than the issue of his reflections on the inner significance of what had happened at the close of the earlier drama. "The King has kild his heart," says Mistress Quickly as Falstaff lies dying. "The King hath

From *Character and Motive in Shakespeare* (New York, 1947), pp. 135–139, published by Longmans, Green and Company, Inc., and reprinted by their permission. Footnotes have been omitted. Ed.

run bad humors on the Knight," says Nym, and Pistol at once responds: "*Nym*, thou hast spoke the right, his heart is fracted and corroborate." None of these worthies would cut much of a figure in a witness-box; nevertheless there is no mistaking the dramatic function of the three consenting voices. The truth of the matter is summed here; there follows the new king's dexterous, necessary but none too pleasant entrapping of Cambridge, Scroope and Gray; then comes the tremendous account of Falstaff's end—and after that we are set for Agincourt and the regeneration and triumph of England. It is of set purpose, then, that the rejection of Falstaff is so resounding, so like a killing. And the reverberation of that purpose sounds here in *Henry* V. What is it? There is an allegorical purpose, Dover Wilson says, and with this I agree. But I think, too, that among the "notions and associations . . . gone out of mind" embodied in this "composite myth which had been centuries amaking" there conceivably lies something deeper, something which belongs equally with drama and with magic.

When Shakespeare makes Falstaff die "ev'n just betweene Twelve and One, ev'n at the turning o' th' Tyde," he is touching a superstition, immemorial not only along the east coast of England from Northumberland to Kent but in many other parts of the world too—one shared by Dickens's Mr. Peggotty (who speaks of it expressly) and the Haidas on the Pacific coast of North America. But there is more of magic about Falstaff than this; and Dover Wilson, whom the editing of Shakespeare has schooled in a fine awareness of the reverberations of English words, is more than once well on the scent. "How doth the Martlemas, your Master?" Poins asks Bardolph. And Dover Wilson comments:

> Martlemas, or the feast of St. Martin, on 11 November, was in those days of scarce fodder the season at which most of the beasts had to be killed off and salted for the winter, and therefore the season for great banquets of fresh meat. Thus it had been for centuries, long before the coming of Christianity. In calling him a "Martlemas" Poins is at once likening Falstaff's enormous proportions to the prodigality of fresh-killed meat which the feast brought, and acclaiming his identity with Riot and Festivity in general.

Falstaff, in fact, is the "sweet beef," "the roasted Manning-tree ox with the pudding in his belly," who reigns supreme on the board of the Boar's Head in Eastcheap—"a London tavern . . . almost certainly even better known for good food than for good drink." There is thus from the first a symbolical side to his vast and genuine individuality; and again and again the imagery in which he is described likens him to a whole larder of "fat meat."

> "Call in Ribs, call in Tallow" is Hal's cue for Falstaff's entry in the first great Boar's Head scene; and what summons to the choicest feast in comedy could be more apt? For there is the noblest of English dishes straightaway: Sir John as roast Sir Loin-of-Beef, gravy and all.

Is it not—I find myself asking—as if the "brawn," Sir John, "the sow that hath overwhelmed all her litter but one," were some vast creature singled out from the herd and dedicated to a high festival indeed? But such festivals commemorate more than the need to reduce stock against a winter season. They commemorate a whole mythology of the cycle of the year, and of sacrifices offered to secure a new fertility in the earth.

Now, anthropologists are always telling us of countries gone waste and barren under the rule of an old, impotent and guilty king, who must be ritually slain and supplanted by his son or another before the saving rains come bringing purification and regeneration to the land. Is not Henry IV in precisely the situation of this king? Dover Wilson avers that it is so, without any thought of magical implication:

> . . . his reign and all his actions are overhung with the consciousness . . . of personal guilt . . . a fact that Shakespeare never misses an opportunity of underlining. . . . We see him first at the beginning of act 3 crushed beneath the disease that afflicts his body and the no less grievous diseases that make foul the body of his kingdom.

Perhaps, then, we glimpse here a further reason why the rejection of Falstaff is inevitable—not merely traditionally and moralistically inevitable but symbolically inevitable as well. And this may be why, when in the theatre, we do not really rebel against the rejection; why we find a fitness too in its being sudden and catastrophic. As long as we are in the grip of drama it is profoundly fit that Hal, turning king and clergyman at once, should run bad humours on the knight, should kill his heart. For the killing carries something of the ritual suggestion, the obscure *pathos*, of death in tragedy.

I suggest that Hal, by a displacement common enough in the evolution of ritual, kills Falstaff instead of killing the king, his father. In a sense Falstaff *is* his father; certainly is a "father-substitute" in the psychologist's word; and this makes the theory of a vicarious sacrifice the more colourable. All through the play there is a strong implicit parallelism between Henry Bolingbroke and his policies and Falstaff and *his* policies; and at one point in the play the two fathers actually, as it were, fuse (like Leonardo's two mothers in his paintings of the Virgin and St. Anne), and in the Boar's Head tavern King Falstaff sits on his throne while his son Prince Henry kneels before him. And Falstaff, in standing for the old king, symbolises all the accumulated sin of the reign, all the consequent sterility of the land. But the young king draws his knife at the altar—and the heart of that grey iniquity, that father ruffian, is as fracted and corroborate as Pistol avers. Falstaff's rejection and death are very sad, but Sir James Frazer would have classed them with the Periodic Expulsion of Evils in a Material Vehicle, and discerned beneath the skin of Shakespeare's audience true brothers of the people of Leti, Moa and Lakor.

If this addition of another buried significance to the composite myth of Hal and Falstaff should seem extravagant, or an injudicious striving after Morgann's "lightness of air," let it be remembered that drama, like religious ritual, plays upon atavic impulses of the mind. All true drama penetrates through representative fiction to the condition of myth. And Falstaff is in the end the dethroned and sacrificed king, the scapegoat as well as the sweet beef. For Falstaff, so Bacchic, so splendidly with the Maenads Doll and Mistress Quickly a creature of the wine-cart and the cymbal, so fit a sacrifice (as Hal early discerns) to lard the lean, the barren earth, is of that primitive and magical world upon which all art, even if with a profound unconsciousness, draws.

BIBLIOGRAPHY

BIBLIOGRAPHICAL AIDS

The body of scholarly and critical comment on Shakespeare is enormous. A helpful introduction to the more important works of Shakespeare scholarship produced in this century is provided by G. E. Bentley, "Shakespeare and His Times," in *Contemporary Literary Scholarship: A Critical Review*, ed. Lewis Leary (1958). The most convenient source of bibliography is *The Cambridge Bibliography of English Literature*, ed. F. W. Bateson, 4 vols. (1941) with the *Supplement* (1957), ed. George W. Watson, which includes material published up to 1955. Work published subsequently can be found in the annual bibliographies appearing in *The Year's Work in English Studies*, *Shakespeare Quarterly*, and *Studies in Philology*.

LIFE IN SHAKESPEARE'S ENGLAND

An extremely valuable collection of studies of facets of English life relevant to Shakespeare's plays is *Shakespeare's England*, ed. Sir Sidney Lee and C. T. Onions, 2 vols. (1916; repr. several times). Tastes, customs, and interests are studied in Muriel St. Clare Byrne, *Elizabethan Life in Town and Country* (1925; rev. 1954) and Louis B. Wright, *Middle-class Culture in Elizabethan England* (1935; repr. 1958). A readable and dependable short history is S. T. Bindoff, *Tudor England* (1950 *).

The standard reference work for all aspects of Elizabethan drama is E. K. Chambers, *The Elizabethan Stage*, 4 vols. (1923). More readable studies are Felix Schelling, *Elizabethan Drama, 1558–1642* (1908; repr. 1959); G. B. Harrison, *Elizabethan Plays and Players* (1940; repr. 1956 *); and T. M. Parrott and R. H. Ball, *A Short View of Elizabethan Drama* (1943; repr. 1958 *). Speculation about the physical features of the theatre for which Shakespeare wrote have interested many scholars in the twentieth century. Though some details are still in dispute, generally accepted attempts to reconstruct and describe that theatre are John C. Adams, *The Globe Playhouse: Its Design and Equipment* (1942; rev. and enlar. 1961); C. Walter Hodges, *The Globe Restored: A Study of the Elizabethan Theatre* (1953); and Irwin Smith, *Shakespeare's Globe Playhouse* (1956). Other aspects of the theatrical conditions are studied in T. W. Baldwin, *Organization and Personnel of the Shakespearean Company* (1927), and Alfred Harbage, *Shakespeare's Audience* (1941; repr. 1961 *).

SHAKESPEARE AND HIS CRAFT

A basic reference work for all matters pertaining to Shakespeare's life and career is E. K. Chambers, *William Shakespeare: A Study of Facts and Problems*, 2 vols. (1930; abridged in 1935 as *A Short Life of Shakespeare*). Standard biographies are those by Sir Sidney Lee (1898; rev. 1925) and Joseph Q. Adams (1923); more recent and easily accessible is Marchette

* Available in paperbound edition.

Chute, *Shakespeare of London* (1949; repr. 1957 *). Good introductions to and background comment on the plays are provided in E. K. Chambers, *Shakespeare: A Survey* (1925; repr. 1958 *); T. M. Parrott, *William Shakespeare. A Handbook* (1934; rev. 1955 *); and Gerald Sanders, *A Shakespeare Primer* (1950). *A Companion to Shakespeare Studies*, ed. Harley Granville-Barker and G. B. Harrison (1934; repr. 1960 *), is an excellent collection of essays (including an extensive annotated bibliography) dealing with Shakespeare's art and career. General critical studies are Mark Van Doren, *Shakespeare* (1939; repr. 1953 *); Hazelton Spencer, *The Art and Life of William Shakespeare* (1940); and D. A. Traversi, *An Approach to Shakespeare* (1938; rev. and enlar. 1956 *). Studies of Shakespeare's language are Miss Caroline F. E. Spurgeon, *Shakespeare's Imagery and What It Tells Us* (1935; repr. 1958 *); Wolfgang H. Clemen, *The Development of Shakespeare's Imagery* (1951); and B. Ifor Evans, *The Language of Shakespeare's Plays* (1952). Many of the difficulties of Shakespeare's vocabulary can be cleared up by consulting C. T. Onions, *A Shakespeare Glossary* (1911; several times reprinted).

THE HISTORY PLAY AND "HENRY IV, PART 1" (EDITIONS, SOURCES, AND CRITICISM)

A good brief account of the English history play is given by C. F. Tucker Brooke in Chapter IX of *The Tudor Drama* (1911); more comprehensive is Irving Ribner, *The English History Play in the Age of Shakespeare* (1957). Shakespeare's history plays have received increased scholarly attention in this century. A helpful survey of this scholarship is Harold Jenkins, "Shakespeare's History Plays: 1900–1951," *Shakespeare Survey*, VI (1953), 1–15. In addition to E. M. W. Tillyard's influential work in this area, of special importance are Miss Lily B. Campbell, *Shakespeare's "Histories," Mirrors of Elizabethan Policy* (1947) and D. A. Traversi, *Shakespeare from Richard II to Henry V* (1957).

Among the many editions of *Henry IV, Part 1*, those by J. Dover Wilson (1946) and A. R. Humphreys (1960) can be cited as distinguished and richly annotated; of first importance, however, for further study of the play are *The New Variorum Edition of Shakespeare: Henry the Fourth, Part 1*, ed. S. B. Hemingway (1936) and the *Supplement* to this work by G. Blakemore Evans, published as the Summer issue of the *Shakespeare Quarterly*, VII (1956). The *Variorum* edition offers the most convenient place (pp. 356–394) to study the chief sources Shakespeare drew upon in writing the play. The complete text of *The Famous Victories of Henry the Fifth* is contained in *Chief Pre-Shakespearean Dramas*, ed. Joseph Q. Adams (1924). Samuel Daniel's *The Civil Wars* has recently (1958) been edited by Laurence Michel. The sources of the play are studied by J. Dover Wilson, "The Origins and Development of Shakespeare's *Henry IV*," *Library*, 4th. ser., XXVI (June 1945), 2–16. The historical background of the play is discussed in W. G. Bowling, "The Wild Prince Hal in Legend and Literature," *Washington University Studies*, Humanistic Series, XIII (April 1926), 305–334; D. T. Starnes, "More about the Prince Hal Legend," *Philological Quarterly*, XV (October 1936), 358–366; C. L. Kingsford, *The First English Life of Henry V* (1911); and J. Dawtrey, *The Falstaff*

Saga (1927).

The bibliographies appended to the *Variorum* and the *Supplement* list all of the important studies of the play to 1955. The following list contains a number of the studies since that date, as well as some earlier ones, all selected as intrinsically rewarding and illustrating various approaches to the play.

Auden, W. H. "The Fallen City: Some Reflections on Shakespeare's *Henry IV*," *Encounter*, XIII (November 1959), 21–31. Interprets Falstaff as a comic symbol for the supernatural order of Charity contrasted with the temporal order of Justice symbolized by Hal.

Barber, C. L. "From Ritual to Comedy: an Examination of *Henry IV*" in *English Stage Comedy*, ed. W. K. Wimsatt, Jr., *English Institute Essays*. New York, 1954, pp. 22–51. Relates Falstaff to the cultural traditions of mirth and frolic associated with English holiday festivals.

Bryant, J. A. Jr. "Prince Hal and the Ephesians," *Sewanee Review*, LXVII (Spring 1959), 204–219. Relates Hal's efforts toward "redeeming time" to the exhortation in Ephesians 5: 15–16.

Boughner, D. C. "Vice, Braggart, and Falstaff," *Anglia*, LXXII (1954), 35–61. Falstaff, a descendant from figures in earlier English drama.

Cain, H. Edward. "Further Light on the Relation of *1 and 2 Henry IV*," *Shakespeare Quarterly*, III (January 1952), 21–38. The two parts are distinct dramatic entities and are not to be regarded as one unit.

Charlton, Henry B. "Falstaff" in *Shakespearean Comedy*. London, 1938, pp. 161–207. A sympathetic approach to Falstaff.

Connor, Seymour. "The Role of Douglas in *Henry IV, Part One*," *University of Texas Studies in English*, XXVII (June 1948), 215–221. Accounts for the change in Hal's estimation of Douglas from "vile" to "noble."

Dickinson, Hugh. "The Reformation of Prince Hal," *Shakespeare Quarterly*, XII (Winter 1961), 33–46. The education of a prince to a realization of his duty and an acceptance of its burden is the theme of the play.

Draper, J. W. "Falstaff and the Plautine Parasite," *Classical Journal*, XXXIII (April 1938), 390–401. The Parasite of Roman comedy as an ancestor of Falstaff.

Empson, William. *Some Versions of Pastoral*. London, 1935, pp. 43–46 and 103–109. Comments on the "double-plot" structure and features of the language.

Goodman, Paul. *The Structure of Literature*. Chicago, 1954, pp. 103–116. The serious-comic structure and Hal's relation to it.

Hemingway, S. B. "On Behalf of that Falstaff," *Shakespeare Quarterly*, III (October 1952), 307–311. The cowardly Falstaff appears on the stage; the martyr is found in the study.

Hunter, G. K. "*Henry IV* and the Elizabethan Two-Part Play," *Review of English Studies*, new ser., V (August 1954), 236–248. Any unity between the two parts of *Henry IV* results from a parallel presentation of incident and not from a continuity of plot or character.

Jenkins, Harold. *The Structural Problem in Shakespeare's Henry the Fourth.* London, 1956. Part 1 is well unified structurally; the two parts are actually two distinct versions of a single reformation.

Jorgensen, Paul A. " 'Redeeming Time' in Shakespeare's *Henry IV*," *Tennessee Studies in Literature*, V (1960), 101–109. An interpretation of Hal's much-discussed soliloquy (I.ii).

Kris, Ernst. "Prince Hal's Conflict," *Psychoanalytic Quarterly*, XVII (October 1948), 487–506. A psychological analysis of Hal and the King in terms of a father-son conflict.

McLuhan, Herbert M. "*Henry IV*, a Mirror for Magistrates," *University of Toronto Quarterly*, XVII (January 1948), 152–160. The corrupt and strife-torn land is the inheritance of the usurping Bolingbroke.

McNamara, Anne Marie. "*Henry IV*: the King as Protagonist," *Shakespeare Quarterly*, X (Summer 1959), 423–431.

Monaghan, James. "Falstaff and his Forebears," *Studies in Philology*, XVIII (July 1921), 353–361. Falstaff as a development from Sir John Oldcastle and Dericke, a clown, in *The Famous Victories of Henry the Fifth.*

Ribner, Irving. "Bolingbroke, a True Machiavellian," *Modern Language Quarterly*, IX (June 1948), 177–184. Cites parallels between the political philosophy of *The Prince* and the words and deeds of Henry IV.

Spivack, Bernard. "Falstaff and The Psychomachia," *Shakespeare Quarterly*, VIII (Autumn 1957), 449–459. A study of Falstaff's allegorical ancestors, the vices, of the morality plays.

Unger, Leonard. "Deception and Self-Deception in Shakespeare's *Henry IV*" in *The Man in the Name.* Minneapolis, 1956, pp. 3–17. The psychological disorders of the main characters reflect the social disorder of the state.

Waldock, A. J. A. "The Men in Buckram," *Review of English Studies*, XXIII (January 1947), 16–23. *Henry IV, Part 1*, like many Elizabethan plays, is a work of many textures ranging from sheer farce to near-tragic; moderns err in attempting to impose a unity of kind where none was ever intended.

Williams, Philip. "The Birth and Death of Falstaff Reconsidered," *Shakespeare Quarterly*, VIII (Summer 1957), 359–365. Supports J. I. M. Stewart's view of Falstaff expressed in *Character and Motive in Shakespeare*, pp. 111–139.

Wilson, Elkin Calhoun. "Falstaff—Clown and Man" in *Studies in the English Renaissance Drama*, ed. Josephine W. Bennett *et al.* New York, 1959, pp. 345–356. Accounts for Falstaff's capacity to earn both our laughter and sympathy.

Zeeveld, W. Gordon. " 'Food for Powder'—'Food for Worms,' " *Shakespeare Quarterly*, III (July 1952), 249–253. Notes the unifying effect of the two phrases ("echo images") in his title in the play.